BETWEEN FORM AND FREEDOM

All involved in the support of adolescence will be delighted to find a new edition of *Between Form and Freedom* with updated references and revised sections. The author's warmth of understanding for this turbulent and often mystifying phase of development is still as strong in this third edition, tackling new and changing challenges, including questions of genderfluidity, eating disorders and media addictions. The author describes how adolescents present either the mask or the volcano as they struggle with identity and self-esteem. There are references to the Waldorf approach to child development and curriculum, but the focus remains on addressing, in an accessible way, the complex landscape of teenage years and the polarities it contains.

Jill Taplin, author of *Understanding the Steiner Waldorf Approach: Early Years Education in Practice*

I found the first edition of this book extremely helpful and have recommended it to many during my years as a consultant… A very good reason for reading this book is that Betty Staley has opened up the window to the changing inner life of the developing child.

Tessabella Lovemore Ph D. Development Director at Elysia Therapeutic Centre

You have a teenager lurking in your house. 'Who stole my child?' You haven't been able to find good advice. Here it is. Thirty-three years since its first edition, this guide is updated by someone who observes, listens, and finds out what's going on in this time of form and freedom. Here is a combination of scholarship with references AND wise-elder advice based on experience AND poetry — as sometimes the turn of phrase of a poem is exactly what will bridge between adult and teen. And Betty Staley understands that these sometimes troublesome characters are there not only to learn from you, but to teach you as well. May your relationships deepen as a result! You might start with the 'In a Nutshell' sections at the ends of each chapter for an overview — very compact summaries, very helpful.

David Tresemer, Ph.D. (Psychology), past president of the Association for Anthroposophic Psychology, editor of *The Counselor... As If Soul and Spirit Matter*, and presently teaching through The StarHouse, Boulder, Colorado

Betty Staley's book is a must have for all parents of teenagers. Her calm wisdom about teenagers and the incredible depth of her knowledge will reassure any parent perplexed or struggling with their teenager. She can enable parents to know how to help their teenager navigate the complex world of adolescence and come out the other side strong in their own identity, participating in life and contributing to others.

Caroline Penney, systemic family therapist and author of The *Parenting Toolkit: simple steps to happy and confident children*

It's a rare book about children or teens that becomes more and more relevant as time goes on. This is not just one of them, it is **the** one. Whenever I am asked by parents trying to unravel their teens behaviour, 'Is that normal?' I have recommended Between Form and Freedom with a confidence that it will give them the understanding they need, to open up a path toward deeper and enduring connection with their child.

Kim John Payne M. Ed Author of *Games Children Play II*, *Waldorf Games for the Early Years*, *The Soul of Discipline*, *Simplicity Parenting* and *Being at Your Best When Your Kids Are at Their Worst*

An excellent book, that is enlightening, inspiring and an essential guide for parents and teachers of adolescents. With a wide range of experience and expertise, Betty Staley offers a wise and practical approach in how we can support developing adolescents to tackle the many changes and current issues facing them in these challenging times of learning to become an adult, such as—power, relationships, self-esteem, alcohol, drugs, body image and social media. Examples from adolescents, nutshell summaries for each chapter, and study questions are interesting and helpful, promoting reflection, discussion and guidance for action.

Robin Steele PhD. Mother of adult children, grandmother of adolescents, retired early childhood teacher, parent educator, psychophonetics psychotherapist and trainer

BETWEEN FORM AND FREEDOM

RAISING A TEENAGER

Betty Staley

Hawthorn Press

Published by Hawthorn Press, Hawthorn House, 1 Lansdown Lane, Stroud, Gloucestershire, GL5 1BJ, United Kingdom
Tel: 01453 757040 Email: info@hawthornpress.com web: www.hawthornpress.com

Cover design by Jason Conway
Design and typesetting by Mach 3 Solutions Ltd (www.mach3solutions.co.uk)
Printed by Severnprint Ltd, Gloucestershire

Printed on environmentally friendly chlorine-free paper sourced from renewable forest stock.

British Library Cataloguing in Publication Data applied for ISBN 978-1-912480-72-2

FSC
www.fsc.org
MIX
Paper from
responsible sources
FSC® C014540

Contents

Betty Staley is an educator, international lecturer, and author of eight books. She pioneered bringing Waldorf education into public schools in the United States, as well as helping to found six high schools.

At the heart of her work is her interest in child and adolescent development, curriculum development, teacher education, and biography.

Dedication

I dedicate this book to the Sacramento Waldorf School, particularly the first graduating class, the class of 1978.

I met these students as first graders when I was their handwork teacher. When I became their seventh-grade teacher, it was not a difficult transition since we had a history of warmth and familiarity. They responded enthusiastically to the curriculum and creatively took up each challenge. The class wrote their eighth-grade play based on the story 'The King of Ireland's Son'. We took it on the road and performed at the Vancouver Waldorf School and on Vancouver Island. At the end of eighth grade, they and their parents wanted the school to begin a high school. I agreed to take up that challenge.

The class was convinced, and probably correctly, that I could not successfully establish the high school without them. They still remember that I gave them an Art History test that took eleven hours. I tried to stop them from finishing it, but they insisted. It took them several days to complete it. I learned an important lesson, and they got to impress me with all they had learned. Toward the end of ninth grade they presented me with a petition that had many questions that I had to answer on the spot. The last one was, 'Do you know what you are doing?'.

They were an exciting group, not always easy, but clearly there to sharpen my skills in teaching and working with adolescents. During their Junior year (11th grade), along with the tenth graders, we traveled to the East Coast by bus. We toured nine Waldorf schools and performed music at each school. It awakened the students to another part of the country, and several now live on the East Coast.

Each year we had a camping or back-packing trip in the beautiful Sierra Nevada, including a terrifying one during their senior year when the brakes on the bus failed as we were driving downhill on a twisting road.

Thanks to Kenneth Melia, our beloved science teacher and bus driver, the bus was brought to a stop, leaning against the side of the hill right before the road continued on without side rails. We sang our way down to a bar, where the students and I stayed while Kenneth and Leon Matthews drove carefully to Visalia to deliver the damaged bus and return with a new one many hours later.

The first graduating class, 'The Pioneers', now 60-years-old, set many traditions at the Sacramento Waldorf School. We have continued to meet for reunions and share our lives, including honoring the passing of two members of the class.

I continued at Sacramento Waldorf School for 14 more years, teaching hundreds of other teenagers. I was advisor to three more classes, and I feel very close to those students as well. I am deeply grateful to the years we shared and continue to share, as well as to my colleagues who were part of the formative years of the high school.

The Sacramento Waldorf School has been my professional home from 1966 to 1992. My children and grandchildren have graduated from the school. September 2020 was the first opening school day in which there was no member of my family either as a teacher or student participating. Without the experiences at the Sacramento Waldorf School, I could not have written *Between Form and Freedom*.

Betty Staley 2021

Acknowledgements

There are many people who have helped to make this book possible. Since it is based on my years of parenting and teaching, I could not have written it without the support of Franklin Kane and Jim Staley, my children Andrea, George, and Sonya, and my colleagues at Sacramento Waldorf School and Rudolf Steiner College.

Julia Connor came up with the title *Between Form and Freedom* for a workshop, and I thought it was perfect for a book on adolescence. I thank her for her permission to use it. Since its first use in 1988, readers have encouraged me to keep the main title, even though subtitles have changed. More recently, the title was used for the first Asian upper-school conference in the Philippines.

Martin Large at Hawthorn Press, Stroud, UK has been a steady supporter over the years, and he has made it possible for the third edition and an e-book to happen.

Preface

I think I've always been a teacher. When I was eleven, I gathered children from my neighborhood on the stoop to teach them. Because my neighbors saw me doing this, a parent hired me to teach Charles, but when we played handball instead of focusing on spelling, I was fired.

I lived in a multi-ethnic lower-class neighborhood in the Bronx, New York. This was before drugs changed life in the city, but drunks loitered on the corners and sometimes chased us, gangs owned some of the streets, and we had to know where to walk and when. School was a haven of safety, and I idolized my teachers and loved learning.

My third-grade class chore was to oversee books in our class library. Stanley had ripped pages in a book, and Ms Knox, a student teacher whom I adored, decided that this was a good time to teach us about the judicial system. She set up a court trial, and I was a witness. The great day came, and Stanley's grandmother, with whom he lived, attended, thinking this was a class play. When it became clear that the students on the jury would decide his fate, she stood up, walked toward us menacingly, and was escorted out of the room. The jury's verdict was that Stanley would not be allowed on class trips for the rest of the year. From then on, I detoured around the street where Stanley lived, hoping to avoid his grandmother.

I don't remember whether our teacher carried out the penalty, but I remember how guilty I felt, as well as disappointed that my adored teacher would do something that didn't feel right for children of my age.

Years later when I substitute-taught in Harlem, an older teacher took me aside and told me, 'Just keep them busy. Don't worry about trying to teach them anything.'

These two experiences, years of working at camps and neighborhood centers, as well as college psychology classes, left me with the conviction that education was flawed. Children deserved better, and I wasn't sure that my becoming a teacher would serve them well.

That changed when Dr Stewart Easton, history professor at City College of New York, told me about Waldorf education. The more he spoke about it, showed me student work, and answered questions, the more interested I became. This was an education that understood child development. A Waldorf teacher would not teach third graders about the judicial system by having them judge their peers.

During Waldorf teacher training I was introduced to the view of child development in Rudolf Steiner's Anthroposophy (or Spiritual Science), and I participated actively in music, art, crafts, and eurythmy. That year changed my life. In the next four years, my husband and I moved back to the USA, I became a mother of two, and I deepened my understanding of Waldorf education.

After a move to California, I began teaching. During 27 years at the Sacramento Waldorf School, teaching handwork, kindergarten, and elementary grades, and starting the high school where I taught history and literature, I was deeply immersed in all stages of child development. I began writing articles and doing workshop presentations in Waldorf schools and in universities.

When I moved full-time to Rudolf Steiner College in 1993, I taught teacher education for 20 years, including summer courses for practicing public school teachers. In addition to teaching future teachers for independent Waldorf schools, my work intensified in diversified educational areas such as heading the committee to develop the first public Waldorf school serving inner-city children in Milwaukee, adapting the Waldorf curriculum for adjudicated youth in Marysville, California, helping establish public independent Waldorf elementary and high schools, and setting up committees for multi-cultural curriculum development.

By sharing conference presentations with Joseph Chilton Pearce, David Elkind, Elliot Eisner, and participating in a think-tank with Ernest Boyer of the Carnegie Foundation, I connected more strongly with the education issues of our time. I gained an international perspective on education by working in Latvia, Russia, Finland, Thailand, Kenya, and Holland. Twice, I was keynote presenter at World Waldorf Conference in Switzerland.

Preface

How does this relate to writing *Between Form and Freedom*? The book has a long history, beginning in 1978 as an idea for a general book on parenting, and shifting to adolescence because of the growing need to understand this age. During the writing of the first edition (1988), my three children and a foster son had reached adulthood, and I had experienced divorce and remarriage, along with step-family challenges.

By the time of the second edition in 2009, the world around families was facing the accelerating challenges of drugs, eating disorders, media, and behavioral disorders. I paid more attention to the middle school age, which was becoming a great concern. I spent five years researching and observing classes, culminating in the publication of *Tending the Spark: Lighting the Future for Middle School Students* (2019).

My interest in human development as well as in curriculum has inspired me to write other books: *Tapestries: Weaving Life's Journey*; *Soul Weaving*; *Adolescence — the Sacred Passage*; *Africa — a Teacher's Guide*; and *Splinters of the Sun: Teaching Russian Literature to High School Students*.

I have written the third edition of *Between Form and Freedom* because new issues such as sexual identity, the autism spectrum, screen dependence, and adolescent depression and anxiety have become everyday issues.

When we bring together neuroscience with the Waldorf approach to child development, we have a powerful way of understanding and helping children and adolescents. Parents, teachers, and counselors have responded strongly to past editions of *Between Form and Freedom*, and have shared how it has become a 'go-to companion'. I hope it will help you also.

Foreword

Can you remember your teens? For me, it was such a roller coaster. There were wonderful highs — being wildly in love, and just occasionally, having that love reciprocated! Being out in the big world on my own terms — climbing mountains, hitchhiking across the country, feeling free and alive under big skies. And also, times of real danger, inner and outer, not knowing who I was, or where I fitted in, or if anyone really cared. Being a terrible worry to my parents, and alone and unfitted to the world. Times of aching loneliness. Then finding caring people who understood me as a young soul just being born, needing to talk, explore, be accepted and valued; raw and unformed as I still was.

Though perhaps roller coaster is a bad metaphor, because a fairground ride is over quite fast and you can get off at the end. With adolescence, it's like there is no going back. You wonder, is this my life? When will it ever calm down again? For parent and adolescent alike, this time of life can scare the daylights out of you.

Betty Staley is something quite out of the box. A wise woman who has been around teenagers for half a century, in tough situations like corrections agencies, as well as gentle ones like Steiner Waldorf schools, and everything in between.

She operates from a tradition within the Steiner world where deep and detailed attention has always been paid to developmental stages, and where there is this profound understanding: that there is an *unfolding* happening, along ancient and organic lines, within the body and mind of a young person. There is a pattern, like the seasons of the year or the growth of a flower into a fruit, and what is really needed is a culture that supports this. Teenagers are doing what comes naturally, and we can provide for this without bewilderment or drama, but trusting and being steady and comfortable as they stumble, struggle, and find their way. And we can even be inspired and rejuvenated alongside them.

Even if you are a totally un-Steinerish person, wary of doctrines or world-views other than the purely mechanistic or secular, you can treat this book as you might a visit to another culture, noticing that there are wisdoms that we have lost, or never had; that within just a couple of pages, your senses are sharpened and your appreciation of subtle changes in your teenager is heightened. Betty Staley has been thinking about and loving difficult teenagers since before most of us were born, and yet her perception is entirely fresh and up to the minute.

Hanging out with her in these pages will make you more open and alive to the young people you love, and that will make many good things happen.

Steve Biddulph
Author of *Fully Human*, *Raising Boys*,
and *Ten Things Girls Need Most*

Introduction

The world adolescents are entering is very different from past decades. The changes have been fast-paced and challenging, and teenagers have to find their way through the maelstrom. At the time when they are entering the search for selfhood, the world around them is making this journey more and more arduous. Parents, teachers, and helping professionals have to be awake, work together, and support communities around children and teenagers.

We have often spoken of the village that is needed to bring consistency, love, and direction to the young people in our care. However, we don't live in villages any more. Our lives are demanding, and there is separation between our families, our schools, and our community. Yet every child has to make the journey through childhood into adolescence, crossing through dangerous times as they make their way into adulthood. How do factors along the way influence the journey, and what have we to do with it? Some factors are protective, appropriate for the stage of adolescent development; but some factors are risks that can threaten the well-being of teenagers. Although there are hazards, our hope is that overall, our young people will be resilient and able to cope with the challenges they meet.

Teenagers are meeting the 21st century. Who are they? What is the nature of their soul life, their thinking, feeling and willing? What is the world that adolescents meet in their families, friends, school, and other relationships? What are the trials they face as they encounter temptations, struggle with body image, food issues, self-esteem, alcohol and drugs, and the onslaught of the media?

This book explores these topics as a way of supporting teenagers in their journey. Children are growing up too soon, making their own decisions about what to do and have. They are pushing away form or structure and blasting their way toward freedom. Unfortunately, they don't yet have the capacities to handle the responsibility that freedom brings. The lack of rites of passage or adult guidance leaves them on their own. However, each youngster has a core of beauty, truth, and goodness that is part of their being.

This *spark* has to be protected in the middle school years and inspired during the high school years so that they will bring clear thinking, compassion, discipline, and idealism into adulthood.

Adolescents swing between form and freedom in finding their center. The great changes expressed in the sacred passage at around 16 or 17 offer them a way to focus on whom they are becoming and how they will get there. In this third crisis of selfhood, it makes all the difference what experiences teenagers have and how they traverse the pitfalls.

Our job as adults is to be present for adolescents through the process, not doing it for them, but indicating different pathways they might choose. We stand by and carefully observe as they rebel against form, seeking as much freedom as they can get. Only as they mature, do they realize that true freedom is different from what they thought in their adolescent years.

Adults are also caught in the conflict between form and freedom, moving from one extreme to the other — being too restrictive or too loose, putting high expectations and pressure, or leaving them too free without guidance. We need to develop trust in the process of growth and act as appropriately as we can.

The reader may wonder why in several chapters I describe the development from early childhood through adolescence instead of focusing only on the teenage years. I believe we gain a deeper understanding of adolescence when we regard the first 21 years as a whole. It is also helpful for parents, teachers, and helping professionals who are working with children of all ages to grasp the patterns that occur in each phase.

My work has been inspired by the insights of Rudolf Steiner, Austrian philosopher and scientist (1861–1925). Steiner's worldview is called *anthroposophy*, or *spiritual science*, and is based on a spiritual perception of the universe. Throughout the book, I offer insights from his work which I find to be particularly helpful. Even if readers are not interested in pursuing these thoughts further, I believe they will find them helpful in working with teenagers.

The work I am drawing upon includes over 35 years of teaching adolescents in Waldorf schools, decades of preparing teachers for high-school teaching, organizing state-supported Waldorf schools, adapting Waldorf education to court and community schools serving adjudicated teenagers, and working with parent groups. I am still active in working with teachers in public and private Waldorf schools, observing in classrooms, and meeting with parent groups. All of these activities have intensified my feelings that this generation is ready for the task ahead of them, but they need our help. I hope *Between Form and Freedom* in its third edition will contribute to these efforts.

As the third edition of *Between Form and Freedom* gets ready to launch, I think (somberly?) of our young people with concern. Now, entering the third year of the Covid-19 pandemic, they are challenged as no generation before. Past wars have been terrible events, casting their shadow on children and adolescents. However, the events of 2020–21 have been a different kind of war.

Some factors that have affected the younger generation are:

- The fears around the Covid-19 Global Pandemic — the numbers of people dying alone, then the polarization around the vaccines and masks, and the hope of overcoming the virus dashed by emerging variants — exhausted many people.
- The issues raised on social media led to questions of, 'What is true? False? What is a conspiracy theory? Who do I believe?'
- The virus had an effect on education. Children and teens were unclear when they would attend school in person or when they would stay at home during lockdown. Graduations, proms, and other celebrations were cancelled. Long periods of isolation affected socialization and personal development.
- Climate change caused shifts around the world — fires, floods, drought, weather shifts. Fears of what the future will bring affected this generation as it comes into their adulthood. Teenagers wrestle with questions arising such as whether they should have children,

whether there is any purpose in planning their careers, or even any purpose in living. Why bother? On the other hand they ask, 'What can we do to make a difference?'

- A series of cultural and political events such as (racial) civil unrest across the United States, the killing of George Floyd, Black Lives Matter, the effects of colonialism and immigration, threats to democracy such as the violence at the US Capitol on January 6th 2021, and the contested history school curriculum, all created a turbulent world for teachers, students, parents and communities to navigate.
- Social media enabled cyber bullying, manipulation through Facebook and Instagram, and the addictive use of YouTube and video games. These affected the increase of mental health issues such as teenage depression and anxiety at levels not previously seen.

As we read this book, let us take these issues and context into consideration.

Note: Teenagers are looking at sexual identity in a new way. Each one asks to be referred to by a specific pronoun. This makes writing a difficult task. I have used 'he', 'she', and 'they' in particular chapters according to the subject. I even varied the pronouns within a chapter so that the images would not be fixed on one identity. I hope this is not too confusing. The reader should feel free to change the pronouns as they seem to fit.

Part I

The Nature of Adolescence

Chapter 1

How do you get to be an adolescent?

Phases in Child Development

> Our birth is but a sleep and a forgetting.
> The soul that rises with us, our life's Star,
> Hath elsewhere its setting,
> And cometh from afar;
> Not in entire forgetfulness,
> And not in utter nakedness,
> But trailing clouds of glory do we come
> From God, who is our home.
>
> William Wordsworth

The child enters life

In this beautiful poem, William Wordsworth shares a living imagination of human incarnation. Our birth is a sleep and a forgetting — yet so often we think of our birth as a waking and the world we have left behind as enclosed in a dark sleep. Ancient cultures spoke of a golden world left behind when the soul descended to earth. The earth, the new home, was then experienced as a land of shadows.

When we are born, we forget the world that has previously been our home. Gradually we come to know our new home — this beautiful planet Earth which sustains us.

Although most of us do not remember our pre-birth state, dim memories live within the soul and emerge from time to time as the child grows and comes to accept the imperfections of the everyday earthly world.

Life unfolds in seven-year rhythms, and each of these life-phases has a special quality. During each, some capacities are lost and others gained, and during the middle of each, the child experiences a crisis.

The child's thinking is very different in each phase, which means that learning is radically different, depending on the child's age. In the first stage between birth and age seven, the child thinks through doing and learns through imitation. Between 7 and 14, the child thinks in images and learns through feelings. Between 14 and 21, the young person thinks conceptually and learns through the intellect.

The first phase: birth to seven

During the first seven years, children's energies are directed to growing, walking, speaking, and thinking, as they establish themselves in the family. The love and care surrounding the young child lead them securely into the world, minimizing the dangers and welcoming them into the human community.

Young children explore the world by imitating the actions of others. They crawl, walk, run, dig, and throw. All the time they are becoming familiar with the earth, their new home. Young children are connected to the world through their will-activity and through their senses. They take in all that meets them through their senses, and imitate what is in their environment.

As soon as someone in the environment is doing something — chopping wood, hammering nails, beating eggs — young children want to do it also. They throw themselves into the tasks with gusto. They also imitate negative behavior — a clenched fist, a slap, or a growl.

Changes in the brain and the young child's emotional state are influenced by the care a toddler receives, and this determines the child's world view, sense of self, impulse control, and the ability to relate to others.

Child-care workers are able to predict troublesome teenage behavior by the gestures and attitude of young children in their care. Already at this young age, these children feel angry, abandoned, distrusting, and trying to survive in a hostile environment.

By the seventh year, this phase comes to a conclusion. The child's physical body is basically complete. The child has mastered the human abilities on which the rest of life will depend — the ability to walk, to speak, and to think.

The second phase: age 7–14

The second phase is the heart of childhood. It begins and ends with a new state of consciousness expressed through physical and psychological changes. The marked physical growth of the first phase of childhood comes to a final expression in the change of teeth — from the uniformly shaped milk-teeth, already under the baby's gums at birth, to the individually shaped second teeth. The second phase ends with changes in the brain, the maturation of the sexual organs, changes in the larynx, a growth in the limbs, and increased activity of the thyroid gland.

During the second phase — from age 7 to 14 — the individual's soul life develops. Children leave the security of the family and venture into the larger world of neighborhood and school. They come to feel at home in the wider circle of their community. They relate to this new world with their feelings, which are expressed in extremes. One hour they are happy; the next hour they are sad. They love you, they hate you. They say 'no'; they say 'yes'. They feel powerful; they feel powerless. Parents are overcome by the rush of intense feelings which the child expresses. The minute parents try to deal with those feelings, the child's mood changes, leaving the adult nursing confused and hurt feelings, unsure what the youngster was actually trying to express.

The child's feeling life is developed in private, in a world of dreams, hopes, and fantasies. As their inner worlds develop, they begin to have secrets. The two worlds — the inner private and the outer public one

— interact, causing tension as children slowly learn to feel comfortable in both worlds.

Because the child approaches the world in this way, the most natural way of learning is through the feelings.

As children experience their new feelings, they show an increased interest in adventure stories. Their imaginations are filled with picture images, and their state of consciousness is a dream state where one image follows another without logical sequence. They relish the swing of emotions they experience while listening to or reading stories filled with terror and suspense. Indeed, the kind of thinking children do during this time is *picture thinking,* filled with vivid descriptions of smells, tastes, sights, sounds, and actions. Out of this kind of thinking, they develop *a sense* for things rather than an *understanding* of things.

Around the ninth year, children experience what is often referred to as the 'nine-year change'. It signals the end of the second crisis of childhood. It is a time when they begin to feel separated from their families and friends, and when they see themselves as outsiders. It is a time of moodiness, when nothing seems to be the way it used to be. As they come through this period and regain balance, they enter the heart of childhood — usually around age 10 or 11.

Because puberty is happening earlier than in the past, averaging at age 12 when girls begin menstruating, and boys experience wet dreams, this period is often shortened, and children enter a time of pre-adolescence, or middle school (in the United States, classes sixth through eighth grade).

The youngsters are no longer children and not yet adolescents. At the same time, major neurological changes are happening, with different parts of the brain affected through growth spurts of neurons, myelination, and frontal-lobe development. Since middle-schoolers have only completed part of their emotional and neurological maturity, it is no wonder that they are erratic and confused. Everything seems new and exciting, but they lack discernment in how to identify priorities or gain control over newly experienced instinctual drives.

Around 11 years of age, picture thinking begins to fade, and children begin to find power in their thinking, enjoying arguing, exploring language, approaching their environment in an objective way, and entering the world of concepts and understanding.

The habits, attitudes, self-image, and social skills they have developed are challenged during this time of chaos. I refer to this period as the 'Vulnerability Gap', when youngsters aged 11 to 15 are at the mercy of powerful forces of advertising, bullying, sexuality, and media. It is a time when teachers, parents, coaches, and other adults working with them need to model behavior of integrity, fairness, idealism, and compassion. As a society, we need to decide what kind of a culture we want to have for the future. Will we leave young people in freedom without guidance? Will we force rigid forms on them? Our challenge will be to help them overcome their instincts and develop what neuroscientist Elkhonon Goldberg called 'the Civilizing Mind'.[1]

The third phase: age 14 to 21

The third phase, 14 to 21, is the 'official' period of adolescence. During this phase, children learn through their intellect. They experience the range of human emotions, ideals, goals, and expressions of personality, and begin to consciously use their thinking to guide their emotional life. With the second growth spurt of neurons, their neurological development is enhanced, and they are able to reflect on their actions, begin the development of executive function, and take hold of their lives. The third crisis occurs at age 16–17. Through the interaction of thinking, feeling, and will, teenagers prepare for the spiritual birth of the individual self, the ego or 'I', somewhere around the 21st year. Childhood is now completed.

In a Nutshell

How do you get to be an adolescent?

- Life unfolds in seven-year phases; in each phase, some capacities are lost and others are gained.
- During the middle of each phase the child experiences a crisis.
- The first phase: birth to 7 — children think and learn by *doing*.
- The second phase: 7–14 — children think and learn through *feeling*.
- The third phase: 14–21 — the adolescent learns through *thinking*.

Chapter 2

Stages of adolescence

The world stands out on either side
No wider than the heart is wide;
Above the world is stretched the sky, —
No higher than the soul is high.
The heart can push the sea and land
Farther away on either hand;
The soul can split the sky in two,
And let the face of God shine through.
                    Edna St. Vincent Millay

The Stage Is Set for Negation and Affirmation

For the youngster, adolescence is new territory, uncharted and unex-
plored. Even parents often feel as if they are trying to navigate this
unknown territory without a map. Imagine how the adolescent feels!

Adolescent development occurs in two recognizable phases which
can be referred to as 'negation' and 'affirmation'. In the first phase —
negation — adolescents want to oppose everything. They want to refute
and criticize the world. In the second stage — affirmation — adolescents try to find their way into the life of the outer world. The polarity
which expresses itself during adolescence is similar to an earlier polarity
expressed when 3-year-olds said 'No' to everything, followed by 4 to
5-year-olds embracing the world with a mighty 'Yes'.

Negation

In the beginning of adolescence, teenagers are searching for their spiritual home, which expresses itself unconsciously as an undefined inner longing for something they cannot yet define. They look for what is wonderful or perfect, and when it cannot be found they feel let down and disillusioned. Then the outer world seems strange and disappointing. As a result, they see ugliness where they had expected beauty. They see human weakness where they had expected perfection. This is frustrating and depressing.

They become defiant, test everything and everyone, particularly anyone representing authority. They oppose everything that is out in the world, and side with the underdog, especially against adults. Most teenagers go through this stage, feeling that adults don't understand them. Some feel the loneliness and isolation more strongly, and think adults are unworthy of respect. Although they may behave quite intolerably to the adult, they are overly sensitive if that same adult should do anything to cause them discomfort. A pained, withdrawn, and hostile response is evoked: 'No one understands me'.

It is not unusual for cynicism to develop out of unfulfilled expectations. Some adolescents never recover from their initial disappointment in the world. As adults, they feel justified in abusing other people to compensate for the previous hurts and disappointments they have suffered.

Because they are still immature and have not developed their executive function, adolescents in this stage have difficulty monitoring their behavior. They react without thinking, may be rude, and in extreme cases are capable of violent action. Such teens can be outrageously rude, set a house on fire, or even pull a trigger. Joining a gang offers them a group to belong to, protection, social connections, and shared feelings of being victims.

Most teenagers go through a time of negation, even if it is mildly experienced and expressed. Teenagers who are introverted may retreat from the world and even harm themselves through cutting or starving themselves.

While these are extreme reactions, many adolescents often have times of feeling removed from other people, and they wonder whether anyone anywhere thinks or feels as they do. They question whether there is a true friend out there for them, and the search for a friend becomes an overwhelming priority in their lives. More than anything, during this time of negation they need an adult who listens, models interest and concern, and has compassion.

The role of the crush

Adolescents feel something akin to the Romantic Era in history, wishing to feel part of nature, as in Shelley's 'Ode to the West Wind':

> Make me thy lyre, even as the forest is:
> What if my leaves are falling like its own!
> The tumult of thy mighty harmonies
> Will take from both a deep, autumnal tone.
> Sweet though in sadness. Be thou, Spirit fierce,
> My spirit! Be thou me, impetuous one!

Because the adolescent's soul has become free with intense feelings, she unconsciously searches for her lost spiritual home — although many young people have deeply religious experiences, which they usually keep private or share with only a trusted few.

The young adolescent longs to meet a kindred spirit who comes out of the spiritual world. How many songs describe the soulmate as an angel or one who comes out of a dream? The soul realizes that he does not yet fit into the physical world, and she yearns for a creature to help them feel whole again.

The search for the spirit expresses itself in the soul life as a 'crush'. In this state, the person being adored does not have to be near. In fact, to adore from a distance is more satisfying because the adored one is not subjected to scrutiny but is held up to be worshiped, with God-like qualities often projected on to the person. A well-known example in literature is Dante's love of Beatrice.

Teenagers model themselves after popular media stars and musicians, but also on people closer to them such as relatives, family, teachers, coaches, and friends. In addition, they tend to choose movie and television stars, rock stars, sports stars, camp counselors, older students, or historical figures. In the USA, more recently Justice Ruth Bader Ginsburg ('the Notorious RBG') has become a favorite because of her long fight for women's rights in the justice system. Greta Thunberg has sparked an idealistic following for her call for climate change. It is always sad to see situations where sports stars have disappointed teenagers because of claims of sexual harassment or violent behavior.

In the crush, the object adored represents perfection. This helps the adolescent deal with the disappointment that the world is not perfect.

Sometimes, a best friend fills a similar role as the adored one, and the two merge their identities, doing everything together. They dress alike, enjoy the same music, share the same observations about people, and cling to each other in the storm of life. In the crush, adolescents feel the reflection of the higher world; 'heaven' is in their hearts. Between age 13 and 15, the crush reaches its greatest intensity, although it may continue on into the late teens.

The crush may be projected on to an activity or an idea as well as on to a person. Teenagers can become fanatically devoted to a game and lose all sense of time. The game may involve a complicated system of rewards and punishments through which the youngsters can test their intellectual skill, or the game may be based on chance, which has its own excitement. They may devote themselves to a sport with similar fanaticism, using every possible moment in the day to shoot baskets, practice pitching, or kick a soccer ball.

Sports have helped many teenagers get through the early adolescent period without becoming too obsessed with themselves. If the adults concerned with the sport create an atmosphere of support, cooperation, and camaraderie, the youngsters can receive great benefit. If, on the other hand, adults foster cut-throat competition, creating pressure on the teenager to win at all costs, they are doing nothing to help the youngster move out of self-obsession, but are in fact intensifying unhealthy self-preoccupation. Some youngsters become addicted to what started out as a crush such as a video game, but they become obsessive and lose connection to everyday life.

. With a crush, something evokes the kinds of feelings that may have been experienced in a far simpler way in the childhood experience of God. That something may be a person — either close-by or unattainable. At some point, however, adolescents can no longer keep the adored object at a distance. They must connect personally. Teenagers fantasize about how the connection will be made, how they and the object of their worship will come together. The youngster may imagine becoming a tragic figure who lives and dies for an idea or a love. Perhaps the teenager will be the only person in the crowd noticed by the cherished singer. This fantasy meeting between the adolescent and the object of adoration carries a storm of emotions which is of great importance for the further development of the individual, and it leads the adolescent over to the second stage of adolescence — affirmation.

Thus, the first love — be it baseball, a cultural hero, or an older person — is often the bridge from the stage of negation to the stage of affirmation at about 15 or 16. No experience will ever have quite the impact on the young person as does this event. Its power lies in the innocence and freshness of the experience. However, the kind of influence this strong experience has on the developing person depends on the way the crush is resolved.

Transition

The 15–16th year is the transition time for adolescents. This usually begins to happen at the end of tenth grade and the beginning of eleventh grade. It can be a dangerous time when teenagers are so dissatisfied with where they are, and they believe it will never change. Life is better elsewhere. They may choose to leave their school, their friends, and even run away from home, hang out with a dangerous group of friends, or harm themselves through cutting, drugs, alcohol, or becoming sexually promiscuous. They feel more comfortable with other teenagers who feel the same way, and they dress like them, listen to the same music, and feel isolated. In some ways, this period is similar to the nine-year change, an earlier time of transition when children felt the loss of childhood. Now they feel a more existential loss, that life itself is not worth living.

It is especially important at this time that adults hang in there, keep connected with their teenagers, find momentary points of contact, and try to support them in their difficulties. Help from outside is sometimes more effective than parents, and professional help is needed. Every attempt should be made to find the right kind of support to help the youngster through this period of isolation.

In many cases, time is the best solution, and maturity, the development of executive function, and a gradual acceptance that the world is not all black or white marks a time of change.

At this time, teenagers are coming out of the extreme of being either too withdrawn or too aggressive, and are beginning to laugh more, to feel accepted, to be accepting, to be friendly and outgoing, to be more communicative, to relate better to teachers and parents, to understand their siblings, and to begin to accept the world as it is.

During this transition they start to question who they are, their identity, their goals, their stance in life. They try out different groups of friends, constantly connect through their phones, explore their sexuality, and feel pressure to conform. Those who are isolated in a group may have a hard time finding where they belong in the social life of school.

One of the problems of the transitional period is the attempt to do too much. In their eagerness to embrace the world, teenagers often take on too many commitments, which they then have trouble honoring, or they take on such difficult challenges that they have difficulty living up to expectations. They try to think about too many things or plan too many activities, and there is simply not enough time to do everything. This exuberance and confidence also leads them to experiment with danger. The 15-year-olds often take risks and test limits, not so much out of insecurity, as a 13-year-old would, but because they want to taste life.

Affirmation

After this time of transition, the way is prepared for the stage of affirmation, which comes around age 16 or 17. The stage of affirmation is characterized by the transformation of love from early sensuality and self-interest to love for another human being and for the world in general, for affirmation is not limited to the love of a person. At this point, adolescents begin to search for ideas, or for a picture of the world with which they can be comfortable. The stage of affirmation is the time when the search for truth begins. Adolescents now search for religious answers, for ideal political systems, and for the next step in their education. They also become concerned about their future careers.

In the earlier period, young adolescents are not familiar with the world. What they experience is discomfort, separateness, hostility, and opposition. This evokes distrust and even hatred from youngsters. Slowly, however, teenagers begin to question, analyze, criticize, and doubt, and gradually the distrust and hostility toward the world is transformed into a longing to do great deeds for the world. The young people come to express joy in the world.

This is often stimulated by powerful experiences in nature. The teenager feels how good it is to be alive, and a period of stability follows in which they feel less tense and less hypersensitive. At the same time, teenagers who are awake to what is happening in the world feel the great burden to do something about climate change, racism, and the political and social mistreatment of children or animals. In order for them not to feel overwhelmed, it is helpful for them to join groups that are trying to rectify these situations. For example, an 11th grade girl chose to do community service in a local food bank and a program for refugee children. She described how much she learned and how satisfying it was to be helping people in need.

As teenagers gain confidence and comfort with themselves, they become more realistic about life. They begin to appreciate their freedom and respect their responsibilities. With that change comes a sense of humor and patience. Relationships with parents and siblings become more comfortable (although teenagers still prefer to be with their friends).

Parents are appreciated and cherished, and adolescents begin to feel free to approach them for advice, feeling less threatened and more able to participate in the give-and-take without losing their identities. Adolescents become more self-reliant and more poised. Life becomes relatively peaceful, and fewer arguments occur. Sometimes older adolescents comment that their parents are becoming smarter or wiser, or at least easier to live with.

As time passes, crushes fade, and in their place come real-life relationships. More immature teenagers may hold on to their crushes for a longer time. At this time, tables turn and the older adolescents become the object of crushes from younger teenagers. It can be amusing to watch eleventh and twelfth graders deal with the admiration of the seventh, eighth, or ninth graders. Not sure how to handle the situation, the older students often try to be sensitive in the way they respond to their youthful admirers.

Late adolescence; 18 to 21

When teenagers step across the threshold of their 18th birthdays, they enter young adulthood and are ready for responsibilities. Learning and maturity now become based on life experience. The focus of their development lies in finding a relationship to their times, to their culture in which they are living, and to the people who embody the ideals and values of their time.

Whether the young adult is working at a job or attending the last year of high school, college or university, there is the need to make a personal mark on life, to see what the limits are, to find one's mentors. It is important during this time to develop social skills, to make strong personal connections with people. These are the years in which the young adult finds career direction, is exposed to new interests, travels, experiments with living arrangements, and works at a variety of intimate social relationships.

Young adults should not make commitments that tie them down. This should be a time of developing judgement, of flexibility, and of forming the picture of one's life. Youngsters who become tied to adult jobs and to family matters before age 21 become responsible adults, but they often take longer to find their direction. They need time to explore, change, and change again.

In my many years of teaching I have especially enjoyed communicating with former high-school students. The changes they go through in the three or four years after graduation are exciting and often unpredictable. Teenagers who were determined to go into one field of study turn 180 degrees and go in a different direction. They find so much that is new and challenging, that is calling to them, that is fascinating. Life, the great teacher, is so interesting for them, and it is wonderful to share their insights.

With the advent of social media, it has been possible to continue connections with those graduates and to follow their lives, their challenges and their successes. I often reflect on a particular former student who told her mother she hated her for making her change schools in ninth grade. Now, as a mature woman of 50, mother of three children, one of whom has health challenges, she expresses gratitude for her mother's wisdom and all that she has learned in her schooling. Students who made fun of school traditions or verses look back at them fondly in their later years and enjoy sharing reflections of their high-school years.

Those who feel tied down have a harder time exploring newer aspects of their personality. They, too, learn from life, but sometimes what they learn is quite discouraging. They may go from job to job, and grow quite frustrated when they find that it is not easy to support themselves. After the initial satisfaction of being on their own, there is a let-down. Why? Rather than discovering new aspects of themselves, they feel stifled and confined. They are not finding out who they are in the world. However, they should never give up on new possibilities arising when they least expect them.

Those who travel, study, work at an apprenticeship, or learn a craft are developing themselves as people. They are expanding their horizons and exploring their skills. Today's young generation has a hard time getting started. The economic recession has affected the job market so that many of them live with their parents and struggle to find jobs. The Covid-19 pandemic is affecting this generation in ways we don't even know yet.

Unlike past generations, many of our younger people, especially those who are well educated, look down on the idea of working their way up the ladder of a career, and want their work to be meaningful from the outset.

Chapter 2 — Stages of adolescence

Yet this new generation of young adults is filled with ideas, ideals, and hopes for the future. Through their ease in working with technology, embracing new ideas, and their ways of connecting with each other, they may have something important to offer society.

Dangers

It they are not presented with ideals or do not have feelings of comfort about their origin, if they do not find a close friend or object of love, if there is nothing that comes to take them out of self-preoccupation, adolescents can be drawn too strongly into the physical-sexual life as their main source of satisfaction. They are encouraged to do this by movies, television, radio, video games, advertising, and the prevalence of pornography. The budding young adult can become trapped into sexual preoccupation through overstimulation from outside. With nothing to balance this preoccupation, adolescents become hard and tough. They are thrust into eroticism or the will to power.

These young people have nothing to lift them out of their despair or sensuality so that their lives become a series of exploits, and few goals other than immediate pleasure or power. It is only in later years when they look back that they may wish they had pursued a different path.

When we study biographies, we can see how one special event, a meeting with a person, an experience with music, a kind word, a book given at the right moment, or an experience in nature, can shake these youngsters loose from the trap, and set them going on a wholesome and meaningful path. Those caught in poverty, minority discrimination, or crime often fall into a despair that drags them down unless they have one of the above experiences to free them.

Others get lost in video games, the internet, or pornography, getting together to replay the games they enjoyed as young teens and eating the junk food they loved at that time.

Drama can be a special help during this time. By stepping into another character, the young person can experience fear, compassion, terror, joy, and humor. In fear, the person breathes in most strongly. In loving devotion, the person breathes out. The rhythm of breathing out and breathing in of emotional experiences helps the soul establish its independence from the body in a healthful way. Through drama, adolescents are able to try out roles, experiment with anger, confrontation, sensitivity, compassion, and sacrifice, and to vicariously experience what happens to people in different life situations.

Another helpful area for teenagers is world events. By becoming familiar with the issues, by learning how different policies and attitudes are formed in response to complex circumstances, they begin to see where change can occur. Rather than becoming cynical, they may develop a hopeful attitude, probably because the involvement itself produces the experience of having an effect on events and circumstances. Although there is much in current life to be disheartened about, there are also great openings and possibilities to make change. Our young people are filled with hope, although they have inherited tremendous challenges.

Interest in the world is also expressed through interest in other cultures. Studying the myths of a culture allows youngsters to understand the ways people think. Studying cultural values provides youth with the possibility to reflect on their own cultural values. Such an interest often leads to greater understanding of humanity and an enhanced sense of brotherhood. We can already see this in their support of indigenous populations, in protests against colonialism, and support for those of different cultures who are struggling to survive.

Adolescents often come up with simple answers to life's complex problems, and adults smile at the naïve optimism that trips off the tongues of youth who want to save the world. However, the idealism of youth sets the stage for commitment and involvement during adult life. Interest in the outer world, in ideas, and in social issues also helps adolescents become free of the control which their bodies still have over them. Rather than being self-preoccupied, they become interested and involved in the outer world. According to Rudolf Steiner, interest in others is one of the first steps of spiritual development.

It is up to the adults who work with teenagers to stay idealistic in a balanced way. Any trace of cynicism dampens their enthusiasm and dams up their energy. Two quotations by Christopher Fry are helpful themes for adults who work with teenagers. The first is the demand for us to be awake and active, from his poem *A Sleep of Prisoners*:

> Thank God, our time is now when wrong
> comes up to meet us everywhere.
> Never to leave us till we take,
> The longest stride of soul we ever took.
> Affairs are now soul size.
> The enterprise
> Is exploration into God.
> Where are you making for? It takes
> So many thousand years to wake.
> But will you wake, for pity's sake!

The second quotation focuses on the greatest gift we have to nourish in our work with adolescents:

> The first of our senses which we should take care never to let rust through disuse is that sixth sense, the imagination. I mean the wide-open eye which leads us to see truth more vividly, to apprehend more broadly, to concern ourselves more deeply, to be, all our life long, sensitive and awake to the powers and responsibilities given to us as human beings.

Adolescence is not a stable time. It is a period of impermanence, conflicting values, new modes, and new ideas being tried out and discarded. It is a period loaded with possibility as in no other stage of life. So much energy, so much promise, so much concern for the future. Because adolescents do not fully experience objective reality until around the 21st year, firmness, understanding, patience, and love are needed from the adults to help them through this chaotic period.

In a Nutshell

Stages of adolescence

- Adolescence is not a stable time. It is a period of impermanence, conflicting values, new ways and new ideas being tried out and discarded.
- Adolescent development includes two phases: negation and affirmation.
- Negation: the adolescent wants to oppose everything.
- Adolescents experience the 'crush' as they model themselves on someone or something that represents perfection.
- The 15th–16th year is a time for transition, often a time of dissatisfaction and disappointment. Give them time.
- Affirmation: transformation of feelings and thinking. Emphasis is on the future
- Around age 18, stepping out into the world. Expanding horizons.
- There are dangers, and there are ways to help.

Chapter 3

The search for the self

What is it about man's being which causes him to strive for questions, for knowledge, for insight, for understanding of freedom? What is the role of tradition, or ritual, and ceremony? Why does man struggle to find meaning in life? Why is he not just content to carry out life meeting the basic needs of survival?

12th-grade boy

I am so grateful for my teachers who were there with interest and care and with time to guide me. They let me explode and allowed me to get a lot of unexplainable tension out of my system. They have radically affected my life and allowed me to see the meaning of so much. They have given me a feeling of real worth and meaning. They have given to me the love of being human and there is no other gift, nothing more noble or beautiful that could ever be passed from one person to another.

12th-grade girl

Who am I? Where have I come from? Is there a God? Is there meaning in the world? These questions become conscious in adolescence and live with us for the rest of our lives. When we feel insecure and separate from the people around us, when we feel spiritually threatened, these questions rise up to meet us. As we develop through the cycles of human life, we undergo change in the way we relate to the world. We become different in ourselves; old capacities fade, new capacities awaken. The old answers no longer satisfy us. As we move from one stage to another, we experience a transitional time when the old approach is no longer adequate, but the new attitude or soul-condition is not yet ripe. Transition periods create discomfort and crisis.

Three major crises

Three major crises occur during the first 21 years, and from then on, other crises continue during adult life, approximately every seven years. Each crisis is an opportunity for developing increased self-awareness and understanding. The Chinese pictogram for 'crisis' has two elements, one meaning 'danger' and the other meaning 'opportunity'. The crisis points in the middle of each seven-year period mark the time when the person makes major steps forward or backward — a time rich with opportunity and fraught with danger.

The third-year change

The first crisis occurs between ages 2 and 4. Until that time, children have experienced themselves as a part of the environment, and there has been no strong sense of separation. Everything in the environment is there to serve the child: to feed, clothe, shelter, love, and support every need that arises. After the second birthday, the child begins slowly to experience themselves as a separate body, and finds that the world may not be there to provide every need whenever they want. The anger that is felt is expressed by the name given to that period, 'The Terrible Twos'.

The child senses that they are no longer the center of the universe, but a separate being, an 'I'. This is manifested in the way that children refer to themselves. Previously, the child may have said, 'Johnnie wants that' or 'Sarah likes cookies'. During this period of transition, however, the mental process itself undergoes change. When the child hears the question 'Do you want another cookie?', a transition is made from 'you' to 'I', and the child responds, 'I want another cookie'.

The early experience of the 'I' is one of the miracles of human development.

The ego or 'I' forms the foundation of later psychological and mental growth. It leads to children's new experience as independent physical beings, physically independent of their parents, their houses, the fields, flowers, animals, and all else that is around them. Having come through this change, children gain confidence in themselves and enter the period known as 'The Fearless Fours'.

All children, except those with severe learning difficulties or those who have deep psychological disturbances, have a similar experience of the 'I'. They may not remember the process of change, but it is reflected in the change of speech, usually by the third birthday.

The experience of the 'I' is unconscious, streaming in from something in a higher region, becoming closer in adolescence, and becoming conscious around age 21.

The nine-year change

Seven years later, between the ages of 8 and 10, the second ego crisis in self-awareness occurs. The child has earlier experienced the physical separation, and now the separation of soul is experienced. Children come to sense that they are their own selves, that they have their own feelings and thoughts. They are not the same as other people; their thoughts and feelings are different. This leads at first to a feeling of loss, and even a concern about death.

They no longer feel what their parents are thinking and, even more, their parents cannot feel what they are thinking and wanting. They see that they have to explain what is going on inside of them, and they have to express their needs and wants clearly. This is very frustrating. It was so much easier when they were little and their parents anticipated their needs.

Out of this, they come to feel soul-loneliness. They yearn for the magic of childhood when small hills were mighty mountains, boulders were forts, animals spoke to them, and the people around them were grand heroes and heroines. Slowly, they are coming to see that the hill is only a hill, the rock is only a rock, and people have flaws. The magic is gone.

As Wordsworth says in his *Ode*, 'The things which I have seen, I now can see no more'. The commonplace has become the normal way of seeing. After every special occasion, one 9-year-old would say, 'Well, that wasn't very interesting'. Events which had been exciting to a younger child now had become too ordinary for words.

Adults may experience something of the loss of the magic of childhood when they return to places of their own early years. Everything is changed: the trees seem so much smaller, the path in the forest is only a scant trail in the bushes. The magic is gone, and the adult, too, is left with a nostalgic longing for what once was.

When children lose the capacity for seeing imaginatively, for seeing the glow around things and people, their focus on the things of the outer world becomes sharper. What was once bathed in beauty and warmth stands cold and unadorned in its objectiveness. It is as if the child's eyes are opening wide for the first time. Children begin to see what they never saw before: They see unfairness, narrow-mindedness, and inconsistency. Their adored adults topple from pedestals, and this upsets them. If parents are not perfect, who can children count on? They see imperfections in their teachers as well, and they feel confused. So they pull back and become aloof because they cannot understand what is happening.

They think about things that are forbidden. They feel temptation and guilt. They feel caught between a voice that encourages them to do naughty things and a voice that restrains them. The youngsters look at the world and see that, as Gilbert and Sullivan put it, 'things are seldom what they seem'. What is supposed to be good isn't always good, and what is supposed to be bad often has an enticing flavor to it.

They see that they can make choices in their lives, so they step out and start expressing what they want. 'I want this. I don't want that.' They try to exercise some control. They find, however, that they don't always get what they want. If they make certain choices, they are confronted with responsibility.

Ah! There's the rub! Choice can become a burden. They slowly understand that this new capacity has a price to it, and they aren't sure that is worth it. They begin to get the message that they cannot have both worlds — they cannot be treated like young children in a little child's world, and at the same time exercise more grown-up decisions. The dawning sense that they are accountable for what they do makes some of them want to crawl back into the safe womb of childhood, while others want to dive prematurely into the exciting teen world and prove themselves worthy.

They become critical of everything around them. Often, only their beloved cat or dog escapes being a target of this frustrated attention. 'I don't like you.' 'You're dumb.' 'You never keep promises.' 'You never let me do anything.' 'You're not fair.' Eight and 9-year-olds who are going through this change become sullen and moody. When asked if anything is bothering them, typical answers are 'No' and 'I don't know'.

The new relationship between the youngster and the parents is often expressed by two questions, 'Are you my real parents?' and 'What was I like as a baby?'. The first question comes from their feeling of separateness and loneliness. They may wonder if they were adopted. Because of this feeling, they often want to escape to the time when they felt safe and connected. They become fascinated with their own childhood and ask many questions. Some begin talking in baby-talk and resume babyish habits like wetting the bed or wanting to sleep with their parents.

The way the nine-year change is resolved has much to do with the way youngsters will enter adolescence several years later. *If* they find ways to gain self-confidence, and *if* they have trusted adults to turn to, then they tend to resolve the sense of separation and make peace with the world.

Parents should not panic when they experience the moodiness of their children during this time. They cannot protect them from the loss of innocence, but they can stand with them day after day as a loving support, helping them find their new relationship to the world.

So often in life when we suffer a loss, we also experience compensation. This is true with the nine-year change. Along with the confusion and frustrations that occur comes an increased ability to do things such as physical coordination, intellectual understanding, and interest in the world. The child has reached a balance between an active inner life and outer ability, which makes fourth and fifth grades (and sometimes sixth grade) glorious to teach. This is the heart of childhood.

Chapter 3 — The search for the self

As we know, life doesn't always go smoothly. If children do not gain self-confidence, if they do not have one trusted adult to turn to, if they cannot find a hopeful relationship, they assume an attitude which says, 'I don't care,' or 'I hate everything'. The despair of many drop-outs or criminals has its roots during this period. This attitude has been referred to as the dropout syndrome, especially for boys. Obviously, most nine-year-olds do not drop out of school, nor do they run away from home, take drugs, or decide that life isn't worth living. Their gestures say: 'Show me'. 'I don't care'. 'I can't do it anyway'. In a few years, they may easily become 12-year-olds who do drop out, run away, smoke pot, drink alcohol, or sleep around.

The 16th–17th-year change

The next crisis, occurring around age 16, has to do with the feeling of spiritual separation. Even though the emotional chaos is mostly resolved and the rate of physical change has slowed down, a subtle feeling of discomfort starts to be experienced. Some teenagers try to come to terms with mortality for the first time. They learn that they have limits, especially limits to their physical abilities. They test their bodies, get too little sleep, ignore nutrition, and abuse their health.

Very often, 16-year-olds are working out the attitudes of loneliness and a feeling of unfairness developed during the nine-year change. As 9-year-olds, they had begun to see the imperfections in others. Now they start to see themselves objectively, experience their own imperfection, and assess their own strengths and weaknesses.

With a new awareness of themselves, they are able to make major shifts in their behavior. The potential for change around age 16 is shown by the numbers of adolescents who do a complete turn-around after experiencing a shock. Their higher self (which may also be called their ego, 'I', or true self) draws closer to their soul and awakens them to the nobler side of their nature.

The spiritual crisis leaves adolescents feeling alone on the planet, and stimulates them to ask spiritual or philosophical questions. Is there life after death? Do angels or other spiritual beings exist? What happens if there's nothing? How can the existence of God be proven? Is there a role for religion or not? They may box themselves into a corner, leaving themselves few options because they want definite answers, or they feel frustrated that there aren't such answers. They may deny the existence of anything spiritual while yearning for proof that the spiritual world exists. They wonder if adults are correct when they make statements of certainty. They are interested in discussing such topics only as long as they don't feel pressure to believe what others are telling them. They realize that they must find their own path, and they engage in serious conversations.

After an initial period of anger and disappointment, they often decide to immerse themselves in the world. They may feel satisfied that while there may not be a spiritual reality, they have found meaning in ideals of human interaction such as truth, justice, and compassion. They identify their heroes and contribute their energy to idealistic actions. They may join a social organization, participate in protest marches, work for climate change, volunteer in non-profit organizations, etc. Or they may convince themselves that the world is completely meaningless. The power of these thoughts may cause deep depression and even hopelessness. Studying literature is a meaningful way of entering dialogue with such questions and exploring different viewpoints.

Some teenagers are not interested in philosophical questions, but prefer their excitement in the physical arena of life. They enjoy thrills of speed and daring, choosing one exciting experience after another. Some confront existential questions when they find themselves in situations such as a serious car accident, a bad decision made while drunk or stoned, facing a pregnancy, being suspended from school, or being in trouble with the law. This becomes a turning point in which they begin to think about how they are behaving, whether they are actually making the choice to behave this way, or whether they are following another person's lead. In moments like these, they may decide it is time to outgrow their irresponsible behavior and grow up.

In this process, they see the importance of choices they are making. They think about their goals, their values. One adolescent said he woke up one morning and realized that if he had started smoking because of peer pressure, he could make the decision to stop smoking. This powerful feeling helped him take responsibility for his actions.

Those who tend to be perfectionists suffer particularly during this time. They set very high standards for themselves, and feel the pressure to measure up to other people's expectations of them. They want to be involved in many activities, carry a heavy schedule, work part-time, and have an active social life. They may also want to participate in competitive sports, practice playing an instrument, be in musical or dramatic productions — all within the space of 24 hours. Late nights and anxieties catch up with them and they sometimes end up sick. The period of convalescence may be valuable because it gives them an opportunity to rest and think about priorities, but they also may feel the added pressure because of missing school. However, the most valuable change that can come out of illness is acceptance that they cannot be perfect and do all things. Choices have to be made, priorities have to be set.

Teenagers in this phase have many painful experiences. The questioning path is a lonely one to tread, but it is the only one that leads to becoming a free human being.

The seven-year stages and points of crisis

Each crisis is stimulated by the youngster attaining a new awareness of themselves. The first comes with the awareness of the self as a separate human being; the second with the awareness that they have an inner life; and the third crisis with the awareness of themselves partaking in life and death, raising the question of whether there is meaning in life.

The crisis usually occurs with the approach of the middle years of the phase. To understand this, it might be helpful to think of a time when we are hiking in the mountains. Our adjustment comes not at the top of the mountain, but as the flatlands start to rise. Our breathing and pulse quicken as our bodies strive to adjust to the strain placed upon them. Once we have made the adjustment we find a new pace, a second wind, and we are able to maintain a steady stride to the heights for a breathtaking view. There we feel a sense of accomplishment. Having had these experiences, once again we take to the path, descend the mountain, and gradually adjust our stride. Our lungs and heart also adjust until we return to our flatland home, never to be the same as when we began. Thus, the adolescent benefits from the inner crisis around 16–17.

Memories of the experience dim, but they can be awakened when a similar experience comes along or when they feel a similar sense of accomplishment. As parents, we may recall it when we are deeply moved or when our own children pass through this period.

The feelings that accompany the crises live unconsciously in their soul lives, working behind the scenes as teenagers encounter people or situations. Each crisis may take several years to resolve, and much of the time they are unaware of anything but a feeling of mild discontent. Many years later, after the crisis period has passed, the mention of it may cause a knot in the stomach or tears to flow. In this way, the person is alerted to the pain still living and possibly unresolved.

The completion of childhood

The childhood of human life is made up of 21 years. For the rest of our lives, we look back to those years for clues to our health, our attitudes, our self-confidence, or lack of it, and our ideals. Often, we find that until we penetrate a childhood experience and understand it, we are stuck in it; but once we come to a clear picture of what happened, we are free to go on with our lives. Coming to a clear picture involves forgiving people for what they have done to us, as well as forgiving ourselves.

Our responsibility as parents becomes greater as we ponder the formative powers we have over our children. Yet we are not the only major determinant. Other people in the environment, heredity, the family's joys and trials, the place and time — all have their influences. However, it is important to recognize that the child's own individuality, the ego coming from before birth and separate from heredity, is a significant influence in the development of the childhood years, and comes to the forefront at around age 21.

What role does this ego have? Perhaps an image may help us. Picture a ship. The ship's design has long ago been conceived, the framework has been constructed, the walls filled in, the cabin completed. Then comes the moment when the captain, who has been working in the background, steps forward. The captain has been preparing for this moment for a long time. How will they take hold of the ship? What crew will the captain choose? Where will they steer the ship? Will the captain be tyrannical, weak, or wise? Will they be respected? Will the captain be responsive to the crew? Will the captain know when to diverge from their course to answer a call of distress?

These are the challenges to the captain of the soul, to the human ego, as it takes place around the 21st year. The parents have completed their major work. Now, as individuals, the young adults have to take responsibility for themselves. The ego is in charge. At 21, young people go forth to seek their fortunes.

In a Nutshell

The search for the self

- There are three major crises in the first 21 years.
- In the third-year change, the child experiences physical separation from the environment and a sense of 'I'.
- In the ninth-year change, the child experiences separation from other people, the loss of the magic of childhood, and faces temptations.
- In the 16th-17th-year change, the adolescent experiences spiritual separation, their strengths and their limitations.
- The adolescent prepares for the awakening of the ego to guide them.

Chapter 4

The birth of intellect

I really finally realized that teachers are people with their own goals and wishes, and have something to say.

11th grade boy

What have we learned from neuroscience?

A new soul force — the force of intellect — is born with the completion of puberty. The young person now begins to form independent opinions based on the experiences of life.

With the benefit of neuroscience let us look back at what is happening in thinking during the whole span of child development. When we are born, we have more neurons than at any other time. The brain is creating millions of synapses every second, which result in the baby identifying color, bringing his hands together, recognizing faces, and reaching his arms out to his parents.

Between the first three months and the first birthday, there is a dramatic pruning of brain cells. Here is where the infant is adjusting to the smells, sights, and sounds surrounding him. An infant in China responds to Mandarin, and a child in Greece responds to Greek. The sounds of other languages are pruned because they are not spoken in the baby's environment.

Over the span of childhood, there are moments of excessive growth of neurons, such as at age 1, 4, 7, 11, 15, and 21. As each part of the brain matures, it is a window of opportunity as each experience of learning changes the neurons. These, in turn, create more synapses and receptors, and determine which neural circuits will be pruned away. After each growth spurt the child needs time for a few years to stabilize in order to support integration for healthy development.

11–12-year period

We can examine this period from two vantage points — from the soul and from the physical changes in the brain.

From the soul point of view, we see a change happening in which the youngster looks back to the great world of imagination, and looks forward to the world of thinking and concept. Some youngsters try to hold on to the past and grasp the last vestiges of the glory of childhood, of characters with magical powers such as we see in the myths of many cultures. They look to super-heroes in modern literature who still have something beyond ordinary human capacities to help the world. They experience changes in their soul life such as loneliness, disappointment, yearning, and confusion.

At the same time, their minds are changing, and cause-and-effect thinking is dawning. They begin to use these awakening skills to understand the physical world through observation and judgement. Something is lost and something gained. It is as if the soul is setting out in a new adventure, leaving the forest with its rich growth and glorious colors behind. In front is a desert land which they have to traverse before finding a new landscape of clear transparent colors and harmonies of sound. They cannot do it alone, and there are temptations lurking, false pathways, and dark moments. We need to accompany them as they grow stronger and gain new capacities to see the shadows and learn to discern what is real.

Their sense of historic time increases; measurement becomes more important as a way of proving physical occurrences, and abstract concepts begin to be grasped. The mythical, imaginative, dream-like perceptions yield to scientific thinking

From the viewpoint of changes in the brain, during the 11–12-year period, children experience the largest growth spurt of brain cells since birth, along with the pruning of unused synapses. What they have repeatedly learned through their childhood years, such as poetry, music, bodily gestures, movement, and language, remains. Those that happened only occasionally are lost. Those experiences that remain are a fountain from which the youngster can again and again draw forth nourishment. The more attention is focused on an activity such as a musical skill, the more energy and information flow through specific circuits and activate them. The more the circuit is used, the stronger it gets and the more space is given to it, influencing the student's musicality. At that point, myelin covers the membranes among linked neurons, and that skill is not pruned. Therefore, it is helpful to start such activities before adolescence.

On the other hand, if unhealthy activities or information are repeated, they have the same effect of remaining as an influence, thus accentuating this kind of behavior. Perhaps the over-emphasis of sexualizing of modern society is affecting the earlier sexual impulses youngsters experience in their bodies.

With the birth of intellect, many things are possible. What a great adventure the human mind is setting forth, to discover, to examine, to consider, to work from within on to the outer world. We must feed this new hunger with worthy examples in order to nourish the newly developing mind. Every moment of learning stimulates the creation of more possibilities. For example, when the child experiences a good feeling or a reward, further development of synapses or connections is stimulated. The flood of dopamine which is released makes learning pleasurable. Learning with joy during this time is expressed by such phrases as, 'Oh, wow! Look what is happening'. 'Let's see if it happens again', or 'That is so great. I wonder if I can be like that.'

However, with these two processes of gaining and losing brain cells going on at the same time, 11–12 year-olds experience a period of instability. So much noise is going on in their heads and hearts that they need time to integrate these new feelings and thoughts. Their minds seem to be going in opposite directions, creating frustration and confusion. The youngster cannot count on anything any more.

In describing new thinking capacities that are emerging, Rudolf Steiner highlighted cause-and-effect thinking as a way children of middle-school age begin to organize the world. Psychologist Jean Piaget spoke of the beginning of formal operational thinking. Both Steiner and Piaget are describing a new capacity of mind in which the 11 to 12-year-olds stand outside their instinctual behavior and the habits of the past, and operate on it or organize it. This is the beginning of being able to reflect on their actions. Children need time, and should not be rushed into another stage of thinking before they have solidified this new capacity of thinking.

Similarities emerge between 11 to 12-year-olds and 2-year-olds, both coming to terms with a new body, new identity, emotions, desires, and thoughts. Because the middle-schooler's brain is only half-developed, they lack the full capacity for thinking and responsible action.

A 12-year-old girl commented on something she had learned when she was 11. 'That was before my brain knew how to think.' The birth of the intellect is accompanied by a great interest in facts about the world. Middle-school children enjoy collecting things such as baseball cards, stickers, sea shells, or stamps, which their new capacity of thinking uses to differentiate, name, or assess the value of each. In early childhood, the intellect was connected with the will; in middle childhood, it was connected with the feelings. Around age 12, it shows the first signs of existing independently of feelings, as when they use cause-and-effect thinking.

In the early teenage years, youngsters begin to feel the power of their attention and discrimination, and may enjoy a subject even though they find it difficult. They begin to read newspapers, pay attention to the news, and enjoy discussions. Many 13-year-olds dig into their homework with a sense of satisfaction and accomplishment. A wide range of interests emerges to meet this new enjoyment of intellectual challenge.

The newly formed intellect, however, lacks discrimination. The young teen uncritically accepts as truth, statements made by adults, older teens and the media, and builds a world view out of the biases and opinions of those around them. This world view becomes the foundation of their judgement. Earlier, the youngster's world view was based on the feelings expressed in the immediate environment, but now the ideas and opinions interest and influence them. Consequently, young teenagers often rely on half-truths and undigested facts when they try to make sense of the world. The power of the intellect allows them to receive information, but lack of experience often results in dogmatic statements that do not hold up under questioning.

These pre-teens enjoy being able to express opinions based on knowledge even though it may be very little knowledge, and it is quite easy for them to think that they know more than they actually do. They fall in love with their own ideas and, like prize fighters waiting to be challenged, they present them to the world. Here we find an interesting contradiction. Having accepted an idea or opinion on the flimsiest of authority, from then on they will permit no contradiction of it. When challenged, they find it difficult to let go of the idea, even if it is obviously absurd. Discussion easily turns into an argument, hurt feelings, and barbed comments, and parents may feel worn out by these encounters.

At this age, young teenagers also sense the power which their opinions have on other people, and realize that they can make or destroy reputations at will. In ways that younger children would never dream of, they test their skill by manipulating parents, teachers, and friends. Cynicism and sarcasm can be used to make fun of other peoples' shortcomings or weaknesses. I used to find notes on the floor, carelessly left by a seventh or eighth grader with ugly comments about classmates. At that time, I tore them up. Now, with the iPhone, young teens post photos or cruel comments about others without thinking of what they are doing. This newly found intellectual power has two sides to it: it can be a reaching-out to new understanding of the world, or it can create painful relationships with others in their community.

Systematic thinking becomes necessary for the soul life to cross the bridge to its next phase. When the middle-school child uses reason to develop concepts out of perceptions, this is a grounding experience. However, one has to be careful because one-sided conceptual education hurries the intellectual faculties. Once the intellectual consciousness is awakened and imaginative thinking is stunted, there is no easy way back. The rich, dream-like world of images recedes, and youngsters learn mainly through the senses and through thinking. They have very little protection from sense bombardment, and are too awake to whatever comes from the environment.

Chapter 4 — The birth of intellect

As teenagers move toward developing *executive function*, they move from concrete to big-picture thinking. In making decisions, they start to consider the larger context of an action, and are able to move beyond getting a reward to opting for positive values. Learning happens through the way intellect is fostered. The more something is repeated, recalled, and understood, the more it becomes part of the youngster's knowledge. As described earlier, the brain plastically remodels itself through these experiences, reflecting the expression, 'Use it or lose it'.

Teenagers learn quickly and hold on to what they gain in memory. If a teenager has difficulty learning, this is a time to identify the areas where help is needed, and offer remediation and special help for learning and emotional issues. However, even though teenagers are learning at peak efficiency, other behaviors are not as efficient, such as attention, self-discipline, task completion, and emotions. They lose concentration quickly and think they can multi-task, when they are not very good at it. Distractions pull them hither and thither. Trying to do their homework while listening to music, or attending to whether their friend is texting them, is a failure.

Because it is hard for them to hold several thoughts in their minds, parents or teachers should write down instructions and directions, and limit instructions to one or two points, not five or six. The other thing young teenagers cannot do well is set limits, e.g. the length of time they will search on the computer, listen to their favorite band, or play a video game. As their excitement peaks, they want to reward themselves with more time. The adults have to step in and limit how much time for each activity. Even though the teens will not like it, parents should know the user names and passwords for all their accounts.

One of the big differences between ninth and tenth graders is that 15-year-olds become better at listening to the thoughts of others. They become more reflective so that a discussion no longer seems like a prize fight. Rather than being in love with their own power of thinking, they begin to be fascinated by thought itself. They respond favorably to philosophical questions, although they cannot concentrate for long.

Their thinking focuses more clearly than before, and they express interest in how things came to be and how they have changed. The power to grasp a thought and develop it grows stronger as their power of intellect matures. An experience during our tenth grade study of ancient Greece is still vivid in my memory. We looked at the questions of the pre-Socratic philosophers. One asked whether the river that we put our foot into five minutes ago is the same river we put our foot into now. One of the students with a smile on his face, made a gesture with his hands and said, 'I leavy!'.

The changes of thinking in the 16th year

Remember the journey of the soul and the changes in the brain that I spoke of in describing the 11 to 12-year-old. Now, the teenager has been crossing the desert and can see beyond. Are those mirages or reality up ahead? By 16, the brain has attained about 80 percent of its power. The prefrontal cortex is the last part of the brain to develop, and with the second growth spurt of neurons, new neural tracks are laid, stimulating the new capacity of executive function. This is the most significant developmental change occurring at this time, based on the maturing of brain function. Teenagers are then able to coordinate and balance the functions of many areas, become conscious, think clearly, assess a situation and reason, remember other events, and pause and reflect on what is going on.

As the soul changes during this time, the teenager's new view opens the world to the expansiveness of the universe. There are no bounds; everything is open. These changes allow teenagers to shape their internal mental processes as they consider, think, and make decisions, including the social processes of empathy and moral behavior.

Then the ego is able to use the physical structure of the brain for executive function, which gives the adolescent the great tool for becoming master of themselves. This allows for significantly more mature responses, leading to the big life questions such as meaning, love, friendship, education, family, and everything else that is part of human life. With this change, adolescents can think outside the box, able to challenge old ways of doing things and solve problems in new and innovative ways. It is no longer only what brings outer reward, but what arises out of creativity and reflection.

The ego is the captain of the ship that organizes and governs the behavior and the awakening thinking of the teenager's capacities such as insight, judgement, abstraction, and planning, and responding rather than reacting. Now, he can assess dangers and risk, consciously make decisions to do something or refrain from doing it. However, let's remember that teenagers are just at the beginning of this new stage. Although they are showing better judgement, at times they are still impulsive, moody, unreasonable, and spacey. They have enough understanding to justify using drugs and alcohol because they think they can handle whatever happens.

By about 17 or 18, adolescents begin to gain perspective. They become interested in comparative ideas, and earnestly strive to formulate individual answers to life's questions. The life experiences being accumulated by adolescents temper the force of their intellect, and start to balance it. Now, more than a weapon, thinking has become a tool which the teenagers can use along with other tools in coming to a conclusion.

It is a tool that needs sharpening over time. Still, at this time, they use and misuse their newly formed intellect, which is the means for questioning the social structure, the human soul, and the nature of life itself. With their enhanced capacities, they can compare, contrast, analyze, and synthesize information. They learn as quickly as their teachers and parents. However, they are still often quick to engage in debate before they have digested the new material. They are not yet ready to acknowledge their lack of wisdom and experience. Their arrogance can be very irritating to adults because another enduring aspect of their new-found intellectual power is that they enjoy finding and boasting about flaws in adult reasoning and identifying hypocrisy in their elders.

As they hone their new capacity, they welcome new ideas, question the world view formed earlier and challenge old prejudices.

The late teenage years: from cleverness to the beginning of wisdom

Between 18 and 21, thinking reaches a new stage. The young adult experiences thought more objectively than ever before as they try to figure out what is real and what is illusion, try to separate their own thinking from that of others, or try to figure out why one person reacts one way instead of another. These are the fascinating changes that go on in the mind of the young adult. Through considering such questions, they begin to distinguish between cleverness and wisdom. They are still vulnerable to indoctrination or dogmatism, but they have more tools at their disposal to use in forming their own judgements.

In college or on jobs, young adults find that they have new strength in their thinking. Problems which they could not solve during their high-school years now seem easier. As one person said after failing math in freshman year of college and taking it again in senior year, 'It is as if something clicked and I understood everything'.

The importance of intellect

Plato described the importance of the intellect in his description of the human soul, which he said was made up of three soul elements. He described the sentient soul and the spiritual soul as two wild horses, pulling in opposite directions. The charioteer holding the rein was the intellectual soul. Through the control of the intellectual soul, Plato felt that human beings could keep in check the pleasures and desires which would pull them into the lower, earthly forces such as eroticism, as well as one-sided spiritual pursuits which would pull them off the earth. In time and with experience, the intellectual soul learns how to control the two opposite needs so that, acknowledged and satisfied, both are able to exist side-by-side in harmony.

The process of balancing the opposites begins in adolescence and goes on during adulthood. It is essential in order to develop maturity and stability.

Chapter 4 — The birth of intellect

Dangers of one-sided intellectuality

Thinking is the gateway to freedom. Yet it is possible — even common for young people — to be sidetracked so that they either become so materialistic in their thinking that they lose touch with their artistic and creative capacities, or they so strongly react to the hardness and coldness of modern materialism that they dissipate their ability to think critically in a cloud of vague sentimentality.

The first danger occurs when the youngster is rushed too quickly into materialistic thought. Adolescents who have been steeped in a view that nothing is real which cannot be physically measured or detected often feel very uncomfortable when asked to consider the possibility of a spiritual dimension to life, or even to work artistically. They wish to reduce all life to cause-and-effect thinking, being more at ease in the factual and objective areas of science and technology.

Charles Darwin went so far in the direction of reducing the world to what he could measure that he experienced pain when he contemplated the world he once had loved. He wrote in his journal:

> But now for many years I cannot endure to read a line of poetry. I have tried lately to read Shakespeare, and found it so intolerably dull that it nauseated me. I have also almost lost my taste for pictures and music. I lament this curious loss of my higher aesthetic tastes… my mind seems to have become a kind of machine for grinding general laws, out of large collections of facts, but why this should have caused the atrophy of that part of the brain alone, on which the higher tastes depend, I cannot conceive.

The second danger is that some adolescents will remain too long in a dream world to avoid dealing with the real world. Because they are uncomfortable relating to logic and critical thinking, they drift into worlds of images and fantasy. Using the imagination as escape, they resist focusing their thoughts or organizing them. They do not like to be pinned down or asked to be objective. They resent anyone who tries to make them bring clarity into their rambling descriptions, often labeling such a person as unfeeling and uncreative.

A variation of the dreamy adolescent is the one who is not living in rich imagery but who simply refuses to take the trouble to be clear. Such teenagers wallow in clichés, sprinkling their speech with 'Well, kinda', and 'ya know'. They share many of the same outer attitudes of the adolescent who is escaping into fantasy, but their resistance to form and rigor comes out of laziness rather than an aversion to the matter-of-fact world.

Development of the ego rests on the balance between form and flexibility in thinking. Such a balance results from the natural maturing of the teenager. In the early adolescent years, the thoughts of teenagers are not their own thoughts. Their thinking is strongly shaped by the images from outside which surround them. Teenagers are at the mercy of those thoughts and lack experience to keep them out. After 16, however, thoughts awaken from within the soul. Adolescents are then able to listen and respond to their inner thought process. They become fascinated with thinking itself, and especially with patterns in thinking.

When adolescents gain control over their thinking and are no longer at the mercy of thoughts chaotically streaming into their consciousness, they bring will into their thinking. Their thinking starts to become disciplined and directed. It has form; it is focused. They can now use judgement informed by experience and intuition rather than the earlier experience based on what brought pleasure and reward.

However, as teenagers become more conscious, thinking can lose its liveliness and spontaneity, and can become dry and abstract. It is a challenge to stimulate feelings which can enliven the thinking. Thinking without feelings can be cold. Here, the reference to feeling should not be confused with sentimentality. Feeling is a primary force of the soul which changes as the person develops through stages. Feelings begin to align with thinking, opening the doorway to wonder.

For instance, many would consider geometry to be the epitome of cold, abstract thinking, but it need not be so. If a student does geometry, alert to the beauty of the forms and lawfulness of it, his relationship to the material becomes transformed and his feelings are filled with awe. Understanding geometry as a key to unlocking the order and beauty of the world leads to participating in harmony of the universe, as Pythagoras stated in the doorway to his studio — 'Let only those who love geometry enter here'. By studying science through working with phenomena, teenagers' thinking is more enlivened than in merely memorizing theories.

A former student explained that while studying in a technical university, he discovered that because he had studied projective geometry in high school, he was able to visualize spatially much more easily than his classmates. Back then, when he was grappling with the unfamiliar language of points and planes, he was actually developing a capacity that would allow him to imaginatively grasp concepts in a new way.

There are many additional ways to awaken livelier thinking. By exploring the deeper truths in mythology, the teenager can develop appreciation for the many levels of meaning in literature. By drawing or painting copies of works of art from different periods, he experiences the change in human consciousness. This experience develops appreciation for the great artistic accomplishments of humanity and gives him a feeling for people of diverse cultures. This also gives him a foundation for exploring his own artistic style.

Through listening to or reading biographies, teenagers can identify with the challenges confronted by men and women of high ideals.

The awakening intellect longs to meet the world, to grapple with ideals, and to feel some sense of mastery over the environment. When issues of substance are presented, the intellect is exercised and developed. It creates the foundation for thinking as a path to freedom.

In a Nutshell

The birth of intellect

- With the completion of puberty, children experience the power of thinking.
- The 11–12 year period is one in which children undergo intense neurological and physical development, as shown in their changes in thinking and feeling.
- Teenagers around age 16 are at the peak of their intellectual efficiency, although they are not efficient in attention, self-discipline, task completion, or handling their emotions.
- Changes in the brain in the 16th–17th year set the groundwork for executive function and new capacities of insight, judgement, abstraction, planning, and thoughtful responses.
- In the late teen years, 18 to 21, they begin to distinguish between cleverness and wisdom.
- There are dangers to coming into one-sided intellectuality, or in remaining too long in a dream world. Balance is important.
- Thinking is the foundation for a path to freedom.

Chapter 5

The release of feelings

A true individual will be the person who reaches highest truth with his
and her feelings, into the regions of ideals.[2]

Rudolf Steiner

Beauty is truth, truth beauty, — that is all
Ye know on earth, and all ye need to know.

John Keats

Early Childhood

The feeling life of the teenager is already influenced during early childhood. The parents' attitude prepares a bond which surrounds the child
with security and warmth. She learns to lift her head, smile, kick, and crawl.
Is the child welcomed into the family? Is she ignored? Is she bonded? Or
is she considered as an unwanted stranger?

The child's connection with the family, with self-image, and with attitudes is developed before the child begins school. Some negative attitudes such as prejudice and bigotry may be harmful to the child. Although
such attitudes can be transformed, scars remain in the emotional well-
being of the child.

Throughout childhood, they are dependent on the adults around
them to form their picture of the world. Gradually with the awakening
of their thinking, teenagers begin to question what they had taken for
granted. By around 21, with the birth of the ego, young adults claim their

own views, although such transformation may take place later in the adult life through personal experience.

When little children are asked how they feel about things, they really can't explain. Many of their feelings are connected with their physical body and with physical needs for food, drink, shelter, warmth, comfort, security, and protection. Children assume that everything in their world is the way it is supposed to be. The child feels the way she breathes — naturally and without judgement. Even in the most adverse situations, children accept what is. I worked with children whose parents were in prison. I expected to find that they carried the stigma of it, but instead, they spoke about their monthly visit as if it were a natural thing, and they looked forward to the next one.

Some children feel that the world is love, and they are protected. I was having a picnic lunch with my three-year-old granddaughter. I mentioned that we might want to say grace before our meal. She asked, 'Why?'. I responded that we might thank God for our daily meal and ask God to protect us. Her response was, 'Why do I need to be protected?' As I reflected on this, I realized that she was embedded in love from her parents and family, and she was right. She didn't need any other help. It was all there in visible and invisible ways.

Not every child has this kind of innocence. Some feel neglected and alone, fearful and longing, angry and resentful. A wise kindergarten teacher told me she could tell by the way children used their hands in play whether they felt the world was good or whether something had been disrupted and would play out in anti-social behavior.

Traumas of war and family dysfunction heighten the feeling of loss. A friend described how during the bombings in Germany, her mother gathered her children into the bomb shelter and told them fairy tales. Even in this difficult traumatic situation, her mother created a bond of love and safety.

How can children understand their feelings? They certainly experience feelings such as pleasure, pain, excitement, and fear. But the child has great difficulty describing, much less understanding, more subtle feelings such as compassion, sadness, gratitude, or joy.

From 7 to 14

During the period from 7 to 14, children live strongly in the life of feeling. All actions, experiences, and thoughts are colored by feelings, most of which are polarities — sympathy and antipathy, love and hatred, like and dislike. When children embrace the world, their gesture is open, and they meet the world with positive feelings.

During the nine-year change, described earlier, children experience a time of separation, when they begin to sense new feelings, some of which cause them to withdraw inward, closing themselves off. They don't understand these feelings. Earlier they had loved their teachers, but now they feel their teachers don't like them, their friends don't like them, and nothing feels right. A typical comment I heard from my class during this time was, 'That's not fair'.

Children lose basic trust that the world is a good and safe place and that people care about them. The world no longer glows with joy and goodness. The child moves from the sunlight into the shadows of anxiety, fear, anger, self-punishment, and conformity. For most children, this stage passes, and after a transition they embrace life again. Teachers who understand this time of childhood can help them find ways to feel good about life again. Parents who understand this period will not panic when their children begin to lose their enthusiasm for life.

The child moves between the inner soul-life and the outer sense-life in a Yes–No movement. Feelings accompany everything children do, yet these feelings are never fixed or stagnant. They are always moving, changing, and influencing them. The world of childhood is the world of flowing color, tone, and sensation — all of which are rooted in the feelings.

Their consciousness is dreamy, and we wish it could continue like this for a few more years. Yet our society pulls children too quickly into wakefulness, offering them constant choice, and stimulating criticism of people around them.

Problems arise when children are hurried, when they feel too much stress, when they lose trust in their relationships, rushing them into the next stage before they have had a chance to integrate their feelings. When that happens, the protection of childhood is over, and the child faces a world which can be unfriendly and sometimes terrifying.

Nevertheless, children still look to adults to guide them, setting standards for behavior at home and in school. Children love stories, and adults can use stories to create a moral backdrop of daily life. Fairy tales present characters who act as guides — the open-hearted youngest brother, the princess who loves the ugly prince and frees him from a spell, those who love animals, and those who bring the treasure back to the community. Fables depict psychological qualities such as patience, cleverness, and 'slow and steady wins the race'.

As children move into the third, fourth, and fifth grades, they love myths from around the world. Here they meet examples of creation, enchanted worlds, and the sacrificial hero. As they move into sixth, seventh, and eighth grade, biographies of real people who meet obstacles in life serve them well, showing how people transform their difficulties into gifts for the community.

In addition to the imaginative ways of guidance, adults also give directions on how to behave in class and at home — be obedient, speak politely, help set the table, clean up after yourself, and listen to your parents and teachers. Camps and religious organizations also provide guidance during these years with ongoing activities and rites of passage.

The highest feelings in the child's soul are experienced as beauty. Beauty is a kind person, a warm, sunny day, a happy moment, a cuddly puppy, holding father's hand, kissing mother goodnight. Beauty is the Yes of the world, while ugliness is No. The child experiences the love of parents as the ultimate beauty.

Feelings in Adolescence

Can you remember uproarious times when something struck you as funny, and you couldn't stop laughing? No amount of stern reproach could stop the giggles. Finally, you had to get up and go for a drink to take hold of yourself. Can you remember crying when you weren't sure what was bothering you? Such experiences begin as the youngster enters the early-teen years. The feelings are surging, and the ego is not yet able to direct them. In the midst of uncontrollable feelings, young people find themselves confused.

During this time, youngsters oscillate between extremes. Within a brief period, they may be alternately withdrawn and aggressive, lethargic and overactive. They are moody and oversensitive. Tears burst forth, small incidents set off big reactions, unpleasant comments are exchanged, blow-ups occur, and a period of general unhappiness results.

When children reach puberty, they have a new awareness of their feelings. This is unlike any experience the young person has ever had before. The change is gradual, but strange and unfamiliar. Feelings rush in and out. The youngster experiences floods of emotions, moods, and desires. Exaggerated feelings well up, and they are overwhelmed by the strange new sensations. Whereas education of the feeling life of children mainly came from outside, young adolescents begin to awaken from the inside. It is like moving into a new city without a map, and the individual has to strike out and find her way. What she knew before doesn't help her now. As with the birth of anything new, it takes time to gain experience and balance. Feelings swing back and forth, changing from moment to moment. Giggles, hysterical laughing, crying, and depression overwhelm youngsters, and they lose control.

Rudolf Steiner calls the new life of emotions the 'astral body' or the 'soul body', expressing the highest feelings such as compassion, honesty, generosity, and fairness, as well as the basest instincts such as greed, selfishness, drives, and impulses. It seems as if the child has stepped into a candy store, and everything is available. Will she be able to handle the temptations? The astral body is also called the star body because it reflects cosmic principles or ideals in the soul life. It is the bearer of the ego until 21 when the ego is freed to do its work. I will use the term 'soul body' to refer to this force-field of emotions.

We could say that the feelings and thinking are still merged in early adolescence when feelings are unconscious. As the ego gradually gains strength, the teenager uses the new capacity of thinking to work on her feelings, consciously moderating them, guiding them, making them more objective, and beginning to make sound choices.

Within the activity of the teenager's brain, feelings are influenced by an increase of dopamine, a neurotransmitter involved in their drive for reward. This leads them to seek thrilling experiences and highs. Without those, they feel bored. They act spontaneously, not taking time to figure out the whole situation, or reflect on the best response. They long for something that will make a great impact on the environment such as turning back climate change or eliminating diseases. Their feeling of power and purpose creates a new level of excitement. However, they learn to take small steps which may not have as total an impact as they had hoped for, but are still significant. When the community recognizes their contributions and celebrates them, teenagers feel affirmed and want to do more.

If younger adolescents are asked to focus on their inner feelings and share them with others, they become confused and find it hard to articulate what they feel. Because they don't realize this difficult time will pass, and life will get better, they may become despondent. They should not be pressured to go inside themselves like this.

As adolescents first become conscious of their feelings, they are confused by them, fascinated by them, and frustrated by them. Giving them time to develop executive function before becoming self-conscious about their feelings allows for healthy integration of their emotional life.

The see-sawing of their feelings coincides with the strengthening of thinking. Both capacities mature markedly around the 16th year. As youngsters develop control over their thinking, they see beauty on another level. Beauty in the world of thought is truth — and the teenager seeks truth. There is nothing more beautiful and satisfying than the moment when they experience the light of truth.

Adolescents stand on the threshold of two existences — the childhood they left behind and the adult world they are about to enter. Should they step forward or should they rush back? Because they feel confused, they usually do some of each. They want to become adults, but at the same time to remain children. One teen demanded to be treated as an adult. When she was called to task for manipulative behavior, she petulantly countered, 'Well, you know I'm just a child. I shouldn't be expected to handle that.'

Steiner compared the freeing of the feelings, the development of an independent soul-life, to a continued experience of gentle pain. When teenagers are preoccupied with this sense of inner discomfort, they find it difficult to direct their interest to the outside world. Teachers and other adults in the community can help them by involving them in community action, whether it is environmental or social, so they forget themselves for a while.

Physical and Emotional Changes

Physical puberty precedes psychological puberty. Because the maturation of the sexual organs brings on physical maturity, the mistaken impression arises that youth have become mature because they can reproduce their kind. However, their emotional level may be years away from maturity. We adults are disappointed by expecting more than the teenager is able to deliver. We grow angry and frustrated with the youngster when the real problem is our own unrealistic expectation.

Emotional maturity develops slowly. Major earlier turning points occurred at about the third, ninth, and twelfth years. With the onset of adolescence, emotional development becomes a major focus of the teenager's life. Emotional maturity has to do with the child's appropriate reactions to the demands of life at a particular stage. A too-sophisticated 9-year-old may appear to be emotionally mature at first meeting, but behind that façade of sophistication, one finds a youngster with the needs and insecurities of a 9-year-old child. On the other hand, the emotionally immature child is living in a past phase. Such children try to meet their needs in ways that were appropriate when they were younger. When a 12-year-old still runs to her mother every time someone frustrates her, or a high-school student responds with name-calling and bluster, she is stuck in patterns she should have outgrown.

One of the great steps toward emotional maturity has to do with separation. Children often unwillingly separate from the secure world of childhood. The separation makes them lonely, but in time, such loneliness may lead them to care about other people. 'If I feel this pain, maybe you do too.' They slowly step out to meet the world. Sometimes, they step out too far and too quickly, and lose their way.

The loss of childhood joy drives some children back inside themselves for protection. Others rush into teenage culture to find solace and reassurance. Most are tossed between feeling confused and feeling understood by nobody. It is to be expected that young teenagers, confused by new and unpredictable feelings and by a changing relationship with the world, will be moody and irresponsible. They seek new relationships with adults. The old relationships which served them well in earlier years do not satisfy them any more, and they don't know how to indicate this in a tactful manner. Adults are confused when a comment or touch that was helpful earlier is now scorned.

The adolescent gradually develops self-confidence, control, and some perspective. Moodiness continues to come and go, along with periods of happiness and unhappiness, but there is a greater ability to handle feelings until they experience a new level of emotional stability. This period that emerges, while not without its traumatic incidents, now includes enthusiasm, renewed energy, and a new enjoyment of people. The teenager embraces life, accepts its contradictions and inconsistencies, and says 'Yes' to it.

In a Nutshell

The release of feelings

- Young children's feelings are connected with the needs of their physical bodies.
- Young children's experiences influence their feeling of safety and loss for the rest of their life.
- During the 7–14 period, children live deeply into their feelings, searching for beauty in the world. Stories are a prime way of experiencing their feeling life.
- Adolescents experience extremes of emotions, and gradually bring them into balance through new capacities of thinking.
- Even though teenagers look like adults, they are immature in their behavior and need time to develop emotional maturity.
- Although moodiness comes and goes, adolescents begin to embrace life and accept its contradictions and inconsistencies.

Chapter 6

Strengthening the life of will

Hold fast your dreams
Within your heart
Keep one still, secret spot
Where dreams may go,
And, sheltered so,
May thrive and grow
Where doubt and fear are not.
O keep a place apart,
Within your heart,
For little dreams to go.
Louise Driscoll

The Young Child

At first, children are active in their will as they begin to unconsciously imitate adults around them walking, running, hopping, skipping, putting on their jacket, eating with a spoon, clapping their hands. I have been getting daily reports from my friend who is a grandmother of a 2-year-old; I'll call him Sam. When Sam visited his grandmother just after his second birthday, they went to a nearby farm. He watched Farmer Steve put on his boots to work in the pig sty. Sam loves seeing Frankie the pig and Patti the cow. When he returned home, he was going out with his father to work in the yard, but he stopped and said, 'Farmer Steve, Farmer

Steve'. They had to go in the house and get his work boots just as Farmer Steve had done. The child absorbs everything in the environment, good or bad, and imitates it with the will. Adults understand that it is important to put their boots on if they are going to be working in mud, but a child does it purely out of unconscious will.

Guiding the child's unconscious will is the task of the parent and early childhood teacher. This is the way habits are developed.

When the child vehemently states 'No', this is the shooting forth of unconscious will. At first, they say 'No!' to everything because their words just dart out without thinking. Similarly, they repeat the word 'Why?' over and over again. Another familiar expression of the young child's will is 'Myself!', said with great strength. Gradually, they are able to differentiate when to say the strong word and when not.

Kindergarten teachers can sense what is going on in the child's life because it is displayed in front of them during the child's play in such expressions as: 'Get down from that chair, I told you not to do that'; 'Let's go to the doctor'; and 'Oh, dear, Grandpa is ill'. On and on, the children play out their home life in gesture and tone of voice. The feelings begin to be awakened. For example, if a child falls on the playground, another child will run over and give a hand to help. This gesture may have begun out of imitation, watching adults do that, but now the feelings stimulate the will, and the child expresses compassion. As children come closer to 5 or 6, they begin to think, as well as feel and will. They might say to the child who fell, 'Shall I get you a Band-Aid?' and 'Will you be OK?',

The 5-year-olds come to the door of the kindergarten and excitedly say, 'Oh, let's play train today. We'll get the chairs lined up, and I will be the conductor. You whistle for the engine to start.' Now, their thinking has a sense of purpose, and they are directing their will.

By the end of the kindergarten year, adults can sense whether children will be impulsive, angry, and spiteful or whether they will be kind, friendly, or cooperative. The power of the child's environment has worked into the gestures of their hands and the expression on their face. Once that is known, the adults begin to try to work with those difficulties which have gone deeply into children's bodies.

The Heart of Childhood

In the elementary school, children continue imitating certain activities of their teacher, but they begin to do more out of themselves. They are given tasks to do in the classroom such as sweeping or putting away paints. When they do this over and over again, they develop habits, and this develops their will. At home, they might set the table for dinner. This also begins to develop their will. When they work in their books, writing letters, drawing pictures, they exercise their will in finishing assignments, in putting away their supplies, and in getting ready for the next activity. Adults can train the will of the child in a militaristic way, but that not only develops the child's will, it also develops fear. The key to developing will at this age is to combine it with the feeling of joy so that they love to learn. All these activities are uniting their feelings and thinking with the will. Slowly, they bring more consciousness to what they do.

A change comes between 8 and 9, when they do less imitating and more directing once they see what has to be done. In the sense of separating from the adult world, they want to do things themselves — so much so that they push away from the adults and find that they are alone. They connect more with the will of their peers than that of the adults.

As they integrate the neurological changes they are experiencing, they become more connected with their thinking and how it affects their will. They plan activities, change what they are doing, figure out the next step. On the playground, we see this age group developing challenging games with complicated rules and setting up jump-rope competitions.

The Ending of Childhood

Around age 11–12, when hormones are shooting through their bodies and their brains are changing with the pruning of neurons, their thinking has the new capacity of *critical* thinking. The challenge occurs because the harmonious integration of their thinking, feeling, and willing of the last few years is now disrupted. The changes are too much for them to handle. Impulses pulse through their bodies; their feelings are scattered;

they can't remember what they were told. Children vary from individual to individual during this time in where they stand in this time of change. Some will have another year to still be a child, others have moved into the next stage, never to go back.

It becomes very important for society that mentors or guides are there during this time. Otherwise, children are reactive, risk-taking, egotistical, and anti-social. This is not because they are bad children, but because their will has become more conscious, without direction, and left to impulses. So they set out to do what admired older teenagers do, or hide, or do what is forbidden. The task of parents and teachers during this time is to guide, by helping children use their new capacity of critical thinking to influence their will, solve problems, delay gratification, and take responsibility for their actions. It isn't easy, and eruptions of emotions and strong will responses lead to slammed doors, hateful statements, and tears.

In my experience, seventh grade is the hardest time when everything is out of balance. Of course, it depends on whether the class is made up of younger or older seventh graders. Adults need to have a sense of humor and perspective to recognize the wonderful potential of these youngsters, challenging them with projects and tasks, and supporting them when needed.

The most important guides are the adults who live by inner authority, willing to stand firm, point to what has to be done, not wobbling in the face of strong reaction, yet being there to help youngsters make up for mistakes and learn to take responsibility. In the face of strong reactions, adults can smilingly respond, 'That's just my job as parent [or teacher]'.

Early Adolescence and the Will

After puberty, everything changes in the will. Because as mentioned previously, puberty is coming earlier, the youngsters are still at the mercy of their impulses. They are swayed this way and that, as if blown by the winds. This is the 'vulnerability gap', creating a challenging time between ages 11 and 14, which I described in Chapter 1.

Because their bodies are changing so much, early teens are overwhelmed. What's going on here? Why is my face breaking out? I keep falling over my feet. I have strange feelings I haven't had before. Nothing is working out right. I'm getting rounder, and my breasts are getting larger.

All they can do to counter these changes is to respond with a powerful surge of will. They take action, strike out at others, break things, join with others in doing pranks, or spend time alone deeply unhappy. There is much that is available during this time to guide the will, such as athletics, drama, team activities, service projects, neighborhood tasks, collecting food for others, gardening, dancing, and many more. Each helps the young teenagers discipline their will, follow through on their promises, and take hold of their body. However, left without guidance their will is taken over by social media, the marketplace of consumerism, and overuse of technology.

It is during this transition that indigenous cultures and religious practices directly work on the will by setting out tasks the youngster has to accomplish, face loneliness or insecurity, and demonstrate particular skills in front of the community. The rites of passage of various organizations and groups are expressions of how the young person is able to guide their will.

Young adolescents choose their heroes and follow their patterns, looking up to those who have made a difference in life, or have a talent in a particular field. 'Can I be like that?' 'Could I ever stand up with courage?' 'Can I climb to the top of the mountain?'

Teenagers and Their Will

In *Observation on Adolescence,* Rudolf Steiner points out that

> …he who acts only out of instincts, passions, urges, and desires and so on does not only have an idea which encompasses all that he does in a given moment, but he performs a deed, a task on the physical level, that encompasses objects and events which he does not think about.

Chapter 6 — Strengthening the life of will

His intentions, his thoughts, thus, are less wide, are smaller than his deeds, on the physical level.[3]

The deeds which are smaller than their corresponding ideas leave such an impression, and show themselves in later life as courage for life, confidence in life, and equanimity in life. To understand this, we can think of raking a lawn of autumn leaves. The deed itself is worthwhile. However, if the idea behind it is to help an elderly person who can't do it by themselves, then the teenager is inspired to do things for others. The idea is larger than the deed itself. Through such actions, young adolescents begin to take hold of their will and direct it.

With the awakening of thinking that comes after 14, the teenager has a tool to consciously guide the will. It is through practicing judgement that teenagers' thinking penetrates the will, slows it down, and thus giving them time to reflect. Through interacting with the world, the teenager searches for a way to make a connection. They choose their response and thus take ownership of their will. So much is coming at them from their outer world. How can they counter it? They have to develop an inner core that withstands the winds that blow, so that they can stand up against what is coming at them. This is a battle between the outer will hitting up against the inner will which is permeated with growing intelligence.

The teenager's task is to participate in life and find ways in which they can contribute. They need to get involved, connect with gardening and farming, business, production, or technology. They need to take part in world affairs, explore climate change, the environment, economic life, social services that help those in need. Each of these experiences disciplines their will — through debate, through volunteering, through gaining ideas on how to make things better and trying them out in the real world. In some schools, high-school students spend one to three weeks each year in a social practicum such as working on a farm or in a factory, with those with special needs, and in a profession that they wish to pursue. Everything they do, especially in the second half of high school, is directed toward the future. 'Who will they be?' 'What will they do?' 'Who will they do it with, and where?'

During a special project week, I worked with a mixed-age high-school group to explore the world of work. We read Studs Terkel's book *Working* and discussed it daily. Every day we visited a different work site, visited the printers' union of the local newspaper, then visited the paper's production room where the newspaper was now being printed automatically. The students met printers who had lost their jobs because of automation. We visited a local home that was being built with beautiful architecture and hand-finished shelves and cabinets. Then we visited a large apartment site where hundreds of units were being prefabricated. In both cases, students spoke with the builders. We visited a brewery and a potato-chip factory, where we followed the raw material from the first step to the final product, learning about factory life and factory issues. In an almond factory, we learned how workers had their tasks changed regularly to keep them from getting bored. Finally, we visited a small bakery, and then a large baking operation. This experience of working introduced the students to the current issues of economics, work issues, individual and mass production. After that week, these issues were not abstract, but were connected with real work in the world.

During this week, other groups were looking at changes in generations. Students interviewed their parents and grandparents, finding it almost comical to realize how different life had been 50 years earlier. Other students worked in food banks or in homeless shelters. Once they interacted with real people, their attitudes underwent a change. It is not only important to visit such places, but where possible to work in them. That is where adolescents' will is engaged.

Love and Life of Will

Another aspect of teenagers' will life is in the realm of love. Love has different aspects: sexual love (*Eros*), love of friends (*Philios*), love of others (*Caritas*, charity), and love of spirit (*Agape*). All of these are brought together in the love of humanity, or brotherhood (or the new term, 'commonhood').

Teenagers are entering this field of human experience, meeting aspects of love as they deal with new feelings of sexual arousal, as they develop deep friendships, and as they give service in their community.

At each step of love, the teenager has to make decisions in how they treat other human beings. It takes time and experience to use their will in an appropriate way. When they bring their thinking, feeling, and willing together in love, their emotional life matures, and they take steps on the conscious path toward healthy adulthood

The path of development of the will in adolescence is from willfulness to mastering the will, laying the foundation for conscious morality.

When they reach their twenties, this journey takes on a new character. The ego is in charge, and teenagers have taken hold of their will and begun the path of transformation.

In a Nutshell

Strengthening the life of will

- Young children are active in their will through imitation of those around them.
- Through imitation, children develop unconscious habits in their behavior.
- In the elementary school age, children begin to use their thinking to plan their activities separately from adults.
- In the middle school years, their will is out of balance and at the mercy of their impulses.
- Adults can guide early adolescents by activities that direct their will toward self-discipline and service to others.
- Teenagers need to find ways of directing their will by participating in life, and contributing to others.
- The journey of the will is to move from self-centeredness to love of others.

Chapter 7

Understanding our sons and daughters

> The maturity level of the boys has gone down 50 percent, and the moodiness of the girls has gone up about that much.
>
> A seventh-grade girl writing to her former teacher

Issues with Gender and Identity

We are living in a time of great change around the question of sons, daughters, males, females, masculinity, and femininity, gender and sexual identity. Some youngsters are becoming aware of themselves in a way not seen before. They claim to be the gender they were born with physically but another gender by identity. The concept of two clear sexual identities is now located on a spectrum, on which each individual is located in a unique place. We may be sitting in a room with adolescents who are straight, gay, binary, transgender, etc. Their experiences are very different from each other, yet each is an individual worthy of respect, understanding, and love.

Generally, a person's sex is biological, whereas gender identity is psychological and may be influenced by culture as well as experienced internally. There is a lack of clarity with these issues, and I have trouble understanding the distinctions myself. Psychologists are also not in clear agreement. I think the most important aspect is that we love our children for who they are, try to understand their feelings when they have questions, and support them in their search for their identity. When I was a young person, the word 'queer' was a negative term, but today homo-sexuals refer to themselves as queer, and there are groups that claim that anyone who is not straight is queer. There are many variations such as genderqueer, gender non-conforming, and so on.

I struggle with the use of pronouns in this book because rules, and what is culturally regarded as acceptable, are changing all the time. In order to offer support to pronoun/identity, I have used 'she', 'he', and 'they' at different times according to the chapter or paragraph. I hope the reader will understand this decision.

The Effect of Society on a Person's Sexual Identity

Society has passed through phases in the last 50 years as to whether or not male and female biological differences defined their strengths, behavior, roles, and responsibilities. Not so long ago, the public view was that males are stronger and more intelligent than females. Women were seen as property of their husbands or fathers and, in some cultures, of their brothers. Women could not own property or have their own credit cards. It was only in 1919 that women in the USA gained the right to vote. Societal roles were distinct. Boys were to be educated for power roles in society, while women were taught to be homemakers and serve the needs of men.

We may think these are old-fashioned ideas, but in January 2020 I listened to a discussion about the film Oscars, commenting that the number of women film directors is miniscule compared to male directors. The journalist commented that the image of film directors is of a big muscular powerful male. Women are passed by because they don't fit that picture. They were there to be sex objects, dress to satisfy men, not compete with them, and be satisfied with what they had. This is still the case in certain parts of society and in some religious belief systems.

The other side of the pendulum swing is that there are no real differences between boys and girls, that it is all a case of conditioning. Except for physical differences, men and women are the same. Instead, the proponents of such a view blamed society for creating the differences through the way children were dressed, the toys they were given, and so on: it was all cultural.

However, since the development of brain research in the 1990s, we've learned that aside from the obvious differences, there are differences in brain structure and function, differences in psychological make-up, and differences in thinking between male and female.

Respect for each person as an individual should be central in all relationships. Differences should not be translated into political or legal power. We are continually uncovering intellectual feats that were done by women who were not given credit for their contributions. For example, the film *Hidden Figures* showcases the accomplishments of three brilliant African-American women who were the brains behind launching astronaut John Glenn into orbit, or the 'Bletchley Circle' featuring British women mathematicians who broke codes during the Second World War. The list goes on and on.

Biological Differences

Girls come into puberty earlier and finish earlier. Being involved in some physical activity, whether individually or as a member of a team, is a good way to build strength, especially bone strength. Some girls who were athletic become self-conscious about their bodies in early adolescence, and refuse to participate. Others start dieting in a way that is unhealthy. On the other hand, becoming obsessive in sports is not healthy for teenage girls who either delay their menstruation, or undergo stressful training sessions which have damaging effects on their bodies. They have fantasies of becoming Olympic gymnasts or dancers, and beat up their bodies mercilessly. Finding the balance between loving participating in an activity and hurting oneself can be a challenge. Other girls may find an outlet in yoga, tai chi, karate, swing dance, or African dance.

As more girls are participating in athletic events, it is important for coaches and parents to be aware that due to structure of their bodies, girls are at risk for certain injuries. For example, as girls compete under the same athletic rules as boys in the same sports, they experience more injuries.

Until 2006, most of the studies about concussions were based on boys. However, girls are at a higher risk of concussions in soccer, basketball, ice hockey, figure-skating, cheer-leading, and gymnastics. Why? The typical female athlete has higher estrogen levels, along with less muscle mass and more body fat, greater flexibility (due to looser ligaments) and less powerful muscles, a wider pelvis which alters the alignment of the knee and ankle, a narrower space within the knee for the ACL to travel through, and a greater likelihood of inadequate calcium and vitamin D intake.

> For example, when landing from a jump, women tend to land more upright and with the knees closer together. And when female athletes suddenly change direction, they tend to do so on one foot (perhaps due to their wider pelvis), while men tend to 'cut' from both feet.[4]

Boys have an advantage when it comes to holding in air. Their hearts grow larger and heavier than girls' hearts. The size of their lungs and respiratory capacity is greater than girls, meaning they can take in more air in a single breath. Their voices deepen more than girls, although girls' voices also deepen somewhat in puberty.

The pituitary gland releases the hormone testosterone, which causes most of the changes that occur in a teenage boy's body, including sperm production, increasing lean body mass and muscle tissues, and stimulating body growth. Although both boys and girls have the hormone testosterone, the teenage boy has to learn to manage up to 20 times as much of the sex and aggression hormone as the teenage girl. He struggles to manage the instinctual surges that pulse through his body. He needs to take hold of the urge toward impulsive risks, aggression, and dominance, and the short-term cycle of tension and release. His greater muscle strength can facilitate bullying, and it must be transformed for the boy to be a successful member of a group.

The pituitary gland stimulates the amount of the sex hormone in the girl's body. This shows itself in developing breast buds and hair in the pubic area and in the armpits. With a high dose of progesterone, estrogen, and prolactin, girls' growth is stimulated, as well as sexual arousal, and the sex organs. During puberty, girls often feel tired as so much of their energy is going into growth. By adolescence, they stabilize and are not as tired.

Girls tend to hear better than boys, as is demonstrated already in infancy. As students, they are more disturbed by noisy and chaotic classrooms. A high-school boy took me aside to tell me that when Steven tapped his pencil on the desk, he wasn't trying to annoy me. He just had lots of energy. He didn't understand why the girls and I were bothered by it. However, the girls weren't just being fussy; they were hearing that tapping more loudly and clearly than their male classmates. Girls also complain that some teachers or parents yell too much.

Differences in Brain Development

According to Leonard Sax, M.D., Ph.D., one of the most significant studies was carried out in 2004 when 14 neuroscientists from three universities (of California, Michigan, and Stanford) demonstrated that there was a dramatically different expression of proteins derived from the x chromosome and the y chromosome in human male and female brains.

> In males, many areas of the brain are rich in protein that are coded directly by the Y chromosome. Those proteins are absent in women's brain tissue. Conversely, women's brain tissue is rich in material coded directly by the X chromosome; those particular transcripts of the X chromosome are absent from men's brain tissue.[5]

This study proved that sex differences are genetically programmed, not mediated by hormonal differences. Males and females get different strengths from their brain — not better, but different.

Girls tend to process information more completely because they connect it with their emotions. They have stronger verbal abilities and are more comfortable with long explanations, interpreting language, while boys do better when they can rely on non-verbal communication or use coded language. However, both boys and girls do better if they can manipulate and touch the problem.

Chapter 7 — Understanding our sons and daughters

Emotional Life of Teenage Girls

Let us remember that boys and girls are on a spectrum. Both boys and girls have a rich emotional life, but they are different. Of course, some girls share more of the male response, while some boys share more of the female response. This is a general statement, and each teacher and parent should explore how and whether these responses are confirmed in everyday life.

Where do these responses come from? In the 1920s, Rudolf Steiner, in the establishment of the first Waldorf school in Stuttgart, gave characterizations of the emotional responses of boys and girls. Neuroscientists have been able to describe specifically how these responses are stimulated within the brain. We want to be aware, however, that it is easy to draw conclusions without looking at the actual behavior of teenage boys and girls. I leave it to the reader to do so.

Girls and women interpret facial expressions better than most boys and men can.[6] This was discovered already to be the case with babies when they were shown mobiles or real faces. The boy babies were more interested in the quiet mobile moving quietly, and the girl babies were more interested in looking at faces. It seems the reason for this has to do with the sex differences in the anatomy of the eye. Through this, girls are more able to answer the question 'What is it?', and boys to answer the question, 'Where is it now, where is it going, how fast is it moving?'.

In girls, the emotional life is far stronger than in boys. Because her emotions and ego are interrelated, girls are very concerned about their identity — who she is and how she is affecting people. The girl typically feels tossed and blown about by powerful emotions which carry her from one situation to another. She finds it difficult to separate who she is from how she feels. She is overly sensitive, and easily gets hurt. She interprets the way statements are made and looks for hidden meaning even when it is not there. She is very concerned about justice and fairness, always ready to defend the underdog or take up a cause and lobby for it.

Girls become more easily conscious of other people's feelings. They are attentive to subtlety and the ins and outs of relationships. She notices glances, body language, and subtle comments between people which may be ignored by boys.

Her active emotional life makes her mature more quickly than boys. She seems to know how to handle social situations, or at least it appears so, in comparison to the boys around her. She exudes self-confidence, although it is often on the surface. This can confuse the boys.

Though of course these are generalizations, typically the girl's sense of ego is not only connected with her feelings but penetrates right into her gestures, including the angle at which she holds her head and the way she walks. Most of what she does is planned. She uses her body to elicit a particular response. She flirts and manipulates. Her behavior can be experienced in cultural context as flirtatious or even manipulative (not that boys aren't capable of such traits as well, of course). Other girls see what she is doing and know how affected her behavior is, but the boys are impressed by it, although they aren't sure what is happening. Not content with gesture alone, girls may use make-up and clothing to express themselves more fully, and eagerly discuss the effect their *look* has on those around them. A girl's preoccupation with appearance can lead to superficiality, but it can also lead to an aesthetic approach — with an accompanying interest in art and design.

Recently during a family vacation, I shared a room with a 16 year-old exchange student. Her preoccupation with her cell phone interfered with my attempt to have conversations with her, until I asked her some direct questions. During family outings she could be sincerely engaged, and then she remembered she needed to take a 'selfie' and pose accordingly. She quickly took on what I perceived as a sexy-model pose, with the appropriate facial gesture, full lips, etc., and she then posted the picture on Instagram. Because I was genuinely interested in her experience, she began to share her insecurities about how many 'likes' she hoped to receive for each photo. After posting photos of herself at the beach, she received some very nasty responses from people she didn't even know. They told her that she wasn't showing enough cheek, only 50 per cent instead of 75 per cent. These responses left her feeling unhappy, and we spoke about it. She's a smart young woman, and she knows that this nasty response is ridiculous, and she should ignore it — but she couldn't. Frankly, except for posting nude, I couldn't imagine how showing any more of her cheek would leave anything left besides a thong.

Chapter 7 — Understanding our sons and daughters

Teenage girls typically need to feel accepted and liked. They want to please, and unless they can summon up the courage to dismiss someone's unkind remark or to stand up for themselves, they can become morose, and even turn the criticism on to themselves.

Girls especially like to do things together — planning, going shopping, sharing intimate conversations. They share what they are going to do and what they will wear. After the social activity is over, they discuss what went on in great detail, including who did what with whom. They talk and talk and talk — planning, scheming, sharing. Their private life is usually out on display — in gesture, in notes that get passed around, in texts, in code, in whispered giggles or eye contact.

The girl's self-consciousness has an inner and outer effect. Outwardly she is very aware of herself, and how she appears to be. This can make her seem sure of herself, even arrogant. However, she pays a price inwardly. Her self-esteem is always threatened. and she is always wondering what kind of an impression she is making on people, how they like her, whether she is being approved of. She never matches up to her ideal of herself. She is too fat, too skinny, too tall, too short. Her hair is too straight, too curly, too thin, too thick. She looks for authority in magazines, on You Tube videos, and in the 'cool' girls around her.

In their teenage years, girls have a particular challenge — to calm their emotional life, to become more objective, to react less impulsively, and to accept themselves. As they are able to slowly separate their ego from their emotions, they start to get balance. This journey goes on into adulthood.

Girls who become involved in deep emotional relationships and parenthood before they are mature have a particular challenge. They haven't yet found their own identity. They have to take on responsibilities before they know who they are, and as they watch peers developing an independent life they may feel frustrated and angry. At the same time, the joy of being loved by an infant, and loving it, brings a special pleasure. So much depends on the kind of support given by her parents and other adult friends. Without support, young mothers struggle to hold it all together, including often having to get a job and support themselves financially. In some situations, the girls' parents have supported their daughters emotionally and financially, insisting they finish school, and making it possible for the baby to be cared for. The question to ask is, where is the boyfriend in this picture? What is the quality of their relationship? What is his responsibility? Or is the girl carrying the burden alone?

The Emotional Life of Teenage Boys

In his book *Raising Boys*, Steve Biddulph discusses a made-up boy named Jamie:

> By age fourteen, the testosterone level is at a peak, and pubic hair, acne, strong sexual feelings and general restlessness may well drive Jamie and everyone around him slightly crazy. For most families, this is the most challenging year of raising boys. Take comfort: if you hang in there and stay caring and firm, it does pass. In later teens, boys become increasingly more sensible and mature. When Jamie reaches his mid-twenties, things settle down, hormonally speaking. His testosterone level is just as high, but his body has become used to this and he is not quite so reactive. Erections are a little more under control! The hormone continues to endow him with male features — such as high cholesterol, baldness, hairy nostrils, and so on — well into later life. On the plus side, the testosterone gives him surges of creative energy, a love of competition, and a desire to achieve and be protective. Ideally, his energies will be channeled into activities and career choices as well as a happy sex life, that bring all kinds of satisfaction and benefits.[7]

Boys tend to have very different adolescent experiences from girls. Their emotional life is much less developed, as their experience of their ego or identity does not become conscious as early. The boy's ego remains independent and aloof, not as easily influenced by his feelings. He matures more slowly than the girl, and the independence of his ego allows him to be more objective. The boy's ego is so strongly connected with his physical body that he identifies with what he does rather than what he feels. He is more concerned with doing things, proving himself

Chapter 7 — Understanding our sons and daughters

in rivalry with his friends, showing that he is not afraid, even if he is. He is interested in things of power such as machines, cars, bikes, planes, and computers. He is fascinated with the way they work. He works out in a gym or lifts weights at home. He does gymnastics, runs, shoots baskets, enjoying a sense of confidence as he masters his body.

He passes by situations, oblivious to undertones, unaware of the drama occurring in front of him unless his attention is called to it. When told about it, he may shake his head in amazement that girls can be so complex or that he could have missed it. Sometimes he is disturbed by the fuss and complications that girls bring to everything. He considers a display of emotions as unnecessary and a waste of time. He is less in touch with his feelings than girls are. Feelings, often complicated and not easily controlled, are threatening, even frightening. He is afraid of being overwhelmed by emotions, and avoids sentimentality, even making fun of it.

> Words and their significant content are taken up unconsciously into his nervous system, and they echo and sound in his nerves. The boy does not know what to do with himself. Something has come into him which begins to feel foreign to him now that he's fourteen or fifteen. He comes to be puzzled by himself, he feels irresponsible. And one who understands human nature knows well that at no time and to no person, not even to a philosopher, this two-legged being of the Earth called Anthropos seems so great a riddle as he does to a fifteen-year-old boy. For at this age all the powers of the human soul are beset by mystery. For now, the will, the thing most remote from normal consciousness, makes an assault upon the nervous system of the boy.[8]

He appreciates straight-forward comments that do not beat around the bush. He wants to know what to expect and what is expected of him. He has no patience with innuendos, and doesn't appreciate being talked to in circles. One young man described how his mother asked him to do the dishes. Instead of saying, 'Ron, wash and put away the dishes', she gave a deep sigh as she looked at the sink and said, 'This place is such a mess'. She waited for someone to volunteer. He was annoyed and amused at the same time, and did not volunteer. Had she been direct, he would have done the task. Boys complain that often their mothers go around in circles explaining something when they wish they would be straightforward and say what they mean.

The boy's patience is taxed by his mother's asking him too many questions or wanting to know what is going on inside of him. Boys do not easily open and share their private feelings — with their mothers, their friends, or anyone else, except in particular circumstances. Especially in early adolescence, they creep inside themselves where they can be in a safe, protected space in their own world. Parents are often frustrated because their sons have retreated into a shell, but it is healthy for boys to do that. They are protecting what is not yet ready to be exposed. Boys keep secrets in their souls. Of course, there are some boys who share their inmost thoughts and feelings with a close friend, but they do not put them on public display as many girls do.

Adults need to respect a boy's need for privacy and not embarrass him by prying into his secrets. It is appropriate for a boy to show some reserve until he has a closer relationship with his feelings.

His romantic relationships tend to be less complicated. Girls become a part of his life, but they don't take over in the same way that girls allow their boyfriends to do. The girls imagine a world inspired by romantic feelings, including trying out his last name with hers to see how it fits, although more women today are keeping their maiden names. Boys keep the relationship in a steadier balance. They compartmentalize different emotions.

Some boys see girls as conquests and approach them as they would a race or competition. The girl is there to be conquered, but not to change his life. They may brag about their exploits to their friends, but they hold back the details.

If a boy's feelings are deeply touched by a girl, however, he is capable of the greatest devotion and love. He will forego many of his favorite activities to be with her. He will miss out on a pick-up soccer game and sit on the sidelines, holding her hand. He will leave his buddies to go for long walks with her. He will talk, letting out secrets he has dared to tell no one. His girlfriend is privileged to get to know a side of him which few others know. If he trusts her, she will be very helpful to him in exploring his feelings.

Boys may have moments of great loneliness, especially if they do not have a strong interest or hobby into which they can pour energy and from which they can gain self-discipline and esteem. This may be anything from weight-lifting, to collecting model planes, to working on cars.

Boys can too easily pass through adolescence being superficial and tough. They need time and experiences that allow feelings to awaken and mature. If this happens, they will have greater depth for the ego experience when it occurs later in his twenties. Beginning at about age 16, the boy's preoccupation with the outer world gradually, almost imperceptibly, gives way enough for him to begin to listen to his inner feelings and questions. Friendships and relationships deepen his soul-life by teaching him to share and understand. Matter-of-factness yields to greater sensitivity. As he becomes receptive to the needs of someone else, he also deepens his awareness of his own needs. This maturity also enables him to develop deeper, more sensitive relationships with girls.

The emotional life of boys is simpler in comparison to that of girls. While the girl's emotional life is more highly differentiated and more delicately organized, that of boys is not all that subtle. Girls can consciously shape their emotional communication. In the family, girls tend to be coquettish with their fathers, playing on their soft spots while pursuing a subtle competition with their mothers. With boys, the reverse occurs as they compete with their fathers and charm their mothers. Rivalry between fathers and sons develops on all levels, from contests of physical skill to rivalry for attention for the women in their lives.

The Teacher and the Adolescent

Differences in the emotional life of the boy and girl have an effect at school as well as at home. It is not unusual to see a girl flirting with a male teacher, trying to charm him into bending the rules or giving her special consideration, or simply looking for attention. The boys see rivals in their male teachers and can feel that they have to take them on.

Teachers have to consider these typical differences in working with their students. Girls are often very astute, noticing details about the teacher, quick to see weaknesses and contradictions. In the name of honesty, they are likely to make a direct offensive comment that hurts. Their manner can be experienced as arrogant and rude. It is best to ignore most of it and to approach the girls with delicacy and lightness. If the teacher can make a comment that refers vaguely to her behavior and then turn away, the teenage girl may take in the message. By contrast, head-on confrontations rarely succeed.

When a boy challenges a teacher's authority, he often does it in a way that conceals what is really bothering him. Losing face is a big deal. He will express his anger in terms of an unfair rule or policy rather than admit that the teacher has hurt his feelings. At all costs, the feelings must remain secret. The boy may lose his temper with the teacher, but if the teacher loses his or her temper with the boy, all authority is lost. What is more effective is humor. However, the boy's upset cannot simply be dismissed with humor. Once the dust settles, the teacher needs to follow up, find out what is really going on, and figure out what to do about it.

At some point, the teacher should step back and gain perspective. It doesn't hurt for the teacher to let the boy know that the action was not very serious, but that it cannot be ignored. A particular example comes to mind. It was tenth grade, and I had given a test on John Steinbeck's *Grapes of Wrath*. After returning the tests to the class, Leo burst into my classroom at lunchtime and shouted, 'I disagree with how you graded my paper. I've checked everyone's test in the class, and my answer was as good or better, but you didn't give me the same grade as theirs.'

I was surprised by his rough manner, but having been through such confrontations with him before, I became calm. 'Really, Leo, you've checked everyone's paper. That's a lot of work. Let's look at your paper and see what you have. If I've made a mistake, I'll change it.' Leo sputtered, 'Well, not exactly everyone's'. 'Leo, why don't you read your answer out loud, and let's see what the issue is.' As Leo read his answers, it was clear that he had not given a full answer. He took the paper back and exclaimed angrily, 'Well, you know what I meant!'.

When I saw him later in the day, we went about our communication in a friendly way. I learned with experience not to bring it up again, and let it pass. It had not been a personal attack, just Leo's way of meeting the world. As he matured, we could talk about such situations with humor and with warmth. Had the teacher been male, the situation might have erupted into a full scale competitive attack.

On the other hand, teenage girls can be very combative with female teachers. In ninth grade, Lily was thinking she would leave the school she had attended for five years. She had gone about trying to convince other girls to leave as well. She had left her Cliff notes on *The Tale of Two Cities* in the room. I picked it up to see whose it was, and I noticed she had a list on the inside back cover of which girls she had spoken to and what they had decided. I showed it to her, and she lashed out at me, denying she had done that. Her self-righteousness was impressive, but the evidence was there. I didn't go any further with it, and she did leave the school. No other girl followed her. A year later, she decided she wanted to return. We put her through several interviews in which she had to convince us to let her return. Having the experience of a semester elsewhere and a different perspective, she realized how much she valued the school and was very convincing. She apologized for her behavior. She successfully completed her high-school years and became a strong advocate for it.

I mention these situations because we cannot judge who a teenager will become based on their behavior during these adolescent years. I could fill a book with incidents, some successful and others not so much, of what a high-school teacher experiences in daily life with teenagers. It is as much a learning experience for us as teachers as it is for the adolescents. In this way, they become *our* teachers. And as a parent, I can say the same thing.

In general, it is harder to have heart-to-heart talks with boys. Boys have feelings just as intense as those of the girls, but they would rather die than let those feelings be known. The girl may blurt out her feelings in a flood of tears, but the boy stoically holds his in. When he does venture into his feelings, he often makes a bad job of it. He hasn't the same knack as the girl. He says the wrong thing and ends up offending when he wants to please. He is comical instead of impressive, crude when he needs to be smooth.

It is worth remembering that there are times when it does go well. Maria was starting to act in a snippy way with me, but I wasn't sure what was going on. She said she wanted to speak with me, so we set a time. Then she directly asked me, 'Why are you in a bad mood when you walk from one room to the other?'. At first, I was stunned by this question. Then I realized what she was getting at. Usually as I walked between rooms, I was getting ready for my next class and was focused on what I would say and do. What she saw was that I was frowning, and with the way girls often interpret what they see, she had come to a conclusion. We were able to have a very sensitive talk in which I could understand what she was saying, and I could explain what was in my mind. That talk created a bond between us that has continued to this day, decades later.

Adam had regularly skipped out of daily school chores which students did at the end of the day. After several days of this, I confronted him with it. First, he gave me a lot of reasons why he didn't need to do it; he didn't agree that the students should do that; it wasn't fair anyway — and on and on. I told him that since he had missed several days' chores, the next day he would stay and paint one of the walls of the room which was scheduled to be done during the next holiday. Adam did show up, and I gave him the paint and brush. His classmates looked at him standing on a ladder painting. 'What are you doing, Adam? Aren't you coming with us?'. Adam replied, 'Oh, I'm just helping Mrs Staley'. He turned to me and winked. I felt this was a success.

Yet another example of the boy's awkwardness at this age is the boy who has a serious comment or suggestion to offer, but who can't do it without wrapping it in barbs. His self-image demands that he pose as the teacher's adversary, but his inner self actually wants to be helpful. The trick for the teacher, of course, is to acknowledge and honor the good impulse and to ignore the package it is wrapped in.

It is important to emphasize again that guidelines such as these must be general. Each student is different and needs to be respected in an individual way. We cannot give recipes on how to treat disciplinary problems, but teachers need to develop intuition in their relationships with students. Nonetheless, I have found that understanding some of the gender differences is helpful.

Beauty, Power and Morality

During the teenage years, youngsters are developing their attitudes to life; in particular, they are developing their sense of morality. How adults work with them affects the way they are nurturing the growth of the teenagers in their care. It is important to help them develop moral insights so that they will be guided from within, rather than respond out of fear of punishment.

Young people, says Steiner, benefit in their moral development from certain images — specifically, the contemplation of beauty, which deepens their moral insight; and the contemplation of heroic struggle in the defense of Good against Evil. This instills in the teenager a yearning to be courageous and noble. They still need explicit guidance on how to behave, but these images do more to develop a deep, personal moral sense than being told by an authority how to behave.

Both boys and girls need and respond to both of these types of moral inspiration, but starting in the early puberty years (sixth, seventh, and eighth grades), girls are especially inspired by beauty which resonates deeply in their heart, and opens a doorway to the spirit. Certain poetry especially touches this longing in the girl's heart. William Blake, William Wordsworth, and, more recently, Mary Oliver are favorites. Also, examples of beauty in action move them, as the example of two women who began a kindergarten on the border for migrant children waiting to be allowed into the USA from Mexico, or the teacher who created a kindergarten on the dump in Sarajevo for children traumatized by fighting.

For boys starting with the early puberty years, the moral use of power makes a deep impression. Their ethical instincts are nourished when they see that heroic courage and commitment are at work in the world. They admire both legendary and historical characters who overcome enormous hardship to battle for a cause. They are also fascinated by the exercise of power through technology, which can be a fine moral image as long as the technology is beneficial to humanity. For example, the musical play *Hamilton* has encouraged boys that despite discrimination and hardship, they could achieve something important. Watching drones being used to fight fires in the Amazon or in Australia can inspire boys to help the planet.

If either beauty or power is out of balance, that can be problematic. Beauty that is overemphasized can be undue concern for one's appearance, and fascination with power can become aggression. These generalizations about boys and girls don't always hold true, and we need to realize that there are boys whose souls are deeply touched by beauty, and girls for whom power is fascinating. Most important, teenagers need examples of beauty and power that can serve as ways of contributing to the world.

Because many young people in our time identify themselves on a spectrum of sexual identity, each person has a unique relationship of masculine and feminine qualities. We may prepare ourselves for a macho son only to find that he is happier cooking or babysitting. Instead of a feminine daughter, we have a girl in jeans, happy changing oil in the car or using a chainsaw.

Teenagers are intrigued by their sexuality, and often express it in exaggerated forms; but as they mature, their sexual identities usually come into balance, and they are more at peace with their identity. That doesn't mean they have resolved all the problems. We live in turmoil today concerning all areas of sexuality, so there are more questions than answers. We seem to be developing toward a recognition of each person's individuality rather than fixing a teen in a particular role. This means that during high school, teenagers are experiencing a sensitive process of finding their identity. In a safe environment, students are more likely to share their identity and welcome the love and support of their classmates. Homosexuality is not the taboo it was in the past, and the variety of identities of LGBTQ (Lesbian, Gay, Bi-sexual, Transgender, and Queer) are unfolding. Some youngsters do not fit the strict categories of homosexual or straight heterosexual.

Often, the feeling that the youngster is different begins in early adolescence, although it can start earlier. The most important guideline is to

Chapter 7 — Understanding our sons and daughters

respect our sons and daughters as individuals, and love and support them as they go through their journey. In some cases, youngsters feel comfortable sharing this; in other cases, not. The teenager should be the one to make this decision. It is most helpful if attitudes cultivated at home have been open and supportive to the question of sexual orientation rather than derogatory. I was deeply touched by a friend who had a terminal illness when he learned that both his daughters were gay. When I asked his wife what his attitude was, she said that he commented that God gives us many ways to love. Unfortunately, he died before he had the opportunity to enjoy his daughters, their partners, and the grandchildren.

In a Nutshell

Understanding our sons and daughters

- We are living in a time with great changes in the area of gender and identity.
- Gender is fluid, and adolescents are engaged in figuring out their identity.
- Our task is to love our teenagers as they go through their search.
- I am myself still learning the nuances of this issue of identity.
- Respect for each person as an individual should be central in all of our relationships.
- There are biological and neurological differences in males and females.
- The emotional life of teenage boys and girls is important to understand at the same time as we understand there is gender fluidity.
- Beauty, power, and morality are signposts of adolescent development.

Chapter 8

Temperaments and soul types

Introduction to the Temperaments

> What would the world be like without the temperaments — if people had only one temperament? The most tiresome place you can imagine! The world would be dreary without the four temperaments, not only in the physical, but also in the higher senses.[9]

Every family is a collection of different personalities. That's what makes life interesting. We learn early that each child is different and must be treated differently. For example, we plan a vacation trip. One child is ecstatic; another is upset because she doesn't want to leave home; another wants to change the route to include only his favorite places. Yet another is agreeable as long as she can have unlimited access to her cell phone. Will we ever please everyone? Each child or teenager needs to be responded to in a way that works with the needs of the whole family, yet meets their individual needs as well.

The traditional 'nature vs nurture' debate presents parents with two views of human nature. One is that children come to us already formed: all we can do is feed, clothe, shelter, and educate them. The second is that children come to us as a blank slate and are strongly shaped by us.

There is a third approach which acknowledges aspects of the two traditional views. However, this approach recognizes as an additional element that each child carries an individual past into the present. The power of destiny is a shaping force in human behavior, and the individual human ego has the power to transform itself.

Individuality develops from two directions — the spiritual and the earthly. From the spiritual side, the human being brings their spiritual essence, their higher ego, which continues from lifetime to lifetime. They also bring talents, tendencies, and capacities that have been influenced by their own past. From the earthly side they bring inherited qualities — family characteristics, race, and gender. On one hand, these inherited qualities limit and define the individuality. On the other hand, the individuality influences what has been brought by heredity.

The temperament is the dynamic in which the individuality and heredity meet and influence each other.

The temperament expresses the relationship of the individual and the inherited nature. The individuality shines through the inherited nature and influences what has been carried from heredity. Although the temperaments provide a helpful clue, they provide only a partial picture. It is tempting to stereotype people according to temperament, failing to recognize that the individuality is far more complex than any category can ever indicate.

Temperaments begin to emerge at around 5 years of age, and are strong indicators of behavior through puberty. Then something new begins to emerge — the soul types. First, I will describe the temperaments, and then introduce the soul types. The integration of the two are helpful in understanding adolescents as well as adults.

The temperaments are expressed by psychological and physical characteristics by four broad groups of people: **cholerics**, **melancholics**, **sanguines**, and **phlegmatics**. There is no good or bad temperament; each has positive and negative attributes. Each person has aspects of all the temperaments, although one or two temperaments are usually dominant. The temperaments come from deep within the human being and express themselves outwardly, coloring the way we react to life, forming our life gesture.

Temperament is influenced by the physical constitution, particularly the bodily proportions. As a generalization, melancholics tend to be tall and slender, sanguines have balanced proportions, phlegmatics tend toward roundness, and cholerics are usually of short, with a solid build. However, as with all generalizations, there are many exceptions.

The melancholic and phlegmatic temperaments are more introverted, self-involved, while the choleric and sanguine temperaments are more outward or extroverted. In the first two, stimulation comes from within; in the latter two, stimulation comes from outside.

The way adults react to a child's temperament strongly influences the child's self-image, way of approaching people, and doing tasks. Hopefully, the positive qualities of the temperament have been nurtured. In cases where this does not happen, the youngster spends much energy during adult life overcoming fears, anxieties, tempers, etc.

During the transition from pre-adolescent years to adolescence, the temperament gradually changes, and a different one becomes dominant. It is striking to see the new personality emerging and to glimpse the coming adult. The real individuality is taking over, and year by year this process becomes more stable as the temperament achieves a balance. Around the age of 21, the ego is born and becomes a major influence in the forming of the adult temperament and in the emotional maturity that follows.

A child and teenager simply live with their temperament, experiencing it to the fullest. They depend on adults understanding and bringing out the best in them. When they become adults, they can consciously work on their temperaments to strengthen the positive aspects. Adults may find that they have one temperament dominating their thinking life, another one influencing their feeling life, and still another one dominating their will life. As parents or teachers become more familiar with temperaments, they have a useful tool for understanding their children, teenagers, or themselves.

Rudolf Steiner calls attention to the study of temperaments as a useful tool for understanding children and for educating in the classroom.

The Four Temperaments

Each of the following sections is a generalized characterization of one of the temperaments. No child will exactly match the description, but each child has enough recognizable characteristics to connect them with a dominant temperament. The dominant temperament most strongly colors the personality, but the presence of the supportive temperaments adds interest.

The basic rule is: Go *with* the temperament, not against it. The child needs the opportunity to experience the world through the temperament and, in that way, achieve balance.

The melancholic temperament

> Why am I always passed by? No one notices what I do that is as good or better than others. It just makes me feel sad.
>
> 11th grader

The melancholic child and teenager often gives the impression of heaviness, her limbs seem to hang with a heavy weight, with shoulders and face drooping. Her head is bent over, her walk is measured and steady with steps seeming to drag her along. She dawdles, closed up within her thoughts, cut off from the world, exuding sadness. Her voice is often soft and restrained. She may hold back, either not completing sentences or mumbling the last words.

She is very conscious of her body, sensitive to how things feel and to the special clothes that feel right. Otherwise, she complains about the tightness around the neck or waist, the scratchiness of a fabric, or an annoying detail in the way the seams are sewn.

Her demeanor is serious, resigned, quiet, and withdrawn, engrossed in the past, reflecting on what she has seen and heard. She is often convinced that a small insult or injury was meant to hurt, and the event stays in her memory. She goes out of her way to look for obstacles which then fulfill her prophecy that life is hard, and people want to make it more difficult for her. We have little hope of convincing the melancholic child of anything, because her viewpoint is fixed.

He imagines all kinds of catastrophes, both in the natural world and in his body. Every little ache is magnified. His general lack of vitality results in being ill and missing events. He complains about not having enough sleep even though he may be the last in the group to awaken. If you ask how he is, he lists his discomforts. However, he gains a certain sense of pleasure in sharing his internal misery. Sympathy is sought and often received. He is self-involved, often worries, and seldom hears what the other person is saying. Though he is very sensitive to any possible hurtful comments, he makes blunt comments, hurting others. It is difficult for him to laugh at himself; instead, he blames others for his discomfort. This makes it hard for him to say, 'I was wrong, and I'm sorry'.

The other side of this is that melancholics absorb the atmosphere and internalize when blame is meant for others. They then feel guilty and punish themselves. This increases the sense that life is a burden. Even when they seem to be having a good time, they will often temper is by saying, 'Well, it wasn't all that good'. Or 'It could have been better'. This disheartens adults until they learn how to respond to it.

There are many wonderful attributes of the melancholic child or adolescent, particularly gentleness, kindness, and thoughtfulness, especially if a person or animal is ill or injured, and she can spend endless hours caring in a most meticulous way. She can be a perfectionist, may throw away her work or rip it up because it doesn't meet her standards. She is capable of thoughtful consideration of an issue, pondering the pros and cons, exhaustive in research.

Often, they are thinkers who gain respect for the attention they give a problem. They come up with original solutions. They also enjoy being responsible for figuring out details, such as mileage covered on a trip, how much money is spent, what items are needed at the store. If someone shows interest in their thoughts, they can be an excellent conversationalist about issues or events. They like to share opinions and often have intelligent and thoughtful perceptions, but they become uncomfortable if they feel someone is probing their inner life.

He is slow to make friends, but often will become the best friend of a similar type of person. He looks at the new day as a time for problems to emerge — all the pitfalls with possibility of failure. He takes impressions so deeply into the soul that he suffers from stomach aches and headaches. The key to the melancholic is to find the appropriate way for him to bring into the light what lives in the dark night of the soul.

Melancholic teenagers can benefit by reading biographies in which people overcome problems or have similar situations. It is good for them to learn that all human beings have to endure and overcome.

We can appeal to the will of the melancholic, to hang on, to persevere. The teacher or parent can give help in the beginning to get them off to a good start, so there is less chance of their becoming anxious.

Many melancholics have an artistic sense, and with encouragement, she can use her creativity in service of others. Special occasions provide opportunities as a reason to make something for another person. This act balances the egoism of the temperament.

Since he craves security, routine is very important. However, he can become rigidly fixed and have a hard time adjusting to change. It is helpful for teachers and parents to help melancholics prepare for change so that it doesn't come as a surprise. Although it is easy to interpret resistance to change as negativity, it is actually masked fear. He can either be so orderly that any threat to him causes annoyance and anger. Or she becomes chaotic, constantly looking for what she has misplaced. A typical response is, 'If everyone would just leave my things alone, I'd be fine'.

Change in family or school is very hard on them. They may take on the responsibility for family problems. They think death or divorce would not have happened if they had acted differently.

Reading can be an escape or it can be therapeutic, particularly if they learn about great accomplishments made in spite of handicaps — for example, the life of Helen Keller. Humorous books also help them to laugh at the world. They often enjoy reading about or watching ridiculous, slapstick behavior which they would not do themselves, but which they enjoy vicariously.

During adolescence, the child's temperament is fading, and the new one is not yet there. The insecurity of adolescence is intensified as they lose their familiar ground. Loneliness, cynicism, and a sense of rejection are aspects of the young adolescent's melancholic temperament. As the adolescent develops, the new temperament comes in more firmly. The wallflower blossoms into a sociable, confident young adult, but echoes of the old melancholic temperament remain as an undertone, providing compassion and sensitivity for others in need.

The sanguine temperament

> I've been thinking about the way I do things. I try to do too many at once, and I don't finish anything. But I like to be involved in everything because it makes life so interesting.
>
> 11th-grade girl

The sanguine during childhood is usually slender of bone and muscle, well proportioned, and supple of movement. She has a light, springing step. Inner happiness shines through her twinkling eyes. Her face is alert and expressive, as features appear to change easily, reflecting her moods. She exudes a sense of well-being and delight in her fine coordination. Her gestures are quick and varied, adding to a general expressiveness. She bubbles, chatters, talks to anyone and everyone. Talking is part of a joy of living.

They live strongly in their nervous system as impressions jump quickly into imaginations. They are quick to grasp and even quicker to forget. Concentrating is difficult. They tend to flit from thing to thing, with scattered thinking. Pictures come and go in their mind and feelings. They live in the images rising and falling away. At times, they feel at the mercy of the changing images and have difficulty remembering what has been read.

He can exaggerate without concern, brushing off criticism. He is sociable, making many friends. It is often difficult to know where you are with a sanguine, as he has many best friends. He brings love and adventure to a group because his love of life makes everything an adventure. His enthusiasm and fantasy often make him the center of attention and the life of the party. With his emotional highs and lows, he is always on the move, constantly surrounded by friends. He can be easily bored, and it is difficult for him to get serious. Despite the fact that he can be charming, his feeling life can be shallow.

In their everyday life, sanguines find it difficult to establish habits, order assignments, or remember due dates. Often this leaves a mess for others to clean up, but their smile is infectious, with lots of promises to improve.

Chapter 8 — Temperaments and soul types

Sanguines are affected by the environment, always trying to fit in to whatever is around them. They need help to relax and simplify their life. It is helpful if they can find a few serious interests underlying all the frenzy. They may explore many interests until finally finding one that will last for a while. It is difficult for them to pay attention, and they need help to do a job well rather than skipping over the surface. As students, they struggle with depth. In their writing they often disregard punctuation and capitalization. Wonderful ideas abound, but they lack form and development. In a classroom they are often very cooperative, responding to approval and attention.

As they move into adolescence, they start to slow down, do better with concentration, while continuing to be cheerful. They often have to make up for the skills they hadn't gained in their butterfly days. They are grateful for the support and patience of adults who insist on their finishing their work.

The phlegmatic temperament

> All things are timely done which are done well.
> Octavius

Good-natured, kind, thoughtful, easy-going — not much bothers phlegmatics. They like to dream and give the impression they are not paying attention. It seems they are not very smart, but that is misleading. They just need time to work things out. They need to put everything in order, look it over, and slowly come to a sensible decision. In fact, most things about the phlegmatic are sensible. They do not like to be pushed to decisions. All things must be considered. The phlegmatic learns slowly, but has a good memory. However, images of past deeds are buried below the surface. When it is appropriate and enough time is given, their memory is stimulated and the image is retrieved.

Physically, she is usually roundish. Her walk is unhurried and easy, and her movements may be clumsy. Everything about her suggests time, time to do everything, and resistance to any haste or compulsion. Her look is calm, even seemingly aloof. Her voice may not have much modulation. She has a tendency to go on and on without much drama in her voice.

Phlegmatics move slowly, lacking vitality, and they would rather stay still and not be bothered. They take it easy and do not exert themselves. It is difficult to get them started, and difficult to get them to stop. They especially love comfort, sleep, and food. They may sigh at times with physical satisfaction at how well everything is going.

He has a love of order, comfortable with habits and routines. He likes life to be predictable with regular hours, large, full meals at the same time every day, and regular bedtime hours. He will tell you that he likes it this way because it makes sense. He doesn't like family or school customs or habits to change, and he will strongly protest when that happens. He exerts strong will to resist change because it frustrates him. He can put up a wall to hold off change, and that can be difficult for those around him.

Phlegmatics often have many friends. Although they may not be exciting, they are dependable, loyal, reliable, steadfast, honest, and truthful. They don't grab the limelight. Often, they have good ideas, but they are modest about bringing them forward. Acceptance and respectability are important. They don't want to make waves, but they like to have excitable people around them so they can vicariously experience situations, as long as others aren't demanding anything of them.

At school, she takes in the material and it sits deep below the surface. She gives the teacher a blank look as if she never heard of the subject. It is hard to remember details. She has trouble completing assignments or showing what she knows. In her thinking, she takes things literally. However, her pleasant manner and evenness makes it nice to have a phlegmatic in the midst of a class of cholerics and sanguines.

In adolescence, his heaviness continues, but his preoccupation with his inner world becomes stronger as he becomes focused on himself, more like the melancholics. Much of what he ignored earlier does start to bother him. He dwells on irritations, and those bother him more.

She wakes up from a sleep and becomes concerned about the way people relate to her, and now she wants to be recognized and appreciated. She responds well to praise. On the other hand, her behavior is complicated as she may withdraw and do very little that is expected, or she can be pleasant on the outside and scheming on the inside. She doesn't place much importance on appearance, and feels frustrated in a group that focuses on looks. A special interest, once cultivated, is the saving grace during this difficult time of transition for phlegmatics.

Be aware of close and overly dependent relationships that may develop between mothers and their phlegmatic sons. The mother tries to protect them from growing up and facing consequences, and they find refuge in the mother's doting. Great patience and creativity are needed with phlegmatics, as they can bring many blessings in adulthood.

The choleric temperament

> Nobody is stepping forward to take responsibility. I guess I'll have to take over the group and make it happen.
>
> 12th-grade student

Usually well-built and muscular, cholerics tend toward stockiness. They exhibit firmness and solidity in their appearance. Their body is filled with energy, they move restlessly, not finding it easy to sit still for a long time. Their eyes move restlessly, scanning the environment. They stand firmly rooted to the earth. When they walk, they stomp on the ground, usually digging in their heels, poised for action. They pace, feel tension and restlessness in their body, and feel caged when they have to stay seated too long.

Her gestures are short, assertive, confident, and purposeful. Her gait has a swagger. She is ready for anything, as she aims in a direction and moves with purpose through the door or down the street. Not easily distracted, she knows her own mind and plows through anything that would distract her.

His voice is strong, often blustery. He easily commands, shouts, filling the room with his voice and presence. His sense of well-being is strong. He takes pride in being healthy and doesn't understand why others are sick or weak. He stoically endures setbacks and is quick to tease or taunt another as a 'cry baby'. He doesn't show weakness or vulnerability easily because he wants to appear tough and independent.

A choleric is like a bull in a china shop. They try to step gracefully, but it is difficult, and they often knock things over or collide with people. Their sense of self is tied up with what they do in life. They are self-centered, pushy, and demanding. It is important for them to be biggest, toughest, and first. Life is a competition either with others or with themselves. They are always fighting toward a goal. If they have to intimidate others to get there, it is justified.

When she wakes up in the morning, she awakes easily, plans the day, sees it as a chance to prove herself, succeeds, and completes the tasks. She feels mastery over situations and people because she senses that people rely on her.

Natural leaders, cholerics have energy to carry out their plans to their end. However, they often feel burdened by life. Impatient with others who are too awkward, too slow, too fussy, or too contemplative, they are glad to tackle jobs and get them done because, who else will do it? They try to shape the environment the way they know it's supposed to be.

A choleric challenges what people say, and she feels that she has to say something about everything. When not listened to she pouts, but overcomes it quickly and goes on. If her honor is attacked, she can be vicious, defending the right, and doing battle-to-the-death. It is difficult for her to accept blame, and she will put it on to someone else. Yet if she realizes it is her fault, she will try to repair the situation, and apologize.

As leaders, they have good ideas, are good organizers, effective in getting people behind them. At times they can bully, but at the same time they also have a sense of direction which attracts others. As the central authority, they are usually kind to followers who hold them in high esteem.

A choleric with sanguine tendency wants to get things done to move on to the next project. They take pride in finishing the task rather than in completing the details well. 'There, I've done it. At least it's done.' They grow impatient when others talk while there is more work to be accomplished.

A choleric with a melancholic tendency directs their attention to details. Everything has to be done perfectly, the way they want it done. Everyone else is imperfect, but only they do it the right way. They redo what others do, re-organizing, checking up on other's work. They worry about the low quality and are convinced the world is headed downhill,

Chapter 8 — Temperaments and soul types

and only they can set it right. They take things personally, exhaust people by demanding explanations, by lobbying for their position, and finding it difficult to compromise.

An argument between two cholerics is a loud, insulting, aggressive experience. When it is finished, they go about their business as before. Although they like the excitement of the encounter, they can have their feelings hurt and carry a grudge for a long time.

They usually enjoy school, feeling satisfaction at getting work completed and being recognized for their good work. They can conflict with other cholerics who detract from the tasks. They are the power for good or bad. Choleric teenagers organize fundraisers, take on projects, follow through, running roughshod over others. Furious when others don't follow through, they rave and rant, intimidating mild students.

Cholerics either say 'Yes' to everything, or 'No' to everything; it is seldom in between. If 'Yes', they get burned out by being over-extended. It is not possible to stop the choleric from accepting responsibility, but a supportive adult can help the choleric set priorities. Giving up a commit-ment is akin to letting a sinking ship go down, so they have to be reas-sured that the job will be done well by someone else. If they don't want to take on the task, their first reaction is usually 'No', because they do not like to be surprised. They need time to integrate the request. Once they can envision what is being asked, they will come up with their own ideas, and so they are willing to say 'Yes'. However, they have an agenda of who and what has to be done, because cholerics have to think it is their idea.

Saving face is important. After an unpleasant situation in which the choleric was unreasonable, adults can help by waiting until the next day to discuss the choleric's behavior. By then the fire has calmed down and they can listen. At heart, they want to do the right thing, but because they are the movers and shakers, they need space around them.

In adolescence, cholerics often develop a sanguine quality. As their emotions take hold of them, they are pulled this way and that. Friends are developing stronger personalities and stand up to them. They experi-ence some of the hurt they have caused, and try to rectify it, becoming more sensitive to others. Some of their energy gets diverted, and it becomes scattered. If their energy become too diffused, they will feel they have failed. Cholerics have to learn to give up control. With maturity, they learn to laugh at themselves.

The Seven Soul Types

When we meet the child in the years between 7 and 12, we meet the temperament most of all. When we engage them in conversation or activity, the quality of that engagement has a great deal to do with whether the child is choleric, melancholic, phlegmatic, or sanguine. During this time, children unconsciously develop a sense of identity. Are they easily pushed around? Do they stand up for truth? Are they supportive of their friends? Some youngsters are born with profound moral convictions which no outer force will dissuade. They have such strong character that even at this age, they leave people feeling uplifted with joy and hope.

As puberty comes to completion, it is not so much that their physical form or their temperament determines their behavior, but another aspect of their soul is awakened and influences the way they act in the world. The astral body or soul body gives rise to strong desires, wishes, hopes, jealousies, anger, and generosity. The world has expanded, and everything is possible to experience. Adolescents will sample each possibility to see how their behavior affects their relationships, until with time and maturity, they are able to handle the choice responsibly. They begin to separate themselves from their parents, friends, and others while they develop a more objective relationship to the world, searching to find what their own beliefs are, and deciding for themselves their core values.

The forces of the soul body can be described as seven soul types, or the planetary types. The soul body is not a physical body, but a body of forces that carries both the lower and higher aspects of the soul life. The soul body is freed when the youngster is sexually mature. Before this, the child's desires were stimulated from the outside, such as, 'I want that toy', or 'I want earrings like that girl has'. At puberty, the soul body penetrates the entire physical body including the sexual organs. Pubic hair develops, breasts develop, voices change, wet dreams occur. With this new activity of the soul body, sexual desires awaken from within.

Along with these changes comes a change in thinking as the adolescent's soul life becomes active. At first, they focus on what is closest to them such as family members, home, school, friendships, hobbies, and decisions affecting their personal life.

As their soul life deepens and expands, they become concerned with wider issues such as climate change, religious beliefs, and social issues such as poverty and homelessness. Issues of truth become central. The meaning of love changes from what feels good to a deeper sense of sharing their life with others.

Each soul type is expressed in the way the adolescents relate to their individual inner world and to the outer world. There are several ways psychologists have formulated to identify types of people, for example, by using the Myers–Briggs personality scale, Enneagrams, or by identifying people as introverts and extroverts. Rudolf Steiner pointed to these seven different qualities or types related to the qualities of the planets.

Each soul type expresses the character of the adolescent as the young person meets the world, shaped by experiences with people and with situations, but their individuality comes from a deeper place within the soul. The essential nature of the person includes noble traits, and moral and ethical qualities, as well as the motivations that guide the person's life. It is built from within the person by the moral decisions they make. Although character is influenced by a person's experiences, it is primarily an expression of the individual, and not merely the effect of training or conditioning. Character traits include loyalty, courage, compassion, honesty, commitment, steadfastness, attentiveness, fairness, and idealism. Each soul type can express these character traits in their own way.

Since the soul is the carrier of the forces of thinking, feeling, and willing, the soul types can be seen as particular qualities or expressions of these. Each person has all seven qualities, some are more connected with the thinking, others with feeling, and still others with willing. During our life journey, we act out of a variety of these soul qualities as a way of describing the relationship between our inner world and the outer world.

The soul qualities are different from the temperament. The temperament is strongly influenced by the physical body. A heavy, slow-moving person tends to be phlegmatic, whereas a thin, wiry, fast-moving person tends to be sanguine. The temperament continues to influence us even after the soul quality reveals itself. The temperament is more difficult to change because it is part of the habits. We can transform our temperament, but it takes strong will of the ego to do so.

We are more flexible in the way we work with our soul qualities since they are not embedded in our physical body, but are part of our dynamic soul activity. It is as if we are actors on the stage, with seven different moods or ways our character can interact with the others in the drama of adolescent life.

During adolescence, the soul types are easier to identify than simply looking at the temperament. First let us explore the seven types, and later we will see how the temperament and soul type interact. As we mature and become more aware of our dominant soul type, we can see how to act out of another type. The ego is the shaper of the interplay between soul types, and guides us in developing our personality.

Reflective Preserver (the Moon type)

This type can be one-sided in either emphasizing reflecting or preserving. Adolescents who are strong Reflective Preservers either don't like change or they like change if they are following others who celebrate it.

Reflective: The person stays on the surface, tends to follow trends, emphasizes appearances, does not express original opinions or thoughts, can tend to glitz and glamor. These are the teenagers who follow fads, and are often the first to show them to the group.

Preserver: The person is systematic, thorough, practical, concerned to document activities, has good memories, ready knowledge of statistics, detail oriented, comfortable in the world of facts, and resists change. These teenagers are happy to be secretary of their class, keep good notes, and remember what was done in the past, but they are uncomfortable when classmates suggest change.

This type reflects the atmosphere around them, finding it difficult to hold a balance between flexibility and order. They can be compulsive in one extreme or the other. However, when balanced and mature, the Reflective Preservers can broaden their perspective through humor and interest. They learn to be flexible when it is needed, and firm without being rigid. They look to depth rather than being on the surface. They bring clarity and focus to a group.

The Social Innovator (the Mercury type)
This type tends to the social side or the innovative side.

Social: They fit in easily with people, enjoy communicating and connecting people with each other. They can be the life of the party and can sell anything to anybody. These are the popular teenagers who know everyone, and everyone knows them. They are great at meeting new students or parents, showing them around, and sharing the fun and excitement of school.

Innovator: They adapt to different situations, are very flexible, filled with ideas, often enjoy stirring up chaos, enthusiastic, even mischievous or unpredictable. These teenagers love new ways of doing things, see new possibilities, and enjoy running for office such as Student Council, but they may not complete the tasks that are started.

When balanced, the Social Innovators bring healing powers, bring what is static into movement, and try new ideas. They are very creative. Every group or organization benefits from their flexibility and enthusiasm.

Dreamy Nurturer (the Venus type)
This type gets lost in feelings.

One-sided Dreamer: They are romantic, with a feeling of being ungrounded. They constantly want to be in love. They tend to be unrealistic, frenzied, will seduce or be seduced. They have fantasies and can be taken advantage of. These teenagers have deep longings, and they may become despondent if they feel things can't be realized. Their dreams can help others imagine what could be possible, even if it is impractical. They need others to anchor their dreams.

One-sided Nurturer: They take care of everybody else, showering love on everyone. They can spend so much time listening that they can't bring closure, don't want to hurt anyone's feelings. They can smother others, be easily hurt, want everyone to be happy, even to being a martyr. They have difficulty with boundaries. One-sided Nurturer teenagers know who is having a hard time, who needs more care. They spend long hours listening to classmates' problems, leaving little time to finish their own work.

The mature dreamy nurturers listen, help, bring aesthetics to the environment, want to bring beauty, kindness, and warmth, yet they know the boundaries. They are able to find outlets for their talents and to serve others. They take a nurturing role in the family and community.

Radiant Balancer (the Sun type)
This type integrates the six soul types.

One-sided Radiance: They shine in every aspect of life, are the center of a group, can become arrogant, considered mature beyond their years, and can resent too high expectations placed upon them. These teenagers are given too much praise and adulation. They do so well that it is expected of them all the time. They sometimes get into trouble just to prove they aren't perfect.

One-sided Balancer: Things come easily to them as they are able to succeed in many areas. It comes naturally to them to organize their assignments, space out the due dates, and use their time effectively. They are able to handle stress. It all seems so simple that their classmates may be jealous of them. Teachers have high expectations because these students deliver what is asked.

When they are mature and balanced, feelings and thinking work beautifully together. They are models, and can accept praise without becoming proud. They understand that they worked hard for their achievements and things have not come easily, although others may think so. Such teenagers are often leaders because people are drawn to them. They are not only pleasant to be around, but they do what they say and accomplish great things.

Active Talkers (the Mars Type)
They are active and forward moving.

One-sided Active: They are impatient to get things done, focus on the future, move things along without enough preparation, often not listening carefully. They can exhaust themselves and others. They often feel they don't get recognized for all they do. For them, life is a battle, and

Chapter 8 — Temperaments and soul types

sometimes they bully, and at other times they respond to being bullied. These teenagers can be challenging to teachers, often asserting that they know better and can do better. They also push classmates around to get done whatever they think is important. Yet because they are good at what they do, others fall in line and obey.

One-sided Talker: They speak strongly, are assertive, and can manipulate or monopolize time. They argue to get their way, exerting power over others. They like competition, wanting to win at any cost. These teenagers take up a lot of time and air, expounding their ideas, forcefully using words to get other students to do what they want. They can see the effects of their speaking and enjoy the results.

Mature Active Talkers are creative, direct, bold, courageous, able to discipline their will, and are excellent leaders. Their energy is concentrated and focused. They can inspire others to join in and work. They have initiative, are independent, and are dedicated to moral action. Teenagers who are maturing in this way are the doers in the school, carrying out ideas, organizing the classes, following up, and getting the job done.

Thinker Organizer (the Jupiter Type)
They live in their thinking and direct their energy outward

One-sided Thinker: They are overly confident that they have figured everything out. They have the big picture, but not the details. They can get lost in the beauty of an idea. Sometimes they think that only they have the truth. These teenagers love the challenge of a difficult subject, can follow the teacher's thinking, feel the excitement when they get the crux of it, and light up in the *aha!* moment. They are cooler than the Radiant type, and they can be judgemental of them.

One-sided Organizer: They grasp the structure of what they are working with, can go too far in following rules, can be arrogant, exploit others, and put people into boxes. Their confidence in their organizing capacity leads them to refuse to be questioned, compromise with others, but try to convince others that they have the answers. These teenagers take on big projects in school such as environmental clean-up, figuring out what each class needs to do, what equipment is needed, and how much time to schedule.

Chapter 9

The development of character

Perhaps all the dragons in our lives are princesses who are only waiting to see us act, just once with beauty and courage. Perhaps everything that frightens us is, in its deepest essence, something helpless that wants our love.   *Rilke*[10]

The whole object of the universe to us is the formation of character. If you think you came into being for the purpose of taking an important part in the administration of events, to guard a province of the moral creation from ruin, and that its salvation hangs on the success of your single arm, you have wholly mistaken your business.   *Emerson*[11]

The Development of Character

Young people in their 20s are distinguished not so much by their physical looks or their temperaments, but by the kind of people they are. Their values, their motivations, and their principles speak to us more clearly than their keen intellect or their latest possession. If we are in a position to hire people, we want responsible individuals who can be trusted to work hard and perform their tasks well. If we rent a house to young people, we need to have character references. If our sons or daughters marry or have a significant other, the character of the intended spouse is far more important than how much wealth or prestige the person brings to the relationship. We expect good character in our elected officials, and are constantly disappointed when they show themselves to be selfish and power hungry.

We may be temporarily impressed by wealth, position, cleverness, and skill, but in the long run it is the character of the person that concerns us. We want to know whether the person can be trusted, whether the person has courage to face their deeds, whether the person lives an ethical life. In short, we are concerned with integrity.

Character develops slowly. In the first seven years, we meet a child and get an impression from their physical form and their gestures. Beneath the physical surface the child is forming a sense of who they are. How have the parents given the child a sense of self-worth, of security, of love? What have the parents or caregivers modeled for the child to imitate? Such an attitude becomes a part of developing character. Already by 6 years of age, the child appears to express a general attitude including being cheerful, angry, loving, cooperative, generous, or competitive.

However, most children do not have such a strongly developed character at this time. Instead, they echo their parents' standards of morality and do not come into their own until later. The young adolescent tends to judge situations by imitating their parents or friends. They may agree and voice their agreement without much thought behind it, or they may take the opposite point of view just to show their independence

During the middle-school years, from 12 to 15, they begin to develop their individual character more strongly. As described earlier in this book (Chapter 1, note 1), this can be called the time of 'the civilizing mind', when the qualities of truth, beauty, and goodness begin to consciously guide them. I described this in greater detail in my book *Tending the Spark: Lighting the Future for Middle School Students*. It is especially during this time that they are influenced by the role models in their community, their schools, and their family, as well as the culture surrounding them.

Character is an expression of the whole personality, and evolves as the adolescent meets the world. It is shaped by experiences with people and with situations. The character defines the essential nature, the noble traits of that person, and includes moral and ethical qualities as well as the motivations that guide the person's life. The character is built from within the person by the moral decisions the person makes and by their standard of behavior.

Although character is influenced by a person's experiences, it is primarily an expression of the individual and not merely the effect of training or conditioning. Although you cannot teach a person character directly, you can significantly influence its development.

Character traits include loyalty, courage, compassion, honesty, commitment, steadfastness, attentiveness, fairness, and idealism. As the ego forms the character from within, it expresses itself in convictions which guide the person's behavior. The great religions and ethical systems of the world have described the force of character by many different terms, such as the conscience; the still, small voice; the inner light; the Truth; the Spirit; the Christ force; the Holy Ghost; the Tao; or the voice of God. The development of character has been considered of prime importance by society, and in the past it has been considered to be the work of the family, church, and community to develop the character of young people

As American society's respect for tradition has wavered, so too has the importance of character. Recently, we have seen ethical values become confused with super-patriotism and big business. Many young people have become suspicious of do-gooders and of those who stand for virtuous behavior on Sunday, but act unethically for the rest of the week.

Two extremes of behavior are demonstrated in many societies. One extreme is a very strict standard of behavior, formed by emphasis on tradition or fundamentalism which leaves no room for the individual to disagree. The other extreme is individualism, a mentality which holds that there are no objective values, and everything is left up to the individual's whim. These attitudes divert young people from realizing the serious task of character development.

Character develops from within the adolescent as a response to what is going on in their community. As the adolescent faces dilemmas involving honesty, courage, and integrity, the opportunities for character development present themselves. But the parental attitudes and the social atmosphere have an important bearing on the way the young person develops. Youngsters who feel a certain inner security are not easily swayed by others and are able to put off rewards and aim for long-range goals. They are able to handle the challenges and find their way amidst temptations and opportunities. Insecure youngsters have more difficulty handling new situations and making decisions that will benefit them in the long run. They want their rewards now, and they need outer forms of recognition and status because they don't feel secure inside themselves.

Examples of Adults Responding to Students' Mistakes

All students make mistakes. However, the way the adults handle those mistakes reflects their moral values and helps the children develop character. This presupposes that the adult cares enough to deal with the issue at all. For example, I experienced two different way of responding to teenage theft.

A 14-year-old student stole flasks from a chemical company. When the teacher took the teenager and the flasks back to the company so that they could make amends, the teacher and student were told, 'Never mind. That happens all the time'. A valuable opportunity to help the teenager work on their character was lost. Instead, they were given the message that what they had done was acceptable.

During a trip to New York, an eighth-grade class had dinner in Chinatown. As the students climbed on to the school bus, they began comparing the ash trays they had taken. The teacher marched the class back to the restaurant, and had each student return an ash tray and apologize. The restaurant manager was grateful for this and explained that although it was common for school groups to take things, no teacher had ever responded this way. The event made a significant impact on these teenagers.

We can help young people develop character by bringing them face to face with themselves and helping them to set things right. By doing this we are communicating that there are objective standards of moral behavior, and we expect youngsters to live up to them. If they are not able to do so out of themselves, we will help them do so. In this way we show them that we care about the way they live their lives, and we awaken in them a keener awareness of their moral nature.

Two girls used their lunchtime to do a 'lawn job' — that is, to make deep ruts on a lawn with their car. The teenagers were identified, and the owner of the property worked with the school and parents so that the youngsters replanted the lawn and did gardening for the owner. This was far more effective for their character development than being made to pay for the damage. The students felt better afterwards that they had been able to set things right.

An example occurred when a faculty member's child, a teenager, challenged the rules, figuring she had special status. The rule was that the assignments had to be in by a particular date unless the student had contacted the teacher and requested an extension. In this case, the student did not do this. The work came in a day late. The faculty (with the student's parent excused from the discussion) sweated over the decision. Every possible excuse was given to avoid enforcing the rule. After all, this was a faculty member's daughter, an excellent student. Taking a deep breath, the faculty followed the rule and gave the student the penalty. The student gained respect for the faculty because it turns out that students had made a bet that the faculty would be soft and not follow through with the penalty.

Often when teenagers get into trouble, they are calling for help, especially for the attention of their parents. If the parents focus on protecting a youngster from the punishment, they often do a disservice to their children. The important question is, how can we make the most of this situation so our teenager learns the right lessons from it? It is not a matter of protecting them from the pain. So often the wrong lessons are learned if the parents are not willing to look at what is happening in their family. Instead, they place the blame on others. Then they seem surprised that their youngsters have trouble accepting responsibility for their own actions. From my experience, I feel that parents often don't realize that when teachers have to discipline teenagers, it is as painful for them as it is for the students.

An example of the teenager's inner desire to lead a moral life is shown when youngsters have to decide their own punishment. They are often much harder on themselves than the adults are. Teenagers know when they are doing wrong, and although they may at first be hostile and lie, in the long run they are actually grateful for the adult's intervention and for the opportunity to learn a lesson.

Chapter 9 — The development of character

One young man always seemed smooth. He never actually got caught or received blame, but he was somehow involved with most behind-the-scenes activities that went on. When confronted, he put on the most innocent look and was in fact insulted that he was accused of lying, cheating, bullying, or whatever the accusation was. Each meeting I called to discuss the problem was tense, and it took persistence to meet him and call him on his antics. As he got older, we were able to speak about difficulties with more directness, and although he didn't acknowledge having been wrong, he did joke with me about it.

After graduating, he wrote me the following:

> First of all, I can't tell you how glad I am that you have been my advisor. I know that might sound silly, but it's true… These past four years I have learned so much from you, not just academically, but about life and people. I'll never forget all the little conferences and meetings I had to go to with you. At the time I hated them, but now I realize how much they taught me. Thank you so much for everything, and I'll always remember you.

Many teachers have evoked similar responses, even if they were not put in writing.

It is nice in retrospect to receive such comments, but while the situation is going on it is quite unpleasant. Not only do they have to face the teenagers' attitude of denial, but in many cases the parents' justifications as well. Those of us who are parents as well as teachers understand how hard it is to have a youngster denied an opportunity or recognition because they have done something thoughtless or just plain stupid. Yet it is an opportunity for a high-school teacher to help teenagers strengthen their ego.

There are numerous opportunities in each community to help youngsters develop their character by facing their misdeeds and helping them set things right. However, it has become far more common for adults to ignore (either out of a lack of caring or out of fear) such actions, and teenagers are running rampant, destroying property, causing disturbances, and even terrorizing adults. The greatest sadness, however, is that these youngsters are not only getting away with what they are doing, but they are doing nothing to develop their character. Unless adults make it a priority to confront errant youngsters with standards of behavior, it becomes harder for those adults who do care to be able to do so. The result is a decreasing morality in society.

Other Examples of Character Development

Character develops in other ways besides making amends for mistakes. For example, parents can praise a teenager for owning up to the truth rather than getting angry about the action. Such praise is a strong message of the parents' values. When teenagers get the message and tell the truth, they are working on moral development. Such practice helps shape character.

Another example is cheating. In schools, there are many occasions when the teenager comes face to face with cheating. 'Should I cheat?' 'Is it really cheating if I just help a friend who didn't get a chance to study?' 'Will I be caught?' 'Is it right?' 'How do I feel about my friends cheating?' The inner struggles the adolescent goes through in making such decisions is forming their character.

One of the most difficult situations I faced was when a very sensitive, sweet teenager allowed others to copy his work. He felt the pressure and yielded to it. However, when the faculty responded with the penalty from the rules in the school handbook, the parent and friends, feeling that the student's entry into a highly prized college would be affected, attacked the teachers. It was a difficult situation, but the student, who was very ashamed of his action, recognized the rightness of the penalty, even though it affected his grade for the course. Three cheers for that young man who was willing to take responsibility for his action!

Adults influence the character development of a young person in several different ways — by personal example, by creating opportunities, and by setting standards for the teenager to meet. When teenagers see adults making decisions to obey their own inner moral standards, it makes a great impression. Even though they may find it difficult to understand in the moment, teenagers are impressed by the effort.

Unfortunately, today character is not valued very highly, and teenagers who choose to act morally are often scoffed at and teased. Because loyalty to a group is ranked more highly than loyalty to the truth, adolescents who make moral decisions are often unpopular with the crowd, and risk being ridiculed. The situation is made even worse when political figures in high positions lie and manipulate, giving youngsters a model for getting away with it.

Adolescents begin facing existential questions such as, 'What will my life be like?' 'What do I want to stand for?' 'What will I sacrifice for?' They are considering different values and priorities. 'Is service more important than money?' 'If I have to go against my beliefs to work in a place, is it worth it?' 'Do I want something enough to cheat for it?' 'Am I being true to myself?'

For example, a 19 year-old college student had always planned to work in nuclear physics, but when he discovered that most of the jobs involved were connected with nuclear plants or nuclear weapons, he felt he had to give up that dream and choose another major.

Making plans for the future also confronts adolescents with character-building opportunities. For example, 'Should I continue my education when I would rather get a job and have a fancy car?' 'Should I choose a career that serves others, or one that makes a lot of money?' 'Should I take initiative or just coast along?' 'Should I help my family so that my younger siblings can continue their education, rather than doing the kinds of things I want to do?'

Character develops as adolescents learn to make moral decisions on their own. For example, a teenager with outstanding intellectual aptitude may decide to work at a menial job or a dangerous job in order to experience what that kind of life is like. Their life may be difficult because of it, but listening to inner principles takes priority over the easy way of life. Such a decision, rooted in the individual's ego, is not the same as rebellion. Such a decision is consciously made because higher values are at stake. When teenagers act out of such impulses, it is very difficult to talk them out of their plans. They are willing to risk loss of approval, financial security, or suffer isolation.

A father was looking forward to his son taking over their successful family business. The son decided, however, to be a teacher.

In another situation, a young unmarried woman became pregnant. Her parents urged her to have an abortion. Her church told her it was wrong. People in authority were telling her what to do. She wrestled with the decision, and finally she decided to have the child and assume the responsibility of raising it. In another similar situation, caught between two strong views, a young woman might decide that she would have the abortion, even though she would be criticized for it. These are painful decisions, which ever way it goes.

A student spoke to a teacher about a classmate cheating in class, even though she knew that she would experience pressure for reporting. She did it in a quiet responsible way, and she was surprised that she was not the target of bullying because of it.

A young man turned in his test to a teacher to be re-scored because the teacher had erred and given too high a score.

Each of us has moments in which we are called upon to test our own character, to be better human beings than we were earlier, to rise to great heights. Or we may give in to greed or laziness, may not follow through on something important, or let a friend down. These experiences stay with us and haunt us, unless we are able to resolve them.

How Teenagers Build Their Character in the Community

Teenagers need to contribute to their community. A part of character development is service. Is the adolescent expected to contribute their efforts to the family, or does every job have a cash value? Does the teenager have an opportunity to help an elderly person or a handicapped person? These are wonderful opportunities which evoke the idealism and good will of teenagers.

Opportunities for developing character occur during adolescence in leadership positions in organizations, in the family, and on the job. In these situations, teenagers have to deal with such issues as handling responsibilities, dealing with repercussions if the responsibility is not met, and denying themselves time for personal pleasure because of the needs that have to be fulfilled. The reward that comes is the satisfaction

Chapter 9 — The development of character

of a job well done. High-school organizations offer many possibilities for such character development, and advisors to these groups should work with teenagers to develop priorities. Such development doesn't just happen by itself.

Another important aspect of character development is the setting of standards for teenagers. Meeting expectations in the family, in the school, or in religious institutions helps adolescents aim for high ideals and develop inner strength. To cultivate ideals, the teenagers must be given a way to implement them. When the standards are not met, the adult has the responsibility to reflect this to the teenager, however unpleasant it may be. No one likes to be told they have fallen short, but it is a benefit in the long run. If the adult sees that the teenager has cheated or behaved irresponsibly in other ways, the adult should act upon their knowledge for the good of the teenager. It does not help teenagers for adults to close their eyes and pretend nothing happened. For teenagers to grow and develop their character, they need the courage of adults to help them face an unpleasant situation and develop from it. The situation may be painful in the moment, but the teenager is setting a direction for their moral life.

To have a profound effect on the development of character means to do something over and over, to engage one's will, to build new habits and attitudes. Giving up a meal once in a while to remind ourselves of hungry people is a noble idea, but it only becomes a part of one's life when this is done regularly, or when actions are actually taken to help those in need. Visiting a convalescent home to cheer up the elderly is a beneficial experience, but only becomes part of character development if, for example, the adolescent goes once a week for a semester, or does something else to incorporate the experience into their life.

A part of character development is maintaining balance between serving oneself and serving others. It means using one's special talents to benefit others and to avoid becoming egotistical and self-serving. Character development doesn't come easily. It takes effort, time, and commitment. In this way, a person influences their own personal evolution.

Personality Qualities and Character Development

Each of us has special qualities in our personalities. The description of soul types in the previous chapter offers many examples of how our personality expresses these qualities. Whether we use them to benefit others or ourselves is an expression of our character. For example, we may be very inquisitive, interested in knowing a great deal about people and subjects. If we are more interested in people, we might direct that quality in an anti-social way by being a malicious gossip. We might love to pursue a subject area by shutting ourselves in a room and becoming a lonely, narrow-minded researcher, the image of the mad scientist trying to gain power.

However, if our inclinations are to bring our talents to benefit others, we would move in a different direction. Our curiosity about people, rather than being used to turn one against the other, could be used to bring about an understanding of people's needs, to understand how one teenager can benefit from one approach and how another responds best in a different way. Our curiosity or our interest then serves humanity. Along the same lines, if we love researching subjects we might discover benefits for society.

We might have the personality quality that wants everything to be in order. We know that when we are involved, things happen. If we are concerned with ourselves most of all, then we want to be the ones to decide how things should be. If anyone disagrees, we might fly into a temper tantrum or slam doors. We might feel unappreciated and frustrated. We want recognition, but no-one is recognizing us, so we feel hurt and angry. However, if we are working to develop our character in a moral way, we can transform this quality so it benefits others. Our sense of order can help a group figure out what needs to be done, and our leadership can inspire others to do what needs to be done without too many commands. This is described clearly in an ancient Chinese statement:

> The highest type of ruler is one of whose existence the people are barely aware.
> Next comes one whom they fear.

Chapter 9 — The development of character

Next comes one whom they despise and defy.
The sage is self-effacing and scanty of words.
When his task is accomplished and things have been completed
All the people say, We ourselves have achieved it.

Tao Te Ching

Another personality quality that can often be a blessing or a curse, depending on what we do with it, is flexibility. On the one hand, the person can be of weak character, and keeps changing to adapt to whatever comes. This person seems very easy-going, but is actually rather spineless. What appears as flexibility is a disguised need to be accepted by the peer group, whatever its values may be. However, this can be a wonderful quality, if transformed and developed morally. Such a person keeps things moving, sharing ideas and keeping things from getting too stuck. They can see what is needed, and are able to change so that new things can happen. This quality then allows the group to heal wounds, see new possibilities, and proceed in a constructive and creative manner.

Each of us has many personality qualities which become the working material of our character development. Beginning in adolescence we become conscious of these challenges, and begin to work to shape ourselves.

Rudolf Steiner points out that there are special times in our lives when our inner voice speaks most strongly, usually in relation to our life's work. These moments occur in an 18½ year rhythm, at about ages 19, 38, and 56. At those moments, we face ourselves in a particularly direct way. We have an opportunity to evaluate what we want to make of ourselves, and see how far we have come. Sometimes we become ill, other times we face terrible loneliness, or we make decisions that turn our whole life in a different direction. At these times the work we have done to develop our character helps us.

Developing character is the great work of human life. We become what we will to become. Whether we believe that we are inspired by spiritual beings or that we develop out of rational ethical sources, the work is still left to our own efforts to shape, to mold, to form what is truly human in each of us. This great work is set out during our adolescent years.

In a Nutshell

The development of character

- Most children do not have strongly developed character in the first seven years. Instead, they echo their parents' standards of morality.
- During the middle school years, from 12 to 15, they begin to develop character more strongly, influenced by role models surrounding them.
- As the adolescent meets the world, their character is built from within by the moral decisions they make and by their standards of behavior.
- The way adults handle children's mistakes influences the way children develop their character.
- Helping adolescents face misdeeds and set things right offers an opportunity for character building. Unfortunately, in many situations teens are not held to a high standard, but are excused from taking responsibility.
- As adolescents begin facing existential questions about who they are and what values they stand for, they begin to awaken their inner selves.
- Opportunities to develop character are in leadership positions, meeting expectations in standards of behavior, cultivating ideals, and maintaining balance between serving themselves and serving others.
- Starting around age 19, and occurring in an 18½-year rhythm, the inner voice speaks, often calling the adolescent to their goal in life.

Chapter 10

The needs of teenagers

Losing the World and Finding the World

Young children live united with the world in an unconscious manner; they have little awareness of themselves in relation to the world. As they develop, however, they become more conscious of this relationship, and lose their earlier unconscious connection to the world and feel drawn into themselves. They experience a shift in identity. We can say they lose the world to find themselves, and with this loss they experience loneliness. Then, out of the loneliness, they reach out from the self to find the world in order to experience unity again, but this is a new unity because they are no longer unconscious.

The tension that develops between the self and the world is a necessary tension of human existence. Because we live in two worlds, the physical and the spiritual, we feel at times pulled in two directions. Where the worlds of body and spirit meet, they create the realm of the human soul. Here, body and spirit weave the tapestry of individual destiny. Consequently, the soul life is always in flux, a present moment hovering between past and future, the crossing point between inner and outer realities.

Adolescents live right in the middle of this tension, unable to find a secure place in the center. Their needs and desires swirl and storm within them, and sometimes sweep them away. It is only when the ego develops at about 21 that most people gain the capacity to take hold of their soul forces and achieve balance in their lives. This capacity begins to form around the age of 17 or 18.

Adolescents seek dialogue between themselves and the world. On the one hand, if the needs of the world become too powerful, teenagers lose their center. They lose hold of themselves in too much activity and intensity, and they are then at the mercy of what is going on outside, and can find little peace. If, on the other hand, the inner life dominates, they may shut out the world, retreat, and become self-indulgent recluses. All human beings have a tendency in one direction or the other, but most healthy people find a creative and tolerable balance.

I am grateful to have read *Beyond Customs* by the English psychologist Charity James.[12]

In grouping these needs, it occurred to me that on one side, the world dominates, and on the other side, the Self dominates. The needs having to do with the world are more commonly the attributes of the success-oriented Western person who lives in the will (physical activity, intensity, affecting the world, belonging, being needed, needing facts), while the needs of the Self are more identified with the attributes of the Eastern person who lives in thought (stillness, routine, rhythm, introspection, separateness, community, and imagination).

> **THE ADOLESCENT'S NEEDS**
> **physical activity < > stillness**
> **intensity < > routine**
> **to affect the world < > to move inward**
> **to belong < > separateness**
> **to be needed < > need to need**
> **facts < > myth and legend**

Just as there is a difference between the Western and Eastern orientation to life, there are differences between the two sides of the individual's soul life. A middle ground needs to be developed where the strengths of the two can interact rather than confronting each other as opposites. The middle is the soul life, the world of feelings, which mediates between thinking and willing.

The Need for Physical Activity and the Need for Stillness

Teenagers are gaining mastery over their bodies, and their ability to feel comfortable in their bodies is an important element in personality development. In that sense, the need for physical activity and the need for stillness are really aspects of the same need. Some teenagers do not want to exert themselves any more than is necessary. Others relish the challenge to use every muscle, delighting in the strains and aches that result from heavy exercise. Others are afraid of physical contact. Fear of being hurt causes them to avoid contact rather than meet it. One can see the differences quite clearly in volleyball games in high-school physical-education classes. Some teenagers go to meet the ball, while others step aside and let the ball drop next to them. Physical activity ideally embodies both graceful rhythm and style. Movement and stillness are in balance.

Physical activity takes many forms and has many benefits. For some, it may be frantic activity to fill time because the teenager is afraid of being alone. For others it is part of the battle to lose weight. For others it is the joy of working together for a common goal, sharing the excitement of achieving it together. For whatever reason, teenagers should have the opportunity for physical activity, whether it be walking, bicycling, running, playing tennis, or any other activity that strengthens their heart and lungs. The current fitness trend has encouraged many teenagers to work out and keep in shape. If this does not become an obsession, it serves a valuable purpose. (Some parents have noticed that they end up mowing the lawn while their teenager spends hours in the gym or on the court.)

The need for stillness is a parallel need. It allows the body the needed rest to replenish forces, and to calm the nervous system. Stillness is also important because creativity is virtually impossible without it. Creativity tends to be born in silence. If our young people are going to have the resources to deal with the world before them, their creativity must be protected and cultivated.

Teenagers tend to operate on nervous energy, not getting enough sleep, overdoing physical activity and experiencing emotions on the edge of catastrophe. Their lives are a dramatic contrast of ups and downs, and their nervous system comes under too much stress. No-one can eliminate, nor should they try to avoid, the tragic-comic highs and lows; but the alternation between tragedy and comedy needs to be rhythmic rather than frenetic, gentle rolls rather than shock waves.

Time is needed every day when the demands of life recede, and teenagers can retreat into their rooms without music blaring or earplugs on. However, this would be true in an ideal world. Today's teenagers almost never have quiet. They are hooked to their cell phones, waiting for the next text, afraid to miss a message from someone or because they are checking on social media. Their need to retreat hardly ever happens, and they are almost never alone with quiet. Oblivious to the outer world, they can bicycle, ride, jog, or fish to the accompaniment of music, podcasts, and social media. Their sleep is also affected by the lack of silence. Many sleep with their cell phones nearby and are connecting with friends in the late or early morning hours, so that they are exhausted the next day. Schools are struggling with the same issues, and have to make clear guidelines in the use of cell phones in classes and on class trips. When they are successful in having a media-free trip, students recognize the benefit, even though they aren't happy about it.

In contemporary society, the need for stillness is ignored, replaced by a hyperactive world of sense impression. It is no surprise to hear about increased nervous disorders and anxiety among a generation whose fear of silence is depriving them of stillness.

The Need for Intensity and the Need for Routine

Teenagers need to have excitement, new ideas, new people, and new challenges. They want to spread their wings and fly, to test themselves in many new areas of life. Telephone calls, time spent with friends and family members, and special activities contribute to the excitement of life. The teenager craves new experiences, and has trouble settling down to anything of a routine nature. However, too much intensity, like too much physical activity, leads to overstimulation and superficiality.

Balance is needed between stimulating activity such as clubs, teams, jobs, social activities, homework, home responsibilities, and family, and a steady, calming routine of everyday life. Amid all the demands that accelerate their lives and leave little time to breathe, a family and school rhythm reassures adolescents that they can count on a few things in life while so much is in turmoil inside them.

Rhythm is important because it provides a structure so that change can occur. Meals are especially important in the teenager's life, and that routine, whenever possible, helps bring stability, even if it is only several times a week. With their busy schedules such as after-school activities, it is reassuring to know that they will have dinner with their family on particular nights or weekends. When they have no idea when they are eating or whether they are preparing their own dinner, eating with the family, or heading to the nearest fast-food outlet, they lack security in one of the basic needs of life. They resent constant change (except when they are the ones initiating it). Of course, teenagers can deal with change and a break in rhythm, but it isn't fair to take advantage of their ability to fend for themselves unless it is necessary. The older they are, the less they depend on the rhythm of their surroundings for support.

Teenagers need routine, but too much becomes boring and they feel they are wasting away. They long for excitement, for changes of pace and place, for a more exciting social life. They daydream, imagining what other places are like and how wonderful their lives would be in other circumstances. This often comes to the fore around the tenth grade, when they may become dissatisfied with their usual situation and look outside. This is an echo of the nine-year change when the magic of childhood is fading, and they become moody and uncomfortable. Some teenagers long for routine, while others long to escape from it.

The Need to Affect the World and the Need to Move Inward

Adolescents need to feel that they count, that what they say and what they do mean something to people, that they can express opinions and bring about change.

They can be invited to participate and contribute ideas in family and school discussion and decision-making, where appropriate. Learning to share ideas and express opinions in a protected space is very valuable, even when it is parents or teachers who are making the final decisions. Being able to plan their own room and arrange it so it expresses their interests and personality are a way of having some control over their surroundings. Having a special area of a school yard or classroom offers the same possibility. Signing up to tutor younger children gives teenagers the opportunity to make a difference.

Schools offer many opportunities to bring about change and affect their surroundings by joining clubs, participating in student government, planning school events, and talking to faculty members about concerns. In the larger community they can write letters to the editor, talk to people in responsible positions, make constructive comments at a job, and volunteer their services.

Joining an organization in the wider community introduces them to ways of governance and decision-making, so they understand that it is not only a matter of winners and losers. Teenagers are needed because they have energy and enthusiasm, and at the same time they need to learn about compromise.

By evaluating their contributions and actions, teenagers learn about their limits. If they feel free to ask important questions, explore different points of view, make statements, and contribute their energy to getting things done, they will be affecting the world. They need to know that they can put their ideals into action and make a difference. Many actions to improve society are being carried by the youth of today, whether it be gun control (in the USA) or climate change.

The other side of this need is the inner side, the need to move inward. To offer the world something of value requires time for introspection. Reflecting, thinking about their aims, pondering values, wondering, comparing, musing, reading, drawing — all offer the teenager an opportunity to enter into a dialogue with their own soul. Such dialogue is the furnace in which ideals are forged. Who is it that lives within my soul? What is most important? What kind of person do I want to be? What do I want to do with my life? These questions can never really be answered from outside. The inner side of the individuality is sensitive and private. It needs nurturing in a special way, unlike any other aspect of the teenage personality.

The Need to Belong and the Need for Separateness

For the adolescent, belonging to a group is extremely important, but it can cause deep anxiety. Each group has its own goals and values, so teenagers need to consider carefully before deciding which to join. Joining a group tells the world what the teenager stands for. Once in a group, it isn't always easy to change and still be accepted.

If teenagers do not find a group they feel comfortable with or which accepts them, they can be miserable. It is easy for adults to ignore the teenager's frustration, but they must understand that teenagers feel pressure. Not to have a group is to feel either that you are alone in the world or that you are so special you will make it alone. Sometimes, however, teenagers choose to stand alone, apart from a group. The choice is not made out of arrogance, but because the situation leaves them no option. Not everyone is a group person. Some are such private people that they are uncomfortable in a group. For them, adolescence can be especially difficult unless they find a close friend.

However, groups can dominate teenagers too much. They impose standards, ways of relating, likes and dislikes. Teenagers may be undergoing critical inner changes, but they will be careful about showing them, especially if these changes include a shift in values or a change in groups. They know that leaving a group will mean instant, major adjustments in their social life.

Adolescents have as strong a need for separateness as they do for a group. They need to think about themselves as individuals apart from the group. They need the opportunity to take a look at themselves to see if they are satisfied with their activities, with the values they have identified with, and with the behavior acceptable to the group.

The struggle between the individual and the group is one of the major struggles of the teenage years. The pressures which a group puts on the individual often determines how the young person will act throughout high school, and this in turn affects choices they make for many years afterwards.

Adolescents struggle with self-esteem. Am I good enough? Why can't I be perfect? To feel good about themselves, they often depend upon a group's feedback. Yet that isn't enough either. They gradually need to develop inner strength to make their own decisions, but only after a painful period of insecurity. Because they are still vulnerable to other people's opinions of them, the effect of Instagram and other forms of social media have a heavy impact on their self-image. This insecurity doesn't just disappear overnight, and most of us adults have gone through similar periods.

Anyone who has been around a teenager who cannot decide what to wear, what to do on Saturday night, or whom to go out with, knows of the insecurity involved. Most teenagers overcome this lack of self-esteem, but some don't. To escape, they conform slavishly to their group or they escape into alcohol, drugs, or video games.

The need for separateness is often depicted as a rival to the need to belong, but both are needs, and it is a mistake to think that they can choose one and exclude the other. Because of the pressures of society and the insecurity of adolescence, the need to belong is stronger for the early adolescent than the need for separateness. After the 16–17-year change, the teenager can deal more effectively with individual decisions and group pressure.

The Need to Need, and the Need to be Needed

Teenagers have an intense need to feel part of their community, whether that is their class, their family, or their social group. Being part of a group lets them feel accepted and approved of. In addition to needing to be part of a group, they need companionship. The need to need, however, goes beyond friends or the group.

Teenagers need to feel that they can ask for help when they need it without being made to feel inferior. Because of the way they have been treated in the past, many youngsters feel that they must have permission to express their needs. In the family, there are many opportunities to reassure them that their needs are important and appropriate. Obviously, when adolescents are doing projects in the house they will at times seek help. How that is given varies from a parent who might say, 'Why are you so stupid?' to another parent who might say, 'Here, let me show you, and then you'll know how to do it next time'.

Adolescents need to feel comfortable needing. If they feel inferior because they have admitted their needs or because they feel they have exposed their ignorance, they are learning a negative lesson — Don't expose yourself. Don't admit your ignorance. Teenagers don't express their needs too often, and if discouraged, they will express them even less.

In a frightening situation teenagers need support, but they often do not express the need out of fear of being called a sissy. The adolescent may be going into hospital or to the dentist for surgery. It may be a driving test or a competitive exam. They may be auditioning for a part in a play or giving a speech to a large audience. Whether they ask for it or not, they need the support of their parents and their teachers. They will be able to deal with a situation better if they know their parents, teachers, and friends will stand behind them. Of course, they will have their share of disappointments in life, but the way the adults respond may determine whether they feel they are a success or a failure.

The need to be needed is a particular problem in modern society. In the past, teenagers were needed and valued for their labor. As they assumed adult roles, they also received adult privileges. Today we have denied adolescents many of the responsibilities they had in the past. They seldom have to leave home at 16, find a job, marry, and begin a family. Instead, childhood actually is prolonged into their 20s. What are their struggles during this time? They have the same struggles as the younger adolescent does, frustration because of dependence on parents, the desire to be accepted as an adult, wanting to make a mark on the world, and the need to get on with their own lives.

Despite the general shift in society, there is still a definite need for the adolescent's contribution to the family and the community. However, many parents would rather pay someone to do a task than take the trouble to teach the teenager the skill. Too many teenagers, especially in suburban communities, have money on their hands which has been given to them rather than earned. They have little idea of its value and may spend it imprudently.

Because society is going through such a radical change, it has been easy to ignore the need of the teenager to be needed. Roles are not very clear. Teenagers see adults acting like their peers, and this is confusing. If adult expectations are cloudy, they are unsure where they are meant to contribute. When adults are clear about their values and expectations, teenagers are more likely to take an active role.

It is important for teenagers to understand their obligations to their families. One rather spoiled 17-year-old girl mentioned that she had to get away for three months in the summer to understand what she received at home. 'I have more freedom now, but I am expected to do certain chores and a certain amount of yardwork. That's fair.'

A family can have different kinds of needs. Chores are an obvious need, but if adolescents are paid for doing chores, they aren't really needed since someone else can do the job as well. Parents should consider what they are doing when they pay their children for household chores. I am not saying that there are not times when a special project should be paid for, especially something that otherwise would be hired out. However, some work should be required, simply because each person is part of the family or community, and there are tasks to be done out of love and responsibility.

If there is an elderly person in the family or nearby, teenagers can do much to help. If they are given specific tasks to do for the person's well-being, it not only gives the teenager something important to do, but it strengthens the bonds between generations. A telephone call, a ten-minute visit, or some other small gesture can mean much in an older person's day.

The need to be needed is especially strong around birthdays and holidays. If teenagers are involved in planning a celebration, they not only fill a need but they are storing up important experiences for when they become parents themselves. If the adolescents are ordered to do things for a family celebration, they may become resentful and sarcastic, and the purpose is lost. The task may be accomplished, but it is an accomplishment of bitterness.

Similarly, it doesn't help to ask a teenager to bake a cake that evening if they already have other plans. It is a different matter, however, if the adult says, 'Next week is Dad's birthday. What shall we do to celebrate it?' One may offer to gather flowers, another to bake a cake, another to cook his favorite meal. A wonderful attitude grows when a family is repeatedly involved in this way over a number of years. Later, after the teenagers have left home, they experience joy when they, too, are remembered in a special way.

The same holds true for the holidays. If the adolescents are brought in to offer their own ideas along with the established customs, they are usually happy to participate. For example, they may be thrilled to hide eggs for an Easter egg hunt although they feel too old to gather eggs. Older children can help in many ways, such as selecting a tree, decorating, supervising cooking, baking, and shopping. Or for Hannukah, they can prepare the menorah, plan small gifts, or make latkes. Even though they may complain at the time, they usually think back to that time with great satisfaction if they had made a meaningful contribution. In school, teenagers are needed in planning special events such as baking sales, proms, or buddy days with younger children.

The world has so much need for the vitality and vision of our young people, and when this need is clearly conveyed to them, the response is outstanding. They yearn to be needed. The need to help hungers in their soul. It is up to us to inspire them. We do them a great service when we find ways for them to demonstrate compassion, tenderness, commitment, and the energy they have to offer.

The Need for Fact and the Need for Imagination

Teenagers crave both facts and imagination. Facts help them establish themselves firmly on the earth. They are relatively unambiguous, and offer the teenager a way to know the world. Young teenagers often memorize lists of batting averages or words of songs. Holding on to facts provides a sense of power and control. Facts give them something to talk about, whereas asking them to express opinions about something they do not understand intimidates them. Facts are safe — the person is right or wrong. Teenagers affirm themselves through the facts they know. Too few facts provide a very subjective view of life. Too heavy reliance on facts deprives them of inner exploration.

Teenagers also crave the world of imagination. Fantasy is one level of imagination and offers an escape route from the greyness of the everyday world or a world that is emotionally demanding. Adolescents, especially between ages 13 and 15, hunger for fantasy. They soak up science fiction, mythology, and adventure stories (including romance), living in created worlds, on other planets, identifying with superheroes, or accomplishing amazing deeds. They yearn for excitement, for magic, for sensational escapes, and mind-boggling plots. Others dwell in the imagination of times past when good and evil were clearer than they are today, and they indulge in games that allow them to play roles and invent plots. These can be done through card or board games, video games, or on the computer.

The human being learns in two ways — in a straight factual objective way and in an imaginative way. Each approach gives a certain kind of information about the world which can be expressed in fact or fiction.

Young adolescents enjoy the content of myths and legends even though they know the stories could not have happened exactly as described. Once they begin to see myths as veiled explanations of truth, they become involved in an exciting inner exploration. Even if they don't relate to myths on the metaphorical level, they may simply find them satisfying and exciting.

When adolescents experience the change of consciousness around age 16–17, they also undergo a change in their relationship to fact and imagination. On the one hand, they seek to expand the world of fact to include an understanding of world events, knowledge of the human being, and a grasp of time and space. On the other hand, they see that facts alone are not enough to satisfy their questions. They crave archetypal images that appear in myth and have their reflection in the human soul. When they grasp the myth as metaphor, they can approach their own struggles as part of the human condition and see how it is part of a universality.

The myths and legends of the world, especially such legends as *Parzival*, *Beowulf*, the imaginative works of Tolkien, works by Ursula LeGuin and many others, and powerful imaginative dramas in such great works as *The Brothers Karamazov* and *The Divine Comedy*, challenge and nourish adolescents when they are taught creatively.

These same feelings also relate to television programs, movies, and video games.

Dialogue

The needs expressed in the adolescent period become the needs of adults on a different level. In the dialogue between the world and the adolescent's own soul, they experience the dilemma of human life. Maturity, or integration, has to do with integrating opposites, or allowing polarities to meet in the middle where a third possibility may arise. The mature adolescent allows for the contradictions while the young adolescent bristles at opposites and labels their existence hypocrisy.

Adolescent needs are expressed in relationship to balancing physical activity and stillness, intensity and routine, making a mark on the world and introspection, wanting to give and wanting to fulfill a purpose, and craving both facts and imaginative fiction. Teenagers define the questions, and then as adults they travel through life trying to answer them. Thus, their lives become quests, and the visions of adolescent strivings provide light on the journey for all the years to come.

In a Nutshell

The needs of teenagers

- Adolescents live in the tension between the physical and the spiritual.
- Through their soul-life, their world of feelings, they mediate between thinking and willing.
- The need for physical activity and the need for stillness: although teenagers are constantly busy, they also need time for being alone, able to replenish their forces and calm down.
- The need for intensity and the need for routine: teenagers crave excitement, with lots of challenge from new people and ideas. At the same time they need routines they can count on.
- The need to affect the world and the need to move inward: one of the strongest needs for adolescents is to make an impact on their surroundings, to change things. At the same time, they need time for introspection and dialogue with their own soul.
- The need to belong and the need for separateness: the adolescent is driven to belong to a group and feel accepted, but they also have a need for time to take stock of their own values.
- The need to need and the need to be needed: adolescents need support as they venture into their school and community, and at the same time they long to feel they are making a valuable contribution in a meaningful way.
- The need for fact and the need for imagination: adolescents feel grounded by their grasp of facts, but it would be a dull world without their being able to escape into imagination or fantasy. Each feeds their soul in a different way.

Part II

The World of Adolescents

Chapter 11

Teenagers and family life

Just having problems with my parents. They're yelling at me.
Don't let your parents get you down.
They love ya, they do. I know that's hard to believe.

11th grade pupil

The Volcano and the Mask

Although teenagers may give the impression that they need more space and push their families away, they still need them and want a connection. Because of increases in divorce, the bonds of blood are loosening, and new configurations are forming. Teenagers need to be in a community in which there are people who have known them for a long time, who have shared experiences with them, who care for them and love them unconditionally, even when the teenagers do not seem lovable. Often, today's biological family is unable to meet these needs, but they are still important to be met in some other ways.

Rudolf Steiner points out that families are not random combinations, but that threads of destiny connect family members. The eldest child usually has a special role in helping create the family. The other children come into an already-formed family and have a different relationship to their parents.

As children reach adolescence, they relate to their parents in a variety of ways, two of which I call the volcano and the mask. In dealing with the adolescent volcano, one senses rumblings beneath the surface and realizes that heat and energy are bubbling there. Spontaneously, the volcano erupts — all kinds of inner stuff is spewed out — and then the volcano cools as the adolescent explosion subsides. If the adolescent is not able to release pressure from time to time, the heat and energy move inward, and the pressure increases until it blows completely out of control.

The mask is another way in which family members often experience the teenager. Adolescence itself is a mask, and teenagers present themselves to their parents and to the world in a series of masks, both comic and tragic. Parents sometimes look at their teenagers and wonder, 'Do I know you?' or 'Who are you today?' 'What will you be tomorrow?' Life at this time is a drama without an obvious director or producer.

The relationship between teenagers and parents becomes an arena for the emergence of the self, and the confrontation can be exhausting for everyone. Some parents see it as a necessary stage to be endured. This, too, shall pass. Many others find this an exciting and rewarding period of life because it is endlessly fascinating. No matter what, it changes from day to day.

During adolescence the relationship between parent and child changes radically. Parents may experience the teenager as a stranger, an intruder, a rival, an arguer about curfews, a critic of the parental lifestyles, and someone who would prefer to be miles away than nearby with the family. They prefer being locked up in their room with friends or even alone, as long as they have their phone with them. There, they can conceal the confusions of life. They may turn to other adults for consolation and intimacy, leaving parents feeling rejected.

Where are the long talks, the shared activities, the family feeling we had imagined would take place once our youngsters became old enough to share our concerns and interests? Where is the appreciation, the consideration, and sympathy we hoped to experience from our soon-to-be adults? Why, instead of running a home, do we mainly find ourselves sharing a house, a car, a refrigerator, and a bathroom, as well as experiencing additional financial challenges?

To the young teenager, parents are fallible, inconsistent, and unreasonable. They mismanage money, time, and relationships. They have lots of answers, but are unwilling to discuss the questions. They concentrate on authority, yet they don't know everything. There are long stretches when adolescents see nothing right about their parents, roll their eyes, or give sighs of frustration, and yet they still need them very much. Under all the outward turmoil, the most important question still is, 'Do you love me?'.

Put another way, the question becomes, 'Do you care enough about me to follow through on what you tell me, even if I fight you all the way?'. Teenagers want the love and respect of their parents, even as they do everything to wear them down. Friendships and romantic relationships come and go, but the parent–child relationship is a constant in a teenager's life. In spite of the tensions, it provides the anchor of stability.

As parents become worn out, they find it easier to give in, to let the teenager go to the all-night bash, to hang around with whichever friends they wish, to choose whatever school, classes, and activities they want. It is difficult for parents to keep up the struggle when their hearts are full of questions. Isn't that what teenagers are clamoring for — freedom? Then why are they so disgruntled? Why aren't they satisfied? Why do they fight for freedom from their parents and then slavishly surrender it to their group?

Parents need to simply accept that teenagers want the impossible from their parents. They want parents to guide, but not to force; want them to give advice but not give orders; want parents to give limitations without punishment; and they want parents to be understanding without expecting responsibility. They want adults around when they need them, but only as helpers, not as authorities.

What is so interesting is that teenagers know this. They know that what they want is unreasonable, but they can't help wanting it. On another level, they don't want this at all. They want parents who talk with them, share experiences, mean what they say, stand up for values, create family experiences, and limit them when they need to be limited. The problem is that most of the time they don't realize that this is what they really want. They see it only when they grow into adulthood and look back.

In a recent *New York Times* article, Lisa Damour goes to the heart of the situation when she describes the puzzling sequence of events. First, teenagers bring the parents their problems. Then the parents offer suggestions, and the teenagers dismiss their ideas as irritating, irrelevant or both. When teenagers bring questions to their parents, they really don't want solutions, they just want to be heard, to vent if need be. It is helpful to get

Chapter 11 — Teenagers and family life

things off their chest, and they don't want parents to analyze the issues and tell them what to do.

> Much of what bothers teenagers cannot be solved. We can't fix their broken hearts, prevent their social dramas, or do anything about the fact that they have huge tests scheduled for the same day. But having a problem is not nearly so bad as feeling utterly alone with it.[13]

What they want most from their parents is a vote of confidence, a sharing of ideas, not solutions, and a recognition that listening with empathy is the great gift parents can give their teenage children.

Siblings

For the adolescent, the family constellation includes siblings as well as parents and any others who live with them, such as grandparents. Teenagers do not only have needs and expectations of their parents, but also of their brothers and sisters. The oldest sibling experiences different kinds of stress than the younger ones. In his book *Brothers and Sisters*, Karl Koenig examines the influence which the place of the child in the family has on the developing personality. The oldest is the first to test the water, to find out what is allowed and not allowed, and to initiate the parents into the world of adolescence.

Compare the experiences of an eldest child with those of the youngest. Is the eldest youngster constantly aware of being an example to the younger siblings? Is the teenager the ready babysitter and co-parent in a large family? Is the teenager given many more responsibilities and privileges because they assume the role of adult earlier than the siblings coming up behind will do?

Does the baby in the family find the teenage years easier because the way has been paved by an older sister or brother? Has the age been lowered for certain privileges? Are they allowed to go along with an older sister or brother to see movies that the eldest would not have been allowed to see?

I've seen several patterns over and over again. The first is the high-achieving oldest child followed by a younger sibling, usually of the same gender, who feels they cannot match the achievements of the older, so they don't even try. To avoid being measured by the achievements of the older one, the younger sibling cultivates a different image, choosing other activities, friends, and interests. But the younger child never feels quite good enough. They secretly long to be as bright, as athletic, as respected, but it doesn't happen. It rankles to have people saying, 'Oh, you're Diego's little brother. You sure are different.'

In another pattern, the oldest sibling is the weaker student, so embarrassed and intimidated by the achievements of the younger and by the competitive nature of the sibling relationship that they become withdrawn and leave the family as soon as they can escape.

In still another pattern, the younger becomes the follower of the older sibling who is not a good influence. It is quite common that teenagers on drugs were initiated into drug use by an older sibling, or even pressurized into being the buyer and seller.

There are many different patterns, and each family has its configuration. In working out an understanding of their biography, adults would do well to consider how their sibling relations affected them, and how they are now treating their children.

Patterns in Families

There is no simple family pattern today. In a group of 20 teenagers, you may only find five living with their biological parents, both of whom are still in their first marriage. Nearly every family today has a different situation — the combination of parents of different genders, same gender, step-parents, natural, step- and half-siblings, grandparents, aunts, uncles, and various cousins — which creates an extremely complicated extended family with complicated emotional relationships. The effect of this on adolescents is different in every case, but the adolescent clearly must find some way to make sense of it.

Because teenagers are trying to understand themselves, they need to take into consideration all of the relationships which affect them. Adults often think that because teenagers are so involved with themselves and their peers, they are not affected by the family constellation. However, the adults are models, and adolescents are trying to see whether they wish to emulate them.

The teenager's situation needs to be sympathetically examined. The youngster needs both parents and loves both parents. When we ask the child to be disloyal to one of the parents, the youngster is split. When divorced parents treat the other parent with respect, their children have an opportunity to develop a positive relationship with each parent. They also feel relieved and thankful. They appreciate that their parents are making the best of a difficult situation. But parents who continually attack one another by word, deed, and innuendo put their children in the impossible situation of feeling guilty whichever way they turn.

Parents' feelings about the divorce affect the way they treat their teen-agers. If parents feel guilty, they often try to make up for it by letting the teens have much more freedom than they normally would have. Parents also use the teenager as a way to make a point or claim power over the ex-partner. Teenagers easily recognize and are quick to take advantage of the situation. However, as they grow older they may come to realize how they were manipulated, and resent it.

Parents often feel that teenagers can handle divorce, but the reality is that they have just as much difficulty as younger children do; they just keep it inside. Teenagers have told me that even though they had adjusted to the divorce when they were young, during adolescence they re-lived the experience, and it was much more painful. As they struggled to define their own identity and become independent, they were forced to come to terms with their parents' relationship and the divorce in a new way. They had to go back, re-experience, and re-examine their feelings about it.

In some cases, divorce prompts one or both parents to experiment with lifestyle, confusing the teenager's sense of stability and familiarity. As they work out their own values, teenagers are often confronted by sharply contrasting values held by their divorced parents. Once again, they feel as if they are in a tug-of-war when they just want things to be the same.

Because teenagers are struggling with their sense of belonging, divorce confronts them with additional problems. The question of what name they will use goes directly to the question of identity. They may choose to use a different name for a number of reasons. If they have been using a step-parent's last name, they may rebel against their parent or step-parent by going back to their biological father's name. Or they may renew the relationship with their father after many years of minimal contact. The new relationship may be celebrated by the teenagers deciding to return to their father's name.

Children of divorce sometimes go looking elsewhere in the family for the love they feel they no longer experience from their parents. They may seek to spend more time with their grandparents or may ask many question about family members in an effort to find their roots. They want to be loved for themselves, and not ignored because their parents have divorced.

Divorce places an additional stress on the adolescent at school. In some cases, absentee parents show little interest in the student's school experience for months or even years, but then arrive unannounced at the school wanting special attention. For the teenager, this adds embarrassment on top of the already-existing pain of having been ignored. In other cases, a parent fails to show up for an important occasion such as a drama production, a significant athletic event, or graduation. In these situations, teenagers never know what to expect.

Divorced parents may have conflicting attitudes toward homework, out-of-school projects, and other school expectations. Such parents commonly use school as another way to make points with each other. In the end, however, they only place additional stress on the teenager. If the divorced parents can possibly agree on what they expect and stop fighting the lost marriage, they can offer support and clear boundaries to their children.

I have sat through dozens of parent conferences in which divorced parents discussed their children with the teacher. Tension, unspoken messages, and poor communication made these conferences difficult for all concerned. When the teenager was present, the parents had conflicting expectations, which created additional tension. The possibility of having a fruitful conference was often better when the step-parents were included.

The most difficult sessions were those in which one parent attended with a new spouse or partner while the other parent was single. The single parent is often dealing with the pain of the divorce (or the relief), while the new couple has begun to build a life together.

Another variety of divorce-induced stress on the teenager relates to money. Divorce often changes the family lifestyle and financial resources. The family home may be sold, the custodial parent and children may have to move into a smaller apartment, and the mother who might have been home, or worked part-time, now has to go to work. The family belongings are divided in two, increasing the teenager's sense of being split, and the family income has to be spread among two households, and at least as many lawyers.

A 16 year-old girl who idolized her father saw him only a few times a year, but she talked about him between each visit. She was his little girl, and she looked at boys on whom she had crushes in a similar way. They weren't quite real to her, and she had great difficulty establishing regular peer relationships with them. After graduation, she moved in with her father. She told me that she stopped idolizing him after six months and began to appreciate him as a real person. After that, she was also able to develop more relationships with boys her age.

A 17 year-old boy was very embarrassed because he had to help his father move out of the house. He felt terrible about having to do this because it left him feeling that he was part of the cause of the separation.

An 18 year-old boy had hoped to go to a state university and had worked hard to qualify. Yet when the time came to ask his divorced father for financial help, he couldn't do it. 'I have to show I can take care of myself.'

Attending university or college can be very stressful in a divorced family because of different attitudes toward higher education, choice of school, financial issues, and even who will attend graduation.

Divorce involving children is a tragedy. There isn't any other word to express it. It may be the best of a difficult situation, and teenagers may even benefit from the divorce, but the trauma scars them. They are strongly affected by separation, the emotional dramas leading up to divorce, and the settlement of divorces, especially child-custody battles.

At the very time when adolescents need to be working on their own relationships, they are absorbed in the destruction of the most fundamental relationship in their lives thus far, their family. During the time they should be breaking away from their parents as a way of gaining independence, they are doing the opposite. They are focused on adult problems, including having to decide which parent to live with.

One of the difficulties for teenagers is that they need parents who guide and limit, who are willing to be disliked, who are more concerned with the teenager's needs than with the teenager's approval. Divorce makes this more difficult. Divorced parents are vulnerable. The parent with custody usually handles the everyday problems, sorrows, and joys. The absentee parent often resents the amount of time the custodial parent spends with the child, and tries to make up for it by entertaining them and by avoiding confrontation. The custodial parent wearies under the load of house-keeping, chauffeuring to lessons and games, earning a living, and the loneliness of parenting, so that additional resentment builds up when the absentee parent takes the teenager on a trip or buys special presents. The absentee parent wants to force intimacy that can develop only in time and without pressure. The custodial parent doesn't want the absentee parent threatening the kind of lifestyle followed in the home.

Teenagers are very smart and see much more than one thinks. It is not surprising to find a teenager who tells the divorced parents to stop playing games and start acting like responsible adults. Or the teenager may step out of a ten-year loyalty to one parent, when new perceptions awaken and maturity arrives, and make amends to the other parent.

In the USA in 2015,[14] 27 per cent of households with children under 21 are headed by a single parent — and that figure is rising. Clearly, the one-parent family is not going away. We need to understand what this means to generations of children. We must find ways to help single parents. Some tend to over-protect their children because they feel vulnerable. It is easy for the parent to create a fortress against the world, trying to keep out hurt and strain. Other parents overload their children with responsibility to help carry the family, especially when more children are involved. Under the burdens borne by so many single parents, it is not surprising when the single parent focuses on personal needs, becomes depressed, and loses track of what is happening in the teenager's life.

In spite of the difficulties, many single parents develop meaningful and nourishing relationships with their teenager. Sometimes the removal of strain from a difficult marriage frees both the adolescent and the parent to have a better relationship, which may provide some compensation for the loss of family life. In other cases, the mutual need strengthens the bond between parent and adolescent.

When single parents raise teenagers, special stresses occur. It is difficult enough for two parents to raise teenagers and to come through with dignity intact. In the single parent's case, the work is not shared — the burden falls on one adult. The single parent, as well as the teenager, is trying to recover from the wounds of the divorce. A family is needed, and the parent is under stress to provide it. In the attempt to be responsible, the single parent is vulnerable to the teenager's criticism, spoken and unspoken, especially if the parent has come to rely on the teenager as a confidant. The parent may have no-one else with whom to share secrets and frustrations, but this creates a gap between the teenager and peers, and increases the emotional burden carried by the adolescent.

It often helps if single parents explore what resources are available in the community to supplement what they are not able to provide. They can invite over the teenager's friends, take them on a trip, or join forces with another single parent and teenager friend. This helps foster a family mood in a relaxed way.

A mother was preparing to take two children camping, trying to recapture the many family trips that had been part of their lives before the divorce. This was complicated as it involved all the gear, the tent, food, as well as driving a distance. Just before they were ready to get on the road, a friend came by. This was another single mom. She suggested that they do it together, and she would need only an hour or two to be ready. The whole mood changed, and now this became an adventure. They shared their skills, and it didn't seem as burdensome as it would have. That evening, as they roasted hotdogs and marshmallows over an open fire, they all agreed that this was a lot of fun.

Joining organizations of single parents may also be helpful because of the opportunity to meet new people and share experiences.

Remarriage

After a marriage breaks up, it takes about three years for the marriage partners to completely separate from each other in their soul life. For the child, however, the bond to their parents continues throughout life. When parents remarry, they generally hope and expect that everything will be wonderful, that the mistakes learned from the past will not be repeated. For the child, and in this case the teenager, the forming of a new family often conjures up memories of the original family, and may evoke anger and blame. Many children never give up hoping that their parents will come back together, but the remarriage of one of the parents usually ends that fantasy.

Once a remarriage occurs, the family constellation is shifted. Children from former marriages become part of the blended family. Relationships with past spouses are different, depending on the family and children. One of the most important issues in remarriage is avoiding criticism of the previous spouse, as this puts the children into a very difficult situation. It is helpful to remember that both parents feel responsible for their children, and they will need to cooperate on big decisions. Of course, adolescents may have a strong influence on these decisions, including who will be the custodial parents.

Step-families

Remarriage has many effects on children. First, the child's natural place in the family is altered when two families merge. Let us look at some examples.

Chapter 11 — Teenagers and family life

- The oldest boy, a teenager, had been catered to, given in to, protected, and favored. With their parent's remarriage, they experienced the loss of authority they had over their younger siblings. In the remarriage, they became a younger sibling to an older teenaged step-brother who was not going to yield that position. This results in strong feelings of anger, jealousy, and the urge to undermine the new parent.

- A young teenage girl who was used to looking up to her older siblings, feeling they must fulfill the expectations of those ahead, now had several new younger step-sisters and brother who looked up to her. Now she must set an example and share space and time with this new family constellation. She is not overjoyed. On the other hand, she feels pride at being able to guide a younger step-sister.

- So much depends on how the teenager feels about their position in the family. A 16-year-old boy resented both his parents and his step-parents because every time he and his teenaged-brothers were shunted off to the other parent, there were unclear expectations. Neither set of adults would commit themselves to the boys.

- A 15-year-old girl disliked her step-father so much that she could not bear to go to biology class because the teacher so strongly resembled her step-father. She had no problem with the teacher, but she explained that she could not have an objective relationship with him. Her mother recognized the resemblance, but she was helpless to solve the problem.

- A 14-year-old boy was delighted when his mother remarried. His parents had divorced when he was a baby, and he had never met his real father. He enjoyed the companionship of another male in the household.

- A 17-year-old boy resented his step-father's expectations. He could not compete with the outstanding academic record of his new step-brother and gave up trying. His step-father's attitude was 'prove yourself' and the boy felt he could do nothing right. He couldn't stand the conversation at the dinner table which centered on 'your children' and 'my children'.

- An 18-year-old girl who had never been able to communicate with her father found an interested listener in her new step-mother. With her step-mother's support, she was able to have a serious talk with her father and overcome years of hesitation. She said it took 18 years for such a talk to occur. She couldn't have done it without her step-mother.

- In another case, two teenaged boys were having troubles. Their step-father's children had not turned out well, and he wanted his step-sons to succeed. He treated them very strictly, hoping that would keep them going in the right direction. Their mother felt caught in between her sons and her new husband. The 17-year-old found it difficult to see his mother in this situation and wanted to move out. He didn't want to make trouble for her.

There are many examples from step-families. Each is unique and has its own time of adjustment. As with single parents, remarriage or new partnerships are now a common part of our culture. We need to build support groups to help step-families survive in as wholesome a way as possible.

Another change that is becoming more common is when a parent comes out as homosexual and chooses a partner of the same gender. Many of the same issues occur as with any new configuration, but this one has the added aspect of relating to two mothers or two fathers.

When the parent enters a series of relationships which do not develop into a marriage, the youngsters go through the loss over and over again. Even if they are not completely pleased with the parent's partner at the time, they share the loss with the parent, the sense of starting again, and the vulnerability of being alone again. The teenager may celebrate that the temporary partner is gone, but they still long for a permanent family.

Despite all that teenagers say in their moments of frustration, they wish to love and be loved by their families. They know that they have been influenced by their mother, father, and siblings, and they sense that they carry their family within them. The challenge they face is how to develop their own individuality in the context of being a family member.

Chapter 11 — Teenagers and family life

In a Nutshell

Teenagers and family life

- Teenagers relate to their parents in many ways, two of which are 'the volcano' and 'the mask'.
- At times the teenagers erupt with emotional outbursts, and at other times they retreat and are hardly recognizable.
- Teenagers want the love and respect of their parents, even as they do everything to wear them down.
- Siblings are an important part of family drama, depending on where the adolescent fits into the birth order.
- Families have many different configurations today because of divorce, death, additional marriages, blended families, and single-parent families. In each case, the teenager has to find their way.
- Adolescents struggle to find their own identity in the context of being a family member.

Chapter 12

Teenagers and friends

When you have a friend, life is worth living.
9th-grade boy

When you have a friend, the sun is shining.
9th-grade girl

Friendship is Essential during Adolescence

Friendship is important throughout life, but at no time is the need as desperate as during adolescence. As youngsters begin to pull away from their parents, they need another anchor, a place of comfort. As long as they have friends, they are not alone in the shaky transition from dependence to independence. While parents symbolize authority, friends symbolize acceptance.

Although friends are necessary, they are also replaceable. In a certain way this gives the teenager a sense of freedom. The feeling that parents and siblings are connected with them for ever helps teenagers to feel secure, but it also can leave them feeling suffocated. They want to try out different friends: friends from school, friends from the neighborhood, friends who share a common interest, friends who help them feel happy, friends with whom they can discuss their problems, friends with whom they can be silly; friends with whom they like to go to the movies, fishing, for a pizza, or for quiet walks.

I remember my own hurt feelings when my 17-year-old girlfriend said that she liked having different friends for different occasions. At the time

I was jealous and thought real friends would do everything together. As I became older, I realized the sensibleness of her perspective.

Friends and Identity

Because teenagers are in the process of finding out who they are, friends play a special role. Together, they can discuss what they like and don't like, whom they like and don't like, and why. Each learns something about life from the other, and each knows that they won't be judged. Together, they explore people, places, ideas, and interests.

'I really like Jean. We have so much fun. We take out fashion magazines and plan all kinds of outfits. We laugh and have such a good time'. 'You can't tell what Carol is like from the outside. She's really very sensitive and is interested in dreams and things like that'. 'We call our group the terrible threesome, and we eat lunch together and read comics and talk about superheroes. No one else understands us, but we like each other'.

An 18-year-old girl was describing her relationship with a classmate:

> We understood each other very well. We knew we were completely different. As long as we stayed on certain topics, we could be good friends. But I never went to her parties or did things with her out-of-school friends, and she would have been bored with my friends. We would never have become friends if I had gone to a large school. But here, we found how much we enjoyed each other as long as we respected the limits of the relationship. We laughed and joked and got along wonderfully with each other. We confided in each other, too. But that was as far as the relationship could go.

A 16-year-old said:

> You have to be careful, when you come to a new school, who your friends are. You become identified with those friends, and that could affect you for a long time. I wish I could have watched everyone from

outside a glass window for a long time before choosing my group of friends. But it doesn't work that way.

Friends provide companionship, which eases the loneliness of life. Having a very close friend is like having a special brother or sister. A 21-year-old explained that he and his friend had been close for years because neither had brothers.

> We became brothers. We affirmed each other's worth as males. We found we shared common views and could teach each other what we know. For example, we learned from each other how to deal with girls. We learned to accept each other and to give mutual support.

When a teenager does not have an older sister or brother to learn from, friends are a fine substitute. Friends tell you what to expect and how to handle yourself. You don't have to pretend with a good friend. You can be yourself.

Friendships are like miniature communities. Teenagers have to learn how to reach out, how to understand, when to forgive, and when to be upset. In other words, many of the same lessons the youngster learned within the family now have to be learned again in a new context. In the family, the teenager can make many mistakes and still be loved, but a friendship is more vulnerable. If teenagers take their friends for granted or treat them as they sometimes treat their families, the friendship may well be over.

In the family, the teenager is one of many. The teenager's needs have to take their place alongside everyone else's. Attention is not focused on the them alone. If the teenager puts on a new outfit or cultivates a new persona, it is noticed, but it doesn't always get front stage. Friends, however, notice everything and usually support their friend in experimenting, within reason.

The parents know that each fad will pass, but the teenager sees the fad as necessity and is supported in this by friends. When I was in high school, I had to have a dog collar around my ankle. It sounds ridiculous now, but it was a necessity then. All the popular high-school girls wore them.

Chapter 12 — Teenagers and friends

Friends tell the teenager whether the jean cuffs are folded correctly, how the shoe laces should be tied or not tied, and what kind of make-up to wear. Friends form a mutual admiration society.

Friends also often act as surrogate parents. They monitor each other's behavior and get through to the friend as no adult can. For example, Frank said:

> Raymond is a creep. He acts like a real jerk. I don't even want to hang around with him any more. People get mad at him because he's so arrogant and condescending. He deserves what he gets. I've told him that, and he does listen to me. No one else can get to him. I'll try again.

Conformity

Friends help teenagers become independent of their parents, but at the same time, they exert a new kind of authority — conformity. Because teenage friendships usually center on school life, it is hard on the adolescent when their friends attend different schools. Such youngsters have a circle of strong friendships in their neighborhood, and another at school. Others have separate circles of school friends and home friends, even though they go to the same school. Neighborhood friends are almost like family members. There are also friendships from shared religious training. These may become very strong if there is an active youth program at the church or synagogue.

In school, friendships can become stressful. To be friends with certain people you have to conform to their expectations. It is difficult to be your own person and have friendships unless the friends share your non-conformist behavior. Even if the teenager chooses not to conform to the group, the pressure is still there. The teenager constantly has to choose, and this takes more energy than most adults realize.

In many schools, cliques dictate what is acceptable and what is not. Teenagers are concerned not to behave in such a way that they won't be accepted by the clique they want to join. The need to be cool and not be a nerd is strong pressure on both boys and girls. Dan may want to befriend Phil, but he won't because of what the group thinks of Phil. Dan is afraid the group may think he is similar to Phil. Only a very securely popular teenager can buck the unspoken code of a group.

Friendships within the clique are insecure as well. There is always the chance that the position of one member of the group will be weakened, or that they will be isolated and pushed out. Blackballing and backbiting make life very difficult for a sensitive adolescent. This kind of political pressure in friendships makes it difficult for honest relationships to exist. However, even though many friendships are fickle, they still rule the social scene. It is not uncommon for teenagers to have only one or two close friends, even though they appear to have many.

In large schools, the cliques are so strong that teenagers have to choose their extracurricular activities carefully to preserve an image. The activity has to be accepted by the group — certain activities are out, they are only for jerks. A 21-year-old was reflecting on her experiences, first in a large public junior high school, then in a small Catholic high school:

> In a small private school, you are already making a choice to be different, and this affects your friendships. They are much deeper. You have fewer people to choose from, and there is an opportunity to get to know people you wouldn't ordinarily connect with. I didn't feel that I was ruled by the cliques as much, and so the relationship was not so superficial.

Of course, the other side of being in a small school is that if the teenager doesn't connect with anyone, life can be miserable.

You have only to walk through a high-school yard at lunchtime to get a feeling for the groups. In many schools, they are based on race as well as lifestyle. Each group congregates in its own special place. The names change over the generations, but some groups have been the jocks, the burn-outs, the preppies, the aggies, the intellectual jerks, the cheer-leaders, the hoods, the stoners, and the loners. The names vary from school to school, but the categories don't change much.

The high-school friendships developed from these times can last for decades. Because I went to high schools in two different American states,

I made very different friendships. Because the first high school was in Hollywood, Florida, a small town where life centered around the beach, school friendships were the center of our lives and we saw each other outside of school. I was part of a group of ten or twelve classmates who shared everything from sleepovers to bike trips to swim team competitions. After leaving in eleventh grade I kept a strong connection with one of them. We are still close friends now, almost 65 years later, and visit when we are on the same coast.

The New York City high-school experience was very different because the school was located in a part of town that was not safe to be in as it grew dark. I also worked three evenings a week an hour away from home. There was a sharper division between school life and social life. I kept in touch with one friend with whom I spent many Sunday afternoons eating pizza and listening to music. We kept in touch for a few years as we went to the same college, and then we lost track of each other. We reconnected after bumping into each other at a graduation of our children, and although we spent a weekend together, the relationship didn't seem to have a closeness any more. Another friendship from this school was cultivated through deep conversations sitting on the steps outside our classroom. We did not do anything together outside of school, and after graduating we did not keep in touch. Now, 62 years later, we have reconnected and find we have many things in common as well as deep mutual affection.

There is something special in these friendships because these are sometimes the only people who actually knew our parents, carry an image of what we were like in our adolescent years, and have followed us in our journey.

Friendships Cross Genders

A platonic boy–girl friendship can be very nurturing for both. Without the complication of romance, the boy and girl can find this to be one of the most meaningful relationships they have. In a platonic relationship, each learns about the other and finds out different points of view.

With more students becoming fluid in gender, teenagers are broadening their viewpoints in this way as well. Here, the atmosphere of the school community is very important. It is heartening to visit a school where students feel comfortable being themselves, as they explore this aspect of their identity. If the school is not an accepting place, students may divide into small groups with specific identities where they feel safe.

A platonic friendship can be very nurturing for both. Without the complications of romance, the boy and girl can find this one of the most meaningful relationships they have. In a platonic relationship, each learns about the other's sex; they find out the male and female point of view. They often act as matchmakers, mother- or father-confessors, and buddies.

Sometimes, the platonic relationship grows into romance, but more often it acts as a stabilizing force in teenage life. If a girl hasn't been asked to a big dance by her crush, or if the boy is not ready to step out into the dating world, they might go together. It also works the other way. If the boy has been turned down, and the girl is not interested in any particular boy, the platonic date allows them both to attend the event and have a good time without worrying about the other's intentions. There is less pairing off today in schools, and groups go out together socially. Or, as has been observed in research, teenagers tend to be spontaneous, using texting to communicate where and when to connect.

When romantic relationships develop, they often affect friendships. The teenager has to parcel out time with friends and with the new partner. Girls tend to be more possessive and jealous of their best friend's time than boys are. Girls feel let down, used, and dumped on when their girlfriends leave them for a boy (or for another girl). They want equal time. Part of the reaction may be jealousy that they don't have a boyfriend of their own. One girl told how excited her friend was when she was beginning to get together with her boyfriend, but once the relationship heated up, her friend became sullen and complained, 'But we never see you'. She said that she was under enormous pressure. No matter what she did, she couldn't satisfy her friend.

Boys seem to be more accepting of the changes without turning them into personal issues. Friendship between two boys can be challenging if they both like the same girl. In some cases, one boy steps aside for the other. Or one of the boys feels guilty because of his secret rendez-vous with the girl. The boys are used to sharing with each other, but they can't talk about this, either because they know it will hurt their friendship or because they are not proud of their behavior. They may resolve it by leaving the choice up to the girl.

Friendship between two girls is also affected if they both like the same boy. Sometimes, a whole group will like a boy, and one girl will plot to make a friend look bad so that she herself will stand out and get his attention. At other times, the girls will celebrate the birth of a romance between one of their group and the coveted young man. All too often, however, the old maxim, 'All's fair in love and war' takes over, and teen-agers are left feeling betrayed and hurt.

Another element that enters into friendships is the accusation of homosexuality. The accusation may be true, but it often is not, and it comes from a lack of understanding or jealousy. Girls with a very close, almost sisterly relationship may be deeply hurt by being tagged lesbians. Likewise, boys who express affection for each other, even in a moderate form, can be isolated as 'fags'. Such incidents may cause deep pain and even lasting harm to those who are being maliciously labeled.

One of the significant changes that has occurred in adolescent rela-tionships has been the acceptance of homosexual behavior. Instead of being secretive, teenagers have come out and shared their new identity. A same-sex platonic relationship can be especially significant, as each teenager is trying to find their way through the new identities. In many cases this is received in an accepting way. It has been very interesting to experience how, in American culture, there has been a faster rate of acceptance of homosexual relationships than of inter-racial relationships, although even that is better than it was in the past.

Parents and Friends

One of the great issues in the teenage years is whether parents approve of their friends. Because friends represent the outer world, parents tend to judge them on whether they fit the image which the parents want their youngster to project into the community. I will always remember a day in which I had parent conferences with parents of two close friends. The first parent said she didn't think that Jim was a very good influence on Ron. An hour later, one of Jim's parents said that he didn't think Ron was a very good influence on Jim. They were both right.

When parents look at friends, they are probably asking what effect this friendship will have on their teenager. Or they may really like the new friend and hope the friendship lasts. Or they may wonder what their child sees in the new friend.

Coming to know the friends is an important way of figuring out what is happening with the teenager. It is surprising to find out why a teenager chooses a particular friend. For example, Alice befriended a difficult, rebellious girl, Dana, who was constantly in trouble. Alice, of course, was constantly defending her friend. In a conversation between mother and daughter, Alice said, 'I don't approve of what she's doing, but I feel I can support her and maybe change her behavior'. From the outside, it looked as if the two were bosom buddies. Once Alice's mother had this insight, she trusted her daughter more, and she was able to show appropriate concern for Dana.

Alice wondered why Dana broke an important school rule. She felt caught between wanting to reflect that it wasn't a good idea, and at the same time, she didn't want to be just another person telling Dana how badly she was behaving and all the things she does wrong.

Naturally, there are times when a friendship seems to be harmful and needs to be limited or ended, but parents should proceed gingerly. Teenagers understandably resent people telling them who their friends should be. This kind of sensitivity is a sore point in family relations. Nonetheless, parents should trust their instincts. If they feel that the situation is very bad, they should have a frank talk with their teenager. However, their credibility may rest on whether they have respected their teenager's other relationships, or whether they have found something wrong with each friend.

In some cases, teenagers, especially the younger ones, are grateful for parental restrictions. For example, 13-year-old Ellen was on the phone speaking to a friend who was describing a party planned for Friday night at the beach. Ellen said, 'Wait a minute, I'll ask my mother if I can go'. Ellen put her hand over the phone and signaled to her mother to say, 'No'. Then she got back on the phone and said sadly, 'Gee, my mother won't let me'.

Parents can get to know the friends by inviting them in, sitting down and talking with them, inviting them for dinner or for an excursion. Otherwise, they may not have much basis for their opinions of their teenager's friends.

There is no question that teenagers can be adversely affected by poor friendships, and sometimes it is so bad that a major move is necessary. I have known parents who figuratively picked up their teenage sons or daughters and took them, kicking and screaming, to a new school. The teenagers hated their parents for doing it. However, in many cases the youngsters were grateful later after they gained a new perspective. In other cases, the youngster's anger sabotaged the parents' efforts, and the new situation did not work out. Changing schools but keeping the old friends is a sure way to abort the new start.

Some parents moved into a new neighborhood to take their teenagers away from a particular group. Some have even changed cities or sent their teenager to live with a relative for a year to break up a destructive friendship.

Teenagers generally move through a variety of friendships. As they mature, so does their taste in friends. They need support rather than criticism as they work their way through their friendships. Because friendships are such a major part of adolescent development, it may be very important if the parent can gain the youngster's trust to speak about these problems. Just as the friend provided a safe haven from parental problems, the parent can be an objective anchor in working through the teenager's problems with friends.

No Friends

Teenagers can be utterly miserable if they have no friends. They feel left out, unloved, and worthless. There are loners in every crowd, and their lot is painful. Wherever they go, they have trouble making friends. They may grow used to it, but it hurts. They may pretend they don't care, but they do. They may put on an arrogant air, but they are only protecting themselves. They complain to their parents and teachers that they want to move, change schools, do anything that will bring them friends. They may even try to buy friendship by inviting another teenager for an expensive weekend or by giving them gifts.

In some situations, the teenager simply doesn't fit into the scene. Even when the fault lies more with the scene than with the youngster, the teen suffers. In another place, the teenager would find someone with similar interests, and friendship would not be a problem. A new school may make a very big difference, giving the adolescent an opportunity for a fresh start.

Once a group labels a teenager as odd, they have little chance to make friends and be accepted. A fresh start, a group outside of school, a job, or a summer program are ways to help them start again.

If teenagers are without friends, they need parent support even more than before. Doing things together, having talks, finding common interests — all will help the teenager during the lonely period. However, parents cannot take the place of friends of their own age, but they can do much to make life bearable and even at times happy.

In a Nutshell

Teenagers and friends

- As adolescents pull away from their parents, their need for friends becomes more important in their life.
- They often go through changes in friendship as their needs and interests change.
- Making friends in a new school can be a traumatic experience.
- Adolescents struggle between conforming to their friends' values and finding their own.
- Friendships can become romantic relationships, both hetero-sexual and homosexual.
- Without friendships, adolescence is a time of loneliness and misery.

Chapter 13

Teenagers and school

... be patient toward all that is unsolved in your heart and try to love the questions themselves like locked rooms and like books that are written in a very foreign tongue. Do not now seek the answers, which cannot be given you because you would not be able to live them. Live the questions now. Perhaps you will then gradually, without noticing it, live along some distant day into the answer.[15]

Rainer Maria Rilke

The Drama of School

Teenagers spend the better part of each day in school. The goal of school is education, and yet the center of the student's life in school is navigating the social scene, dealing with anxiety and depression, and handling issues from family situations. Schools are very complex institutions, and even good schools struggle to provide a scene of healthy interaction, learning, and individual growth. Below the surface of the classroom is a dynamic drama which challenges young and older teenagers on a daily basis.

To some extent it has always been like this. Yet the powerful influences that shape the contemporary teenager's life are beyond a school's ability to control them. Thanks to social media, advertising, internet, competition, consumerism, and changes within the youngsters themselves, schools have become complex, stressful communities.

One of the issues of social media has to do with multi-tasking. The more students multi-task, the less attention they devote to any one activity. Most students multi-task when they are doing homework, i.e. they speak on the phone, do instant messaging, watch TV or the iPad, listen to music or surf the Web. Very little single-minded attention is given to their homework.

There are many reasons why teenagers are having such a hard time moving through this transition into adulthood. Lack of time, unrealistic expectations, fear of not being successful, feeling unsafe at school, being bullied, distractions, social pressures, and using substances to get through the day — all point to the fact that modern society is failing its children. It is a problem in schools that have the best facilities, the most successful of teachers, and adolescents who have everything they could want. It is also a problem in schools that have poor facilities, exhausted teachers, students who come from dysfunctional homes, poverty, and worries about caring for their families.

There are things that can be done to reach out and help, to recognize risk factors, and to offer services to support young people to work through these hindrances. Let's look at a few issues.

There are many different kinds of schools, depending on their neighborhood, student population, and resources. I am choosing two examples of different student groups.

Two Different Schools

In her book *Doing School: How We Are Creating a Generation of Stressed out, Materialistic, and Miseducated Students*,[16] Denise Pope interviewed adolescents in a successful high school to gain their perspectives on their goals, their relationship to their teachers, and the curriculum. The group of five students was diverse, and represented what the guidance counselor considered 'some of our best and brightest'. This school, located in a wealthy California suburb, has everything going for it — one of the lowest dropout rates in the state, small class sizes, outstanding teachers, high acceptance rates at highly recognized colleges, and impressive test results. This is the best of public education.

What she found was that the students worked hard, worried a great deal, were anxious, and lived in a constant state of stress. I had the opportunity to sit in a faculty meeting with Denise Pope after she published the book and discussed her findings. What she found, and what became the theme of our discussion, focused on the disconnect between what a school hopes to offer and what the young people thought they were getting out of it. The phrase 'Doing School' meant that they understood that the system they were part of was not particularly interested in their passions or deep thoughts, but it was a management problem they had to master if they were going to do well. One would have expected them to speak about their favorite subjects, or particular classes that challenged their thinking or awakened new insights. Instead, they explained what they were really learning was to go through the motions rather than engaging.

They focused on what they had to do to gain high grades, how they had to learn to impress their teachers, figure out how to argue for the grade they thought they deserved, and figure out the unspoken rules for them to outdo others and come out on top. If they didn't succeed, they would consider this a failure, and would be depressed.

Perhaps the student Kevin said it best: 'People don't go to school to learn. They go to get good grades which brings them to college, which brings them the high-paying job, which brings them to happiness.'

Good grades and high scores are the targets rather than learning to think, solve problems, and consider what is most valuable in their lives. Every aspect of school was a competition, every day was a battle between having enough time to get all the work done and getting enough sleep. In order to do this, students had to sacrifice their outside interests, connection with their families, and aspects of their social life. In other words, they were in a race which justified unhealthy choices, manipulation, and compromise. Whatever they chose to do was directed toward how it would look on their college applications, and whether it would push them ahead of other students.

In contrast to schools in which wealth and high academic standards propel students to looking at school as a stepping stone to college, a good job and a high income, I visited a charter high school in Sacramento. This school, the George Washington Carver School of Arts and Sciences, founded in 2008, has a very different student body.

Chapter 13 — Teenagers and school

I interviewed Dr Allegra Alessandri, and we reflected on the early years of the school and the challenges that she and the faculty have faced. Sacramento is a hub of Waldorf schools, public and independent, and therefore has a strong community support for this approach to education. When the Sacramento City Unified School District went through a reorganization of high schools, the Waldorf community responded and Carver was established. The school was originally an American Choice small high school which was failing and on the verge of closing when Dr Alessandri and a few faculty members moved in to try to transform it.

The population of 250 students (sometimes as high as 300) are 60 per cent white — 30 per cent of them are Eastern European, reflecting the low-income neighbourhood around the school; 15 per cent African-American, 12 per cent Latinex, and others which make up the difference. The percentage of Special Education students is 25 per cent, which is higher than the district average. Some 50 per cent of the students receive free and reduced lunch.

When Dr Alessandri took over the school, it was a disaster. The district had provided a beautiful campus with well-endowed facilities. One day early on, she walked into a brand-new lab and saw the students unscrewing hardware on the lab tables, systematically dismantling the new classroom. She had never worked in public schools before, and each day was traumatic. She felt scared, and she had panic attacks from the stress. She hung on to the essence of education, as well as her years as a Waldorf teacher. She brought together a group of public-school teachers who had already been committed to this approach. They worked past the daily fights, the stealing of cell phones, and the graphic language. But her weapons were kindness and love, smiling on the outside and screaming and crying on the inside.

One of the difficult girls looked at her from the side, and said, 'Why are you always smiling?' Startled by the questions, when she felt so unprepared, Dr Alessandri blurted out the truth: 'I have always worked with teenagers because I love them.' Sharing her commitment helped transfer the student's view of her, and she began earning the respect of the student body.

One of the transformative moments occurred during an assembly. The teachers tried to prepare the students to participate in the program. After all, they were in a publicly funded Waldorf school, and assemblies are part of the program. The Spanish teacher stood up with four volunteers to recite the poem they recited daily in Spanish. Then one by one, others joined. That was the beginning of the strong community life that has become a defining aspect of the school.

The other major event was when a group of boys who had graduated eighth grade from Alice Birney Public Waldorf Methods School entered Carver in ninth grade. They were known as the 'Whetstone boys', named for their class teacher who had taken them through their elementary years. These were confident, creative, strongly ambitious students who took the lead and helped create a student culture and healthy social life. When students from Alice Birney were in all four of the high school grades, they acted as a yeast which shaped the student body.

Day by day, Dr Alessandri and the faculty shared the vision, asking each other what they could bring from Waldorf education that would relate to this community and situation. The strong collegiality and interest in the diversity of the students sharpened their enthusiasm. The school applied for all kinds of extra funding to deepen the curriculum and methodology, as they met their goals of social and environmental justice and creating active citizens.

What kinds of students were choosing to attend Carver? After thinking a bit, Dr Alessandri replied:

> They are creative at-risk students who would not be comfortable in other public schools. Many have suffered trauma and loss. They were free thinking, exploring their identity, needing a school where they could express creativity, explore who they were, and find community support. Many had a school history of being bullied by other students and were forced to conform to the rules set by the school. What they experienced at Carver was a place that fostered warmth, safety, engagement in the curriculum, and relationships with the teachers as mentors as well as authority figures. Here they developed healthy relationships with adults which, in turn, helped them imitate appropriate

Chapter 13 — Teenagers and school

adult interaction and grow into adulthood. The teachers' goal was to develop relationships with the youth, so that they would be inspired to take responsibility and use their personal agency in their maturing.

Because of the poverty level, the school has free breakfast for all, snacks available all the time, as well as free lunch for those who specifically qualified for it. Readily available are backpacks, soap, and clothes, and other things for families in need, as well as human resources such as social workers to meet with parents or students.

Through the nearby Folsom Lake Community College, classes are offered on the Carver campus for credit, and students also earn credit in their regularly assigned classes from the local state college. Those students who, because of poverty, would not have considered this next step carried enthusiasm from the psychology class into their other classes, and they could now imagine going further and applying to college. The professor teaching the class loved the creativity, curiosity, and the love of learning these Carver youngsters expressed.

In closing my interview with Dr Alessandri, I asked what were the strongest problems her students faced. Immediately, she responded:

> Anxiety and depression. Some don't even have the strength to come to school. I feel such empathy for our youth. They are overloaded with information They are under attack through social media. Trolls are luring them into prostitution, pornography, vaping, and gangs. If they can get the teenagers addicted, they feel successful. The students who are most addicted to social media are usually those with learning issues. There is less cyber bullying going on at the high-school level, because it is more rampant in earlier grades. We used to deal with students sending out naked photos all day long. There is much less of that now. The main issue is vaping in the bathroom.[17]

I reflected afterwards on the concerns Denise Pope expressed about the upper-class students, focused on getting good grades, but not necessarily engaged in their learning, and Dr Alessandri's students who are grateful for a safe place where they can explore their identity, engage deeply in their academic work, and drink in the warmth of a community that believes in them. In both schools, teachers were working hard to meet the needs of the students, trying to stimulate them to engage in learning, and face difficulties from the societal pressures that were distracting them from being able to grow up and enter the larger world. Even with a different profile of students, adolescents of both schools are struggling with anxiety and depression.

Examining the challenges in these two very different schools raises important questions for a society that wants to celebrate talent and innovation, educating students for a democracy, and taking on the important issues of our time. Does this super-competitive approach have anything to do with developing passion about ideas, taking risks, and exploring new directions? It seems not. Instead, students are learning to be cynical, pursuing the easy 'A' with as little effort as possible, pursuing narrow goals, focusing on making money and gaining power over others.

Not all the students who are at risk are at such a high-pressured high-achieving school as described above. There are other issues as well.

Today's teenagers are the most anxious and depressed ever. According to health surveys, about 10 per cent experienced 'a major depressive episode with severe impairment', according to the US National Institute of Mental Health. This is defined by at least two weeks with little sleep, energy, and low self-esteem, and an inability to participate in life's activities, including school.

Encountering Stress

Can students who are struggling with poverty, homelessness, and lack of financial resources overcome their anxiety in order to face the usual adolescent challenges of psychological growth? How can they focus on the next step in their education if they cannot imagine themselves attending college classes, or no-one ever suggested it to them and helped them through the process? Without the strong support of a school, they often hit a dead-end and give up.

Chapter 13 — Teenagers and school

One concern is the growing suicide rate. According to the US Centers for Disease Control and Prevention data.[18] An incredible one in six high school students reported 'seriously considering suicide' in 2017, including nearly one in four girls and almost half of gay, lesbian, and bisexual students ('As Suicide Rates Climb Among American Teens, Educators Need to Ask and Listen').[19]

A 2019 CDC report shows the number of young people dying of suicide jumped by 56 per cent between 2007 and 2017, outpacing any other group. The reasons given range from social media and smart-phones, bullying, and lack of community, and societal issues such as a family history of mental-health issues, firearms at home, and untreated substance-abuse disorders.

Students climb on to the school bus, walk, ride their bike, or drive to high school. They wave to their friends, go to their lockers, and sit in class. It looks benign. This is the time when teenagers should be developing independent judgement, clarifying their critical thinking skills, being on fire with new ideas, but instead they have entered into a whirlwind of social media trauma, nasty looks, power plays, and meanness. 'Young people can't learn when they are preoccupied with their social lives and don't have faith in the adults to create and maintain a fair and just learning environment.'[20]

How do teenagers learn to cope with this situation, knowing that at any moment a classmate may be shaming them on their phone?

Schools are trying to meet these situations in many ways — teaching ethical use of technology, offering classes in social and emotional skills, offering exercises in mindfulness, and training counselors to be aware of risky behavior and reaching out to students in need. Students are helped to thrive in schools where teachers know something of the students' family situation, connect with parents, focus on students' supporting each other, and work to build a community. We shouldn't be naïve and think that these efforts will take care of all the issues, but they are a start. Let's also remember that teenagers today are living with questions of their own identity, with questions of whether the planet will survive their adulthood, and whether there is a place for idealism in this tough world.

Middle Schools

The problem doesn't start when students enter ninth grade. It begins much earlier, and is especially intense in middle schools. During this delicate time when early adolescents are fragile, when so much is going on in their soul development and brains, they need time and space. By schools accelerating their programs so that high-school subjects are taught as advanced classes, pressurizing young teenagers to make choices that will affect their next four or five years, by encouraging extra summer programs to get ahead of others, the message is that 'It's never enough. You can always do better.'

It's never enough to enjoy playing a sport, but it becomes important to take extra programs to qualify for high-school teams. Yet high-school coaches have told me that it is difficult to fill their teams as the youngsters are burned out, having started playing sports when they were in elementary school. These are not the old pick-up basketball or soccer games in the neighborhood. Everything today is organized, with emphasis on winning.

It is wise, of course, to offer opportunities to explore new areas of interest such as drama, extra physics programs, school newspapers, dance, etc., but the message is not that they need to do everything to build a resumé to get into the 'right' high school and the 'right' college, but because they want to expand and explore new parts of themselves.

Parents with greater financial means often fill their children's free time with these kinds of pressures, hoping to give them a heads-up over others. Some parents struggle with living vicariously through their children. with what the child accomplishes reflecting on the parents' self-worth. We experience this when we read Facebook posts and see the latest achievements of children who have gotten used to performing for the benefit of their parents. It is refreshing when someone posts something about enjoying children who are just being children, rather than being the best at something.

Parents want more and more feedback from teachers on how their children are doing, they want to know that the child is happy and does not have to be upset to redo an assignment or accept a punishment for a wrongdoing. Other parents have no time to even think about these things as they are so exhausted just working to take care of their family. Volunteering has decreased in schools as parents are working and can't help out in classes, go on trips, and get to know the teachers and other children in the class.

The relationship between parents and teachers has been highlighted during these days, as we are facing the pandemic of the corona virus. Parents are under stress working from home at the same time as they are supervising their children who are distance learning. On the one hand, it gives parents a greater understanding and appreciation of the role of teachers, and on the other, there is concern over whether their children are being challenged enough in their learning.

The stress generated by the corona virus has opened up the inequity between students in different schools and different neighborhoods. The greatest problem in some schools is whether there is ample food for the day, or whether there are the devices needed for distant learning. In others, there is the concern of whether the students will fall behind other students who are in competition for entrance into a particular university.

Teachers are under tremendous stress and they can't meet the problems alone. They are already under pressure to meet expectations set by school boards to help middle-school children with a wide variety of special needs, as well as meeting the needs of all other children in their class. Some school districts require constant training of teachers to be able to teach the latest new program or include technology in areas where they don't feel it will serve the children. Schools have been experimental places where the latest trends are inserted into the classroom backed by big contracts of large sums before they have been assessed to be helpful. Teachers are leaving the classroom in great numbers, looking to other careers.

What used to be the parking lot gossip is now hostile commentary on cell phones, creating an antisocial atmosphere among parents as well as teachers. It is really hard.

At its heart, modern society does not trust childhood development. It rushes children from the time they are born, urging faster, faster, faster. Parents and teachers who don't agree with this attitude try to create alternative approaches. They search for schools and teachers who are committed to providing education for young adolescents that will transform this race to nowhere. They search schools within schools, charter schools, private schools. They move to different neighborhoods so their children can attend a better school. Often those schools are full and enrollment is through lottery. It is a job to be a parent today.

Middle school is an important time to recognize the physical and psychological changes that are going on, offering exciting projects, exploring new possibilities, guiding youngsters in taking responsibility, setting rites of passage, celebrating with the community in which every child has a place to be recognized. Giving them this kind of space and time has tremendous benefits as they pass through this vulnerable period, building up resistance and strength for the next big step, that comes in high school.

High School and the Teenager

I regularly observe in high schools, meet with students, and work with teachers. Despite all the challenges, the quality of many of the young people today is extraordinary. They still have hope and intention, and dream of making life better for all. Their capacity for empathy is impressive. But it's tough out there. The messages in the media, advertisements, song lyrics, movies, violent sexual images, and games work against social harmony, brotherhood, and love.

Schools struggle with the influence of technology. More schools are attempting to keep cell phones out of the classroom, even though students argue about how necessary they are. Parents also expect that they should be able to be in touch with their children during the school day, even during class-time. Students may argue that they can concentrate better if they can listen to music while solving math problems or translating other languages. They are very clever about hiding their cellphone earplugs under their hoodies

No one can meet the challenge alone. Parents look to the schools to solve the problems, and at the same time want the school to provide the best for their individual child. Parents feel the pressures also, always feeling they are rushing to the next thing. I was amused reading an article some years ago in the *New York Times* magazine section advising families to eat dinner together at least once a week, even if it's take-out. It's not easy for parents. They themselves don't have time to reflect, to slow down the rush, and get to know their children. Many parents struggle with parenting, unable or unwilling to be authorities in their teens' lives. They are tired and often give in to their children's arguing or pushing to do something or buy something that they think will make them cool.

I have visited schools which have consciously decided to create a healthy community among the students, hold back from constant competition among them, provide opportunities to try out new experiences in which they may not get the top grade, and learn skills of self-regulation and self-evaluation. Some counselors try to tone down the anxiety about getting into the 'right' colleges, showing students and parents that there are many choices and many ways of getting a good higher education. Another approach has been to encourage students to take a gap year after graduation, a time to mature, to follow an interest, do community service, travel, or work.

The quotation from Rainer Maria Rilke that begins this chapter is speaking about something deeper, more meaningful than urging students to ace the test or outdo someone else. Rilke is expressing to a young poet that it takes time to live with a question, time for solitude, time to find meaning. It can't be rushed. Many students would not understand his message because it seems old-fashioned. But those students who intuitively grasp the message are the ones who sense that adolescence is a moment in time that needs to be protected and nurtured. They can relate to it and give examples of what happened when they were able to live with a thought until something revealed itself. These are *aha!* moments that open up windows of the mind and soul.

In a Nutshell

Teenagers and school

Although the key reason for being in school is to get an education, the reality is that the main part of the school experience is social engagement.

- Examples of two different high schools provide unique experiences of teenagers' goals and social configurations.
- Pressures on teenagers in school range from expectations of achievement, future plans, family situations, competition, and effects of technology and social media.
- Parents need to understand how middle-school students develop physically and psychologically, without putting heavy pressure on teachers to accelerate learning, offer extensive extra-curricular activities, and give instant feedback.
- A challenge in every high school is finding the right balance in the use of technology.

Chapter 14

Waldorf education

The Ringing of the Bells
To wonder at beauty
Stand guard over truth,
Look up to the noble,
Resolve on the good.
This leadeth us truly
To purpose in living,
To right in our doing,
To peace in our feeling,
To light in our thinking,
And teaches us trust
In the working of God,
In all that there is,
In the width of the world,
In the depth of the soul.
                    Rudolf Steiner

An Alternative Approach to Schooling and Teenage Development

During the twentieth century, a number of attempts to develop an educational system based on a view of child development were established. Some notable examples are the progressive schools based on the teachings of John Dewey and Maria Montessori. The free-school movement drew its inspiration from the work of A.S. Neill and his experimental school, Summerhill in Suffolk, UK. Waldorf education, based on the view of child development put forth by Rudolf Steiner, has become a world-wide movement.

One of the important aims of Waldorf (or Steiner) education is to develop a curriculum which supports the stage of development of the child. The children's developmental needs in a particular class may evoke changes in the curriculum to suit those children. Steiner called attention to the need to understand the ideals of education and then to develop flexibility to deal with practical situations. Thus, within Waldorf education there is a tension between the ideal and the real; learning to compromise is a necessary part of life.

In this chapter I will introduce the reader to Waldorf education. Because this book focuses on adolescence, I will give a brief introduction to the scope of Waldorf education, followed by examples drawn from the high school.

History of Waldorf Education

Waldorf education had its beginning in Germany during the chaotic period following the First World War. The centuries-old social order based on a fixed class system and privilege was rejected in many countries, and a new social order, respecting the integrity of every human being, was emerging. Rudolf Steiner had been speaking all over Europe to thousands in packed lecture halls, to night-school classes for factory workers, and to groups interested in Spiritual Science or Anthroposophy, of the need to transform culture, based on a new view of the human being.

In his lecture 'Education of the child in the light of Anthroposophy',[21] Steiner laid out his fundamental ideas on education. He was deeply concerned about the need for cultural transformation in all areas of life, and he was given the opportunity to put his ideas into practice when Emil Molt, manager of the Waldorf Astoria Cigarette factory in Stuttgart, asked him to design a curriculum and methodology based on the anthroposophical view of the human being for the children of the factory workers.

Steiner gathered a faculty of twelve people who had not been teachers, but who came from various professions and were familiar with the anthroposophical view of child development. Over the next two weeks, he gave three lectures a day, in which he laid out an educational approach based on this view. The first Waldorf school was dedicated and opened on 7 September 1919 in buildings of the Waldorf Astoria Cigarette Company.

The school for factory workers' children flourished, and soon it was opened to other Stuttgart children at the request of people in the community.

In 1922 when the oldest students were preparing to enter the tenth grade, Steiner worked with the faculty to gain insights into the needs of adolescence. These talks, published as *The Supplementary Course*, and more recently as *Education for Adolescence*, are still studied as the basic principles of Waldorf high-school education.

Each Waldorf school is an independent organism, dedicated to the educational principles of Rudolf Steiner, and adapted to the particular country and its students.

Basic Principles of Waldorf Education

Every man passes personally through a Grecian period.

R.W. Emerson

Waldorf teachers strive to understand the human being as body, soul and spirit. This view of child development, with the seven-year rhythms and critical periods of ego development, has been described in earlier chapters. The fundamental approach of the teachers is to study and develop educational methods based on child development. Using this view as a guide, teachers shape the curriculum and methods to meet the developmental needs of the age. Since specific children or situations may call for unique solutions, the teachers work together to find these solutions.

Steiner taught that human beings have passed through stages of evolving consciousness from ancient times to the present and that these stages closely parallel the psychological states which a child passes through. This is referred to as the evolution of consciousness.

The Lower School

Waldorf education begins in the kindergarten years where the children enter into a world of play, color, music, drama, festivals, gardening, and practical life. When they leave kindergarten, they move into the lower or elementary school with a reverent and loving experience of nature and humanity.

Children in the lower school experience their learning through their feelings. The study of history, literature, science, grammar, and geography evolves out of a feeling for the subject in which they experience the joy of learning. The content is experienced in many sensory forms and in many mediums before the intellectual concepts are formed. In this way, the youngster's experience of the world is multi-dimensional and has breadth and width. The children make their own books, write their stories, and draw pictures exploring the subject of the main lesson.

Each subject develops from the first grade through the eighth grade, building on what has gone before and unfolding in a way that is interesting to the child of a particular grade because it addresses the inner changes that are going on.

The children in a class form a community and travel the journey from childhood into adolescence together with their main teacher for five, six, seven, or eight years. Their main or class teacher teaches them for the first block of time every morning in which they study one subject intensely for three or four weeks before passing on to another one. The main lesson subjects alternate between the humanities and the sciences.

After main lesson is over and the children have had snack, there are other lessons — painting, drawing, singing, playing musical instruments, eurythmy (a form of movement working with tone and poetry), arithmetic, writing/reading practice, crafts, gardening, and games. Here they meet other teachers who join them on their journey, sharing special skills with the class.

The children develop in a natural way through the grades. Some learn quickly and others need more time. Rather than being labeled or graded by how much they know or don't know, the emphasis is on developing an appreciation of each other's gifts, working on skills, experiencing the wonders of the world, and building a strong community life.

In addition to the subjects I mention for each grade, the children study world languages, painting, drawing, sculpting, form drawing, eurythmy, games, handwork, and crafts.

First and second grade

During the first and second grade, the child is still very dreamy, living out of imitation, and experiencing the world as a unified whole. The Waldorf approach to reading, writing, and arithmetic has been treated in great detail in other books; and since we are concentrating here on adolescence, I will only briefly mention that the emphasis is on the oral approach, on developing a strong appreciation of language, vocabulary, and story-telling, out of which the alphabet, sounds, and words are introduced. Emphasis is placed on painting, drawing, and writing leading to reading (as was experienced in human history). A strong foundation of sounds, visual forms, and context is built so that reading is an experience of meaning rather than one of isolated skills. Arithmetic is taught in a very active way, developing all four processes of addition, subtraction, multiplication, and division, using concrete objects, recognizing patterns in number series, and mental math. The children are active, moving and doing rather than being pressurized to remember.

Third grade

The 9-year-old has left behind the glow of early childhood when they experienced the world as perfect. Like Adam and Eve in the Old Testament, the child has been eating of the Tree of Life. But there comes a time when that is not enough. The child yearns for something else. Temptation enters, and the youngster eats of the fruit of the Tree of Knowledge of Good and Evil. As children go through the 9 to 10-year crisis and become self-conscious, their eyes are opened to the evil of the world. They leave behind innocence and are cast out of a Paradise-like state of being. Like Adam and Eve, they must go forth on the earth, learn to grow their food, clothe and shelter themselves, and experience the joys and sorrows of being mortals.

As in the Old Testament, they go through many temptations and disobey authority (God, parent), worshipping the Golden Calf and idolizing material wealth.

As part of studying the Old Testament, children might learn Hebrew prayers and carry out the ritual of the Passover meal, complete with the proper questions, food, and songs. In this way, they experience the customs and spiritual relationships existing between the Hebrew people and God.

The Waldorf teacher understands the change of consciousness which the 9-year-old is experiencing and works with the curriculum to meet these needs. They have left behind the experience of earth imbued with spirit. With the Fall, with the growing awareness of self, children feel separated from their spiritual origins and now have to become familiar with the earthly world. They must become earth-citizens. But it must go far beyond hearing and telling. They must grapple with practical life, so they are involved in farming, house-building, cooking, and clothing. They work with the soil, plant seeds, cultivate, and harvest. They gather what grows wild such as apples or grapes. They cook and bake what they have harvested and 'break bread together'. If possible, they learn to milk a cow, make butter, and gather eggs from chickens. This gives them an ecological basis on which to have conversations later.

They learn about the local building materials, and how houses are constructed. They might mix mortar, make bricks, lay a pathway, or build a playhouse for the kindergarten children. One class made their own nails with the help of a parent who knew blacksmithing, and another built a rain shelter for the whole school. It is important that the children make something useful for others.

They learn about clothing, the fibers and cloth that comes from plants, cotton and flax; those that come from animals — silk, wool, and leather; and those made by human inventiveness. They might gather plants and make dyes, or watch a sheep being shorn. They may also learn stories and poems about the plants related to clothing (such as 'Little Lamb' by William Blake), learn to use a spindle, perhaps a spinning wheel, card wool, and do simple weaving.

All of these subjects are used in the teaching of arithmetic — measuring standard units of linear, liquid, weight, time, money, and musical measurement and notation. Each teacher or school will choose how to teach all of these subjects, depending on where they are located, what resources are available, and what skills are offered by the parent community.

These are only a few examples through which the third-grade curriculum meets the third-grade child.

Fourth grade

Fourth graders tend to have a great deal of energy, and their teachers challenge them to stretch themselves and try new activities. The children focus on the place where they live. They learn basic geography, beginning with their own school, neighborhood, city, and state. They learn the history of the people who came to that area, what their vocations were and their customs.

Having come through the third-grade experience of landing on the earth, they will study stories of loss and gain. This could be done through the Norse myths, the Kalevala, the Native Indian tales, or those with similar themes from other cultures. A new type of character has entered in these stories — the Trickster. The children become aware of this quality within themselves and they relish stories in which the Trickster-type wins and then gets caught. It offers wonderful opportunities for discussion and humor.

The holistic approach now changes as the children strengthen what they've learned in earlier grades. Now they study more specific subjects. In natural science, the emphasis is placed on the study of animals in relation to their environment; in mathematics, fractions are introduced, reading continues both in group and individually, and they write stories as they work on grammar and language skills.

Fifth grade

The 10 to 11-year-olds pass from spatial consciousness to time consciousness, meaning they no longer perceive the world as a random series of images, but begin to see it chronologically. As they study history, they gain an idea of what it means to speak of a 30-year change or 50 years ago. The fifth-grade curriculum bridges history from the ancient world — China, India through ancient Persia, Mesopotamia, Egypt, and Greece. It spans mythology to history, as children hear about the great figures who brought the religions and cultures to humanity — the Buddha, Zarathustra, Moses, Osiris, Prometheus, Socrates, and Plato. They learn about geography and the everyday life in these civilizations, the way the people worked and played, how they built their homes and tilled their farms. In some schools, the ancient cultures of South America or Africa would be included.

The capacity for thinking develops in a new way as mythical thinking gives way to historical thought. The Greeks were the turning point because they were interested in why things happened. Using reason, they were fascinated with thought, and developed the laws of drama, government, philosophy, mathematics, physics, and music. As the first conscious historians, they interviewed people and recorded the results.

Fifth-graders make their own books, filled with vivid descriptions of these historical figures. They make maps, trace journeys, illustrate narrations, make models of buildings, and learn to measure as it was done in each of these civilizations. Their citizenry of the earth is more fully established, and they learn not only to work on the earth as human beings, but to think as human beings. In science, they focus on ecology based on the plant life, and in geography they expand to the whole country or continent.

Sixth grade
In the sixth grade comes a deeper descent into matter, as the youngsters either have begun or are approaching puberty. In Waldorf schools in the West, Roman civilization is studied. Here the student traces the simplicity of early Roman life, the change from kingdom to republic, the concern for honor and integrity needed to keep the republic pure, and then the decadence that set in as spiritual corruption took over the soul life. They study various aspects of the Roman Empire, such as the cosmopolitan unity that arose out of expanded citizenship, the *Pax Romana*, which made it a time

of great accomplishments, and the disintegration of Roman character as the spiritual core of Roman culture dissolved. As slavery increased, laziness, cruelty, decadence, and self-indulgence also increased, and were experienced in the gladiator fights and Roman orgies.

In Eastern countries, the curriculum would focus on cultures with similar contributions and challenges.

Sixth-graders are passing through similar inner experiences. The honor and purity of earlier years gives way to a fascination with grossness, laziness, and self-indulgence. The golden age of childhood is passing, and the changes of puberty cause the students to focus on themselves. When they experience the mirroring of their changes in the descriptions of the Romans, they can awaken to the importance of moral discrimination.

Six-graders study the rise of Christianity which occurred in the far eastern corner of the Roman Empire, the crucifixions and stonings, the slave uprisings, the persecutions of Christians, the toleration of Christianity by the emperors, and then the establishment of Christianity as a state religion as the northern tribes were making their way into the Roman borders.

Islam and the study of Muhammad bring an understanding of the richness of civilization that was taking place in Baghdad and Damascus, as well as the Islamic kingdom in Spain with the three Abrahamic religions of Judaism, Islam, and Christianity sharing their achievements in science, mathematics, music, medicine, poetry, and philosophy. The way that these achievements were brought into Europe stimulated the Renaissance. The Crusades bring a meeting of the different cultures of East and West, shaping the medieval period.

The teaching of science mirrors the new capacity of formal operations, as Piaget calls it, which becomes accessible to most youngsters of this age. They are able to grasp cause-and-effect thinking for the first time. The curriculum of the sciences is formally introduced, and students study astronomy, geology, acoustics, light, color, heat, magnetism, and electricity. Through repeating experiments, they get to test what they observe and what it tells them of physical laws.

They use decimals and fractions to do business math as they connect with modern life. Geography connects them with the rest of the globe, as over the next three years, they study the history and geography of South America, Africa, and Asia.

Seventh grade

In the seventh grade another important change occurs. The development of the Renaissance period parallels the development experienced by 12 to 13-year-olds. Here, the pre-adolescent shares with the Renaissance figures the question of authority, the fascination with exploration and experimentation. The Renaissance artists wanted to be recognized for their own work rather than being an anonymous part of a group. The scientists wanted to be able to observe for themselves rather than rely on ancient authorities.

The leaders of the Reformation wanted to find their own relation to God rather than going through a priest as an intermediary. They began to see themselves as separate from the rich heritage of customs and traditions, and experienced doubt and questioning. Young teenagers, like their Renaissance counterparts, want to burst out from restrictions that bind them. They will come to realize, as the leaders of the Renaissance and Reformation, that freedom of choice and freedom of opinion come at a cost — leaving behind the familiar territory of security and stability.

The science curriculum carries through the year with the introduction of physics — light and optics, sound, heat and cold — chemistry, and physiology. Students are using their new conceptual thinking to understand what it is they observe. World geography continues around the globe. If South America was studied in sixth grade, Africa might be studied now. It is important that students studying these cultures learn about the great achievements that existed there before the Renaissance explorers came to Africa and set up competitive trade with the Arabs, or the great achievements of the indigenous empires before the Conquistadores came into South America.

Students learn about their bodies in physiology and nutrition, becoming aware of choices they have in taking good care of their bodies and minds.

Eighth grade

The eighth-grade consciousness is a continuation of the seventh, with emphasis on the modern world, especially the industrial revolution and its effects on history. In most American Waldorf schools, United States history forms the bulk of the history curriculum, including current events and government.

Science expands to anatomy, chemistry, and physics. In some schools, eighth graders have an introduction to the computer as part of the industrial and electronic revolution. Geography continues to include Asia, as well as a world picture of meteorology. Mathematical concepts are expanded to include an introduction to algebra.

The curriculum acts as an overview of what they have studied in their earlier years, but now they are more individually responsible for their observations, their thinking, their ability to write clearly, and to read and discuss many different kinds of literature.

The Waldorf High School / Upper School

When the youngsters finish the eighth grade, they pass over the threshold into high school. Here, many of the same subjects are taught, but in a completely different way. In the lower grades, the teaching was through feelings, through dramatic stories, and through imagery. Subjects are now grasped through presentation, discussion, reflection, experiences, and thinking, but the artistic is not forgotten.

Rather than teachers relying completely on standard textbooks (although some may be used), they choose material that particularly relates to the students in the class. They describe biographies and events, create assignments that allow students to explore the subjects in various mediums, and make evaluations based on the special nature of the ninth, tenth, eleventh, or twelfth graders. (Years 10, 11, 12, and 13 in UK.)

Instead of a class teacher to shepherd the class through the lower-school years, there is a community of specialists who teach the students out of their expertise. One or two faculty members act as class advisors or sponsors over their four high-school years.

The high-school curriculum

The Waldorf high-school curriculum is based on the understanding that each subject has a special place in the life of the student. For example, through science the adolescent learns to observe natural and mechanical processes. Through world languages the teenager learns to enter into the thinking of another culture and to communicate. In the study of mathematics, the student experiences the wonder of form and pattern in number and nature. Through art the students develop inner sensitivity to living processes, and through crafts they learn to bring an aesthetic sense to the practical world. In music, students develop an individual sense of tone and have a social experience of sharing musical works and productions. Through movement, students continue their study of eurythmy and physical education. The subjects become the stuff of the world through which is woven an integrated view of the universe.

In Waldorf education, each child is seen as gifted, worthy of the enrichment from all subjects in the curriculum. Opportunities for electives are present in the curriculum in each school's plan. In general, students are offered a broad view which includes the humanities, the sciences, and the arts. Of course, each high school also fulfills governmental requirements and what is needed for enrollment in university. This differs in each country. Students can then choose what to specialize in during the next stage of their education.

The concept of the main lesson continues from the lower school into the high school, but the content and the form are different. After main lesson, the rest of the day includes a wide range of subjects such as mathematics, world language, English skills, literature, choir, orchestra, art and craft, eurythmy, gardening, computer skills, and physical education. An attempt is made to work out the daily schedule so that the subjects that require the most intellectual focus are placed in the morning.

The original Waldorf school curriculum was put together by Carolyn van Heydebrand and Karl Stockmeyer, from indications Rudolf Steiner gave in lectures and meetings with the teachers of the first Waldorf school. There was freedom for individual teachers to build on the guidelines and add their individual creativity. Certain subjects will be found in all Waldorf schools, but there are also individual differences based on the location of the school and the special interests of the faculty and community. Much has happened in the hundred years since the curriculum was developed, and teachers continue to bring the curriculum up to the present time to meet the new generation of students, weaving their own history, geography, and culture through the classes. For more detail, I refer the reader to *The Tasks and Content of the Steiner-Waldorf Curriculum.*[22]

The special nature of each high school year
Out of Rudolf Steiner's unique gift of the evolution of consciousness in relationship to education, the curriculum is related to each year of the high school and to the psychological development of the students. Just as children in the lower school experienced the recapitulation of cultures in their development, a similar parallel exists in the high school. There is a key theme related to each stage of adolescence.

The ninth grade
Ninth graders have left the second seven-year phase behind, and as happens in most life phases, the first year carries with it something of the old. Eighth graders have arrived in modern times; they have become contemporaries with others of their age. As they come into ninth grade, there is a strong feeling of the present time. They want to be involved in what is happening now, to be citizens of the modern world. As yet they do not have much understanding of it. The curriculum is woven around the themes of power and strength — for example, in history, the study of revolutions and power struggles such as Civil Rights; and in physics, thermodynamics. The key word is 'what?', concrete descriptions of objective facts.

At the same time, ninth graders are focused on the structure of the physical body, while in geography they study the physical body of the earth — its continents, mountains, volcanoes, earthquakes, etc. They also study chemistry.

Over the course of the four years, students study an aesthetic curriculum in which they explore a particular art form as a window to history. In ninth grade, they study History through Art, and History through Drama.

Students learn the way art was expressed visually from the ancient world through the 17th century (to be brought up to modern times in further lessons). Seeing and discussing different standards of beauty over the ages helps ninth graders see that there have been various standards. They also learn that they are capable of producing beauty, and they gain confidence in their capacity to produce it.

In History through Drama, students study the changes in drama over time, from Greek drama which was meant to have a cathartic effect on the audience, to individual drama in modern times.

Ninth graders are also busily involved with wood, clay, drawing, and calligraphy. Some ninth graders are trying to make an impact on everything around them. They have trouble being still and concentrating, and for them the arts provide a healthy challenge. They have to learn to respect the particular medium and materials, to live with the process. Other ninth graders may be hesitant, afraid to make a mistake. For them the arts provide an opportunity to step into the unknown and take risks.

The tenth grade

Tenth graders have come to the next step in maturity. Feeling fairly comfortable in themselves, they become interested in process, in development, in metamorphosis. The key word is 'how?'. How do things happen, how do governments form, how did the Word come into being? Whereas the ninth grader needed stability, the tenth grader responds to that which is in motion. In geography they study the fluids, water currents, water power. In biology, the fluids of the body, circulation, the endocrine system, reproduction. In chemistry, the organic processes of fermentation and distillation. And in physics, the world of mechanics.

The idea of finding out how things work is important in this year. Steiner was especially keen that the teachers would develop practical lessons, including surveying, first aid, typing or shorthand (today this could be coding in the computer lab), technical crafts such as weaving and mechanical drawing.

In history, they go back to the ancient world and see how rivers and climate affected ancient settlements; they trace the evolution of societies from ancient India to the Hellenistic period in Greece. Where they have learned about ancient Greece in the fifth grade through myths, biographies, geography, and the meeting of the small group of city-states fighting against the powerful Persian army, the study now is about the powerful ideas in the meeting of East and West, the birth of philosophy, and the shaping of Western culture through Greek ideas.

Socrates was put on trial for corrupting the youth of Athens because he questioned traditions, and sought to find the meaning of the true, the good, and the beautiful. His student Plato introduced the Analogy of the Cave — the imagination of spiritual reality and earthly illusion. Finally, it was Plato's student, Aristotle, who opened the gates of modern thinking with his emphasis on categorizing knowledge and seeing the laws of nature, drama, logic, and politics, and of thinking itself. These topics are chewy, and students can sink their teeth in and test their own thinking.

The tenth grader is experiencing many of the same changes. Out of the previous image-like thinking, pure concepts begin to be formed and grasped. Working with these ideas helps youngsters bring form and order into their thinking as well as balance, movement, and grace that so imbued Greek sculpture and architecture.

In literature, they study the Word in the epic, lyric and dramatic poetry of the Iliad or Odyssey, of Greek drama and of the Old Testament, and perhaps the sacred literature of various religions.

Many other subjects are included in the tenth-grade year, and of course each school has its own special courses. For example, many schools in the United States include American literature that is appropriate to each grade, such as nineteenth-century American authors Hawthorne, Emerson, Thoreau, and Whitman, Zora Neale Hurston, and John Steinbeck; English authors such as Blake, Wordsworth, Coleridge, Byron, Keats, and Shelley are studied. Their language, imagery, and their biographies stimulate discussion.

The eleventh grade
Most eleventh graders are going through the 16-17th year change. The mysterious inward journey of the soul is mirrored in the curriculum through the question, *Why?* In history, the great religious questions are addressed in the study of the Roman Empire, the birth of Christianity, the development

of Judaism and Islam, the development of the Roman Catholic Church, and the Reformation. Just as the Renaissance personalities questioned traditional authority and asked 'Why?', so do the eleventh-grade adolescents. It gives them satisfaction and insight to see that the questions they ask are the questions of their age. It is exciting to know that to challenge the accepted customs is valuable and necessary for the development of civilization.

Seventh graders respond strongly to the Renaissance because they are experiencing rebellion towards the physical authorities in their lives, but 16–17 year-olds experience rebellion in their souls. For example, the doubt mirrored in the Reformation is not doubt of whether the authorities have vested power, but existential doubts such as whether there exists the soul, a spirit, God, and eternity.

The emotional or soul life of the adolescent is going through a profound development during this time, and one of the courses taught is History through Music. One major aspect of music through the ages has been an expression of the meeting between the soul and the divine. Listening to music of the different historical periods and coming to appreciate and understand it helps youngsters develop an inner listening. They see how different musical styles emerge at different times and places.

Just as history through art in the ninth grade fed the craving for imaginative visual images, and history through poetry helped the tenth grader relate to language, history through music in the eleventh grade feeds their craving for tone.

In literature, the study of *Parzival* mirrors the inner journey from foolish young knight to the Grail knight, from naivety to mature wisdom. Many schools introduce eleventh graders to the great works of Dante, with his picture of sin and redemption. The study of Shakespeare reveals the insight of the modern condition in characters such as Hamlet.

The world of the heavens is studied in astronomy, and the sub-earthly power of electricity and magnetism is studied in physics, quantitative laws and atomic theory in chemistry. Projective geometry opens the students to a new imagination of space.

The eleventh grade is a turning-point in the adolescent's Waldorf experience. Out of the richness of the courses, teenagers are put in touch with their inner resources and higher selves.

The twelfth grade

The theme of the twelfth grade is freedom. The main question asked is, 'Who?' — meaning, 'Who is behind this doctrine?' 'Who is working through that personality?' 'Who is really speaking?' Through these questions, young people confront questions of destiny, of good and evil, of meaning. Twelfth graders analyze and synthesize thoughts. They can look at an issue from many points of view, finding the common elements and the central issues. Waldorf teachers bring example after example for the students to explore and think about.

Some examples from literature studies are the works of the 19th-century Russians, Germans, and Americans. By reading Dostoyevsky's *The Brothers Karamazov* or *Crime and Punishment,* the student comes to understand how a Russian considers the deep questions of life. In Melville's *Moby Dick,* there is the struggle of the American soul with evil, and in Goethe's *Faust,* the German approach to science and spiritual meaning. Adding authors from African, Asian, and Latin American cultures as well as African-American literature, and making sure women writers are included, expands their view of the world. In each of these studies an understanding of the particular culture is considered, but more than that is the realization that the issues addressed are universal. The greatness of these writers is that they have soared beyond their nationality and have given to humanity an artistic expression of questions facing human beings everywhere.

Twelfth graders grapple with the issues of their times. Before they leave school they step into the present. Their teachers examine with them the issues of the day — problems of economics, politics, social issues, nuclear chemistry, modern art, debates over evolution, and so on. The history through art of the twelfth grade is the study of architecture in which the students examine the expression of thought in physical form. What is the gesture of an Egyptian pyramid, a Gothic temple, an Art Deco bank, or of a high-tech office building?

Everything twelfth graders study is done by the adolescent penetrating the world — reflecting, shaping thoughts, discussing, sharing. In mathematics, the young adults have passed into the abstract world of trigonometry and calculus, in English classes they work with precis and

Chapter 14 — Waldorf education

research, synthesizing viewpoints, and analyzing a theme. In their world-language study, they delve into literature, exploring similar themes to their English literature studies — the battle between good and evil and the nature of freedom.

The twelfth graders can reach way back in their education into the imaginative first-grade world of the fairy tale, and bring the powerful shaping forces into creative writing. They experience the sweep of history through thousands of years, and see patterns and threads working in human and national biographies. They see the development of human life — from the kindergarten children they pass every day to their teachers who are quickly becoming contemporaries. They are able to understand the paradoxes of life without losing sight of the ideals. Their eyes are on a distant shore while they prepare to leave their school-home and bid their school-mates and teachers goodbye.

In a Nutshell

Waldorf education

- Each Waldorf school is independent, based on the educational principles of Rudolf Steiner, and the schools differ from community to community, from nation to nation.
- The curriculum is based on the developmental stage of the child/adolescent and is reflected in each grade.
- Children's consciousness changes over the course of the elementary school, and each grade meets this change in the approach to teaching, as well as the subjects taught.
- The high school offers more freedom to the student, as well as a greater exposure to teachers from different specialties.
- Each high-school year has a special quality, reflected in the curriculum and in the teachers' educational approach.

Chapter 15

Teenagers and the arts

The poet, the artist, the musician, continue the quiet work of centuries, building bridges of experience between people, reminding man of the universality of his feelings and desires and despairs, and reminding him that the forces that unite are deeper than those that divide.

John Fitzgerald Kennedy

Art itself is the fruit of free human nature. We must love Art, if we would see how necessary to a full humanity it is.

Rudolf Steiner

We use the arts to remake ourselves.

Elliot Eisner

The Power of Art

We live in a world that is splintered. The spiritual life is separated from the scientific and artistic life. We classify knowledge and experiences into neat compartments, but the soul of the human being fights against such fragmentation and cries out for unity, for inter-relationship. Because the newly awakened soul-life of the adolescent is open to all that works upon it from the environment, fragmentation is particularly painful. Art is the healing remedy for fragmentation.

The ancient Chinese character for art looks like this:

I have often discussed this character with ninth-grade students. We can imagine that the upper stroke is the heavens, the lower stroke is the earth, and the crossed figure in between stands for the human being, perfectly balanced between earth and heaven. If a person is too strongly connected with the earth, they are trapped. If the person is too connected with the heavens, they are 'spacey'. Art is the dialogue of the human being with the heaven and the earth.

In the following poem, Rudolf Steiner describes how the arts are a gift to the human being who longs to be connected with the spiritual world. We spoke this every morning during the History through Art class.

> On a primeval day,
> The Spirit of the Earth
> Approached the Spirit of the Heavens,
> Pleading thus:
> One thing I know and that is, how to speak
> from out the human spirit.
> But now I beg to learn
> that other speech,
> whereby the great World-heart
> knows how to speak to human hearts!
> The Spirit of the Heavens, then, in mercy,
> Bestowed upon the pleading Spirit of the Earth
> THE ARTS.[23]

Art becomes the saving grace for human beings cut off from their spiritual origins and suffering from the loneliness of the human condition.

Teenagers understand this image without any difficulty. They, too, feel cut off from the spiritual links they felt in childhood. By a living experience of art they are able to reconnect with the celestial light which they once saw around all living things. When human beings feel whole again, they are able to use their energy to enliven and transform social life. Lacking the feeling of wholeness, they feel empty and strike out at what is around them as well as at themselves.

Importance of the Artistic Process

When we are engaged in artistic processes, we have a conversation with our inner being. We are not so concerned with the product of our work as with the process, which puts us in touch with the spiritual in us. In most activities of daily life we respond to the outer world, but art allows us to awaken our inner eye and inner ear to imagination and inspiration. It helps us understand our thinking, feeling, and willing, and to gain insights into who we are and who we are not. It helps us explore the qualities as well as the quantities of life.

As teenagers experience the many-textured levels of artistic process, the diverse ways of coming to an answer, the richness of metaphor in language, in rhythm and melody, of the living quality of form and space, their capacity for imagination deepens and their inner soul-space expands. A transformation of the commonplace stimulates their consciousness and sense of existence.

The inner life of the adolescent craves art as a way of connecting, of conversing, of creating. Out of the inner conversations comes judgement. When we create something artistically we stand before a mystery, something unknown. We feel that something alive is present, and that we are the means for it to come into physical form. As adolescents develop sensitivity to the creative process, they sense that they are midwives to something being born. Although this is an intimate experience, it is also an objective one. As they work with stone or wood, tones or words, they must respect the laws of the medium. They must honor the material even as they impose their own will on it. In this way, they approach the artistic process as the philosopher approaches truth — as a beholder. When adolescent artists have a dialogue with their artistic work, they come to love it so much that they become one with it. They experience the artistic process at a time of quiet contemplation and communication. It resembles a conversation between the lover and the beloved. This is the power of art.

The power of art was so beautifully expressed by Rainer Maria Rilke in *Letters to a Young Poet*:

> There is only one single way. Go into yourself. Find out the reason that bids you to write; find out whether it is spreading out its roots in the deepest places of your heart; acknowledge to yourself whether you would have to die if it were denied you to write. This most of all,—ask yourself in the stillestt hour of your night: must I write? Delve into yourself for a deep answer, and if this should be affirmative, if you may meet this earnest question with a strong and simple, 'I must', then build your life according to this necessity; your life, even into its most indifferent and slightest hour must be a sign of this urge and a testimony to it.[24]

Art and Observation

Surrounding teenagers with works of art allows them to experience the power of creative expression. When they admire what is beautiful, they experience the creative powers that live and weave in nature and in creative activity. They develop an appreciation of subtlety and nuance. They feel uplifted by the creative energy that went into the work. When teenagers admire the beautiful form of a Greek vase, The *Pieta* of Michelangelo, the *Holy Family* of Rembrandt, or a painting of Maori design, they develop a love of truth. It is not easy at first for young teenagers to appreciate the form and color of a painting or sculpture, but as they try, a new capacity is awakened that helps them see the beautiful. They exercise a new 'muscle', which gives them soul strength and endurance.

Drawing and painting are other ways of seeing. When teenagers are able to spend hours copying the works of the Great Masters, they come to know their works in an intimate way, and they never forget them; they take them inwardly. As they explore their hidden talents, they find they are capable of producing beauty as well as admiring it. Even the most rumbustious teenager, if given an opportunity, feels calmed and awed by the grace and uplifting quality of great art. I have seen tough youngsters transformed by this process. It is as if the edges of a roughly cut gem are polished to reveal the glory of the human being — the higher self.

Van James, an experienced international art teacher, writes:

> Perhaps the single greatest support and encouragement for a student's painting, in fact for any skill, is the teacher's constant trust that the student can do remarkable work. However, it only works if this trust in the student is actually a knowing, a certainty that with effort and engaged will, success can in fact be achieved.[25]

Teenagers should come to know about the artists' lives as well as about their works. The lives of the artists appeal to the teenager's fascination with the drama of life. The agony of Schumann, the struggle of Beethoven to deal with his deafness, the sensitivity of Emily Dickinson, the despair of Van Gogh, the quickly burning flame of Keats or Shelley, the persistence of Turner, the elegant simplicity of Georgia O'Keefe, the disappointments of Coleridge, the tragedy of Melville, the fire of James Baldwin, or the power of Dostoyevsky — all appeal at different stages of adolescent development. Because adolescents are envisioning their own destinies, they have a special empathy with the creative process and struggles of artists. Perhaps the extra sensitivity of the artist's soul life is mirrored in the teenager's own inner life.

For ten years, I worked with teachers at a court and community school and in juvenile hall in Marysville, California. The teachers became interested in adapting Waldorf methods to this group of students of 14–18 years of age who had come from dysfunctional families, struggled in school, had low self-esteem, were repeatedly getting into trouble, and were considered to be 'throw-away kids'. At first, the students were suspicious of the good art materials that were given to them, the lessons in drawing and painting, and the opportunity to illustrate their history and science lessons. However, over time they connected with the experience, and showed talent that surprised them as well as their teachers

Chapter 15 — Teenagers and the arts

and parents. Previously, they had limited their artistic expression to graf-fiti carried out at night at forbidden sites.

Art and its Relationship to Feeling and Thinking

When the teenager's life is permeated with the artistic impulse, their soul life is exercised. Wonder, awe, fear, sadness, laughter, pain, happiness, and compassion stimulate the breathing of the soul.

In their plays, the ancient Greeks applied this knowledge of the healing influence of rhythm by presenting three tragedies followed by a comedy. Memory is intimately bound up with feeling. An idea or concept enliv-ened by feelings is carried into memory. We remember those ideas best which are connected with strong feelings. The art of drama has this power.

Because their souls are so receptive to the power of art, adolescents experience their own soul life even through such elementary artistic exercises as color exercises in painting or vowels in eurythmy. The power of true art is so strong that even its simplest elements can transform. For example, when teenagers work with music and poetry, the ideal aspect of the art touches their souls; they feel lifted out of themselves and united with pure artistic powers. This is what lies behind the ecstatic smile and the big, awe-filled '*Wow!*' that they so often express after an intense, artistic moment.

Art helps us to explore ideas in a non-verbal, non-linear way. Because it does not limit us by pragmatic dos and don'ts, we can explore the byways of our minds, and all things become possible. In this process, youngsters learn to take risks. Doing this in the artistic realm gives them courage to try it in the conceptual world.

A twelfth-grade girl expressed the difference between Western and Eastern thought in a fascinating way. She spent weeks creating a large urn, pouring her love and care into it. She fired and glazed it, marking it with the Japanese character for life, and glazed it again. She brought it to class where her classmates and teachers admired its beauty. She stood at the threshold of the room and said, 'I will now demonstrate the attitude of non-attachment to things'. Then, she dropped the urn. We sat in shock as the urn smashed into dozens of pieces. At that moment, she achieved a deeper experience of the concept of non-attachment than any research paper would have given her.

By working artistically, the teenager's intellect is awakened and the will is activated. The human will is so strongly attacked by the overdose of sense impressions flooding in from the environment and by the impersonal nature of fast-paced modern life that many children instinctively protect themselves by withdrawing and becoming passive. Their will becomes weakened and they lose control over their own lives. When will activity is brought into the thought life, however, it enlivens it. In this way creative thinking can occur. The role of art in activating the will is essential. Teachers give special attention to this by addressing the various capacities of the teenager's observation, memory, and imaginative thinking. All of these are enhanced through the artistic process, and that is why it is so necessary that teenagers experience and understand art.

The artist does not progress in a straight line, but makes leaps in abilities and understanding. Moments of inspiration and insight are unpredictable, and must be regarded with appreciation and wonder. We cannot plan for them, but once they occur our lives are changed. The teenager who has this experience is put in touch with the inner sources of imagination and the unconscious world of archetypes.

The childlike forces of imagination do not continue into adolescence in the same form. At about the 14th year, the soul of the child moves inward to a protective inner space, safe from the onslaught of new feelings. At about that time the imaginative forces also withdraw. As in a cocoon, the soul lives in darkness until it is ready to burst its shell and emerge into the light of day as a butterfly. The forces of fantasy which previously lived in imagination had not been the child's own. They had come from the surrounding world and from the spiritual-soul sphere. They came *to* the child rather than *from* the child. In adolescence, these forces are transformed into forces of intelligence or into practical abilities. When imagination arises after puberty, it has a new quality, that of individuality.

The youngster arrives at an independent imagination from within the soul. When adolescents have an opportunity to work with art and to respond individually to it, their soul lives are quickened and their imagination stimulated. An atmosphere of individual freedom is essential if teenagers are to appreciate and enjoy art, and if they are to create artistic works. This does not mean that the student is left totally free. The teacher should limit subject matter, but choices should be offered so that the adolescent helps shape the work. For example, if the class is doing watercolor painting, the teacher may call for a scene including trees and water, but then let the students work out the placement and color. Or students may be asked to draw in the style of Michelangelo or Picasso, but they may choose from among ten or twelve of the artist's works.

Steiner made a great gift to education when he called attention to the arts as agents of healing, balancing, and nurturing. Our utilitarian society sees it as frill or enrichment, but Steiner pointed out that art is essential to the well-being of the child, adolescent, and adult. Because of this, art in its many forms constitutes the backbone of a Waldorf school, and the central art is the art of teaching.

We have seen the growth of recreational art classes being offered as part of community education. Art classes are offered to the elderly, to people with disabilities, to prisoners, to children, and to over-stressed professionals. Art is so popular because it brings balance to our hectic lives, but it does much more than that. If we understand the healing aspects of art, we would honor it more in our daily lives, and art classes would not be the first ones eliminated when budgets are tight. Music, poetry, literature, speech, drama, movement sculpture, painting, drawing, and architecture allow the soul opportunities for expression, exploration, and self-discipline.

Art and Curriculum

When Rudolf Steiner introduced the curriculum of the original Waldorf school, it was built around those courses which lead to an understanding of art and those dealing with the study of the language and history. These courses remain as part of the Waldorf high-school curriculum. They are often referred to as the Aesthetic Courses.

In the ninth grade, art is explored through the history of visual arts of painting, drawing, and sculpture. It is also explored through the history of drama. In tenth grade, the Aesthetic course deals with history through poetry. In the eleventh grade, the focus is on history through music. In twelfth grade, students study history through architecture. In all these courses, students experience the changes in consciousness through the particular art form. This is enhanced with their original explorations in the art and sharing it with the community.

Crafts as Power

In addition to the powerful role of the arts in adolescent life, crafts are also significant. When the artistic approach is applied to the everyday world, to the dishes we eat from, the clothes we wear, the furnishings in our homes, we imbue our surroundings with beauty and care. When teenagers become proficient in crafts, they develop skills, self-discipline, a feeling of purpose, and a sense of worth. To make a well-formed plate from clay and take it through the entire process until it is ready for the table; to card, dye and spin wool and then use it for knitting or weaving an article of clothing or a household item; to make a bookcase or a chair out of carved or cut wood; to print calligraphic invitations or posters; to bind a book or make a stained-glass window; or to do any one of a variety of other crafts is a major accomplishment.

Teenagers who have these experiences develop confidence, concentration, skill, and appreciation for work done by hand as well as done by machine. Their judgement is sharpened and their integrity enhanced. Appreciation for handwork also creates an understanding and appreciation for technology. Pride in craftsmanship and quality is needed in both handwork and technology, and certainly there is a need for improvement in the quality of mass-produced items. At the same time, there is an interest in 3D print techniques introduced today.

The word 'craft' once meant power or magic. It is not surprising, then, when those who take hold of a craft develop power in their lives. When teenagers feel that they have meaningful power in their lives, they are less apt to seek it in anti-social ways. Working with crafts such as woodworking, carpentry, and metals offers an opportunity for students who would want to prepare for work in the trades, or seek an apprenticeship.

Music and the Teenager

> What happens between a teenager's headphones? Today's kids aren't listening to the bands you liked at their age — you already know that. Young people tend to use music as a way of defining and sharing their sense of self, identity, or 'personal brand'.
>
> Rebecca La Clair [26]

One of the most significant areas of a teenager's life is music. Each generation has had its music, its songs and singers. Fans have fainted at concerts and been swept away. Yet the music of today's teenagers has a different quality to it. This difference has to do with loudness and beat; it has to do with the effects of electronics; it has to do with the anger, drugs, and violence that permeate the words and the lifestyle.

For many teenagers, listening to music is a way of identifying with the peer culture. Young adolescents may not know what they like, but they want to have group status. There is status in knowing the latest thing, and they don't want to be left out. All they know is that this is 'our music'. That is understandable, and we see how as they grow older they become more knowledgeable and more selective about the groups and songs they choose.

Listening to radio, cds, streaming, iPods, or any of the latest technologies is an important part of becoming a teenager. To the young teen sprawled out on the bed for hours, each song has a special meaning. Listening through earphones brings the sound into a much more intimate relation than hearing it from speakers in a room. It feels as if it is coming from inside. There is almost no place a teenager can go without being accompanied by music, whether riding a bike, walking, running, driving, eating, or doing homework.

Music expresses emotions.

At the highest station, the auditory cortex, just above your ears, these firing cells generate the conscious experience of music. Different patterns of firing excite other ensembles of cells, and these associate the sound of music with feelings, thoughts, and past experience.[27]

Lyrics that describe the teenage experience give words to the longing for a relationship, losing a relationship, feeling rejected, hoping for love, and wanting the future to be bright. Some music is politically focused, describing poverty, racial discrimination, and unfairness. Music also expresses anger and frustration, loss and despair, homelessness, confusion, and yearning for the stability of childhood. Another genre of music expresses the rage of a generation of children who feel abandoned, angry about the break-up of marriage, of the father who walked out or the father the youngster has never known. Larger themes are included such as climate change, war, human trafficking, and immigration issues.

Just as music has an effect on teenagers, it also mirrors teenagers' experiences. Reading the lyrics of many contemporary songs paints a picture of the challenges of present-day culture and its effect on children and adolescents. Music of the Broadway show 'Hamilton' has not only captured the attention of adults, but of all ages. The fact that Lin-Manuel Miranda conceived of the production in rap with a racially diverse cast makes the themes contemporary, as well as the lyrics themselves. It stimulates teenagers to connect with the foundations of American history.

There is no question that marijuana and other drugs are commonly part of the contemporary music scene, but that is not new. Sex and drugs have been strongly identified with teenage music since the late 1960s. Parents should be aware of this if their young teens are attending rock concerts or other large musical gatherings.

Rock stars have become an accepted part of our culture. Constant publicity leaves us feeling that we know them. Not all take drugs, however, and many rock stars today do not even drink. Rock groups project an image of being very powerful, and teenagers think they can take on some of the power of the group they identify with. (It is similar with fans of sports teams, politicians, and the like.) This is referred to as the 'positive mania syndrome', reminiscent of primitive beliefs in which the tribal member takes on the power of a god by wearing a headdress or by drawing certain symbols. So teenagers participate in 'air bands', wear tee-shirts with grotesque pictures spread across their chests, and leave a trail of graffiti depicting the logos of their favorite rock groups on their books, school lockers, and in public places, enabling them to feel bigger and more powerful than they feel when they behold themselves as solitary beings.

Electromagnetic forces pulsing through rock music affect not only the listener's nervous system but also their soul. In addition to hearing rock music as they go to sleep, many youngsters wake up to it, never giving their nervous systems a rest. Jurgen Schriefer, a distinguished musician and music teacher for over 20 years, has said that heavy listening to rock music even harms the quality of a person's voice. According to Schriefer, the music hardens muscles in the back of the throat, reducing the quality of the singing voice.

In a distorted way, rock musicians understand something very important about our times, namely that the will is the key to the soul of the modern adolescent. If we work with the will in a positive way, we awaken devotion and service; but an overdose of rock music can cripple the will, making devotion and service very difficult.

Teenagers are drawn to different styles of music. As a generalization, teenage boys tend to listen to music highlighting frustration, rage, and despair, while girls prefer love, tenderness, and relationship. Some musical styles support resistance to authority, others describe personal problems at home or at school, loneliness, or feelings of inadequacy. Others stimulate relaxation, create a happy mood, calm insecurities, and provide rhythm to dance to. Teenagers express interest in many styles of music in addition to contemporary rock, such as rhythm and blues, New Wave, punk and reggae, Country, Western and folk, religious, and classical music.

Whereas the choice of music by itself will not cause a teenager to choose destructive behavior, those experiencing social alienation, disturbances at home, or a feeling of hopelessness are especially vulnerable.

Another symptom of the huge impact of music on modern youth is the fact that teenagers today, far more than ever before, build their sense of identity around their music preferences. Until recently, students grouped themselves into categories that had little to do with music. They were identified as jocks, preppies, etc. Those categories remain, but now there is an additional identity based on what kind of music a person listens to. A student is expected to know whether they are New Wavers, punk, heavy metal fans, or soul-music fans. There is the music of the inner city and the music of the suburbs. You are what you listen to. Only as teenagers become more self-confident can they buck this single identity and admit they like different kinds of music.

Music and the Soul

Music used to uplift the soul. Now it is generally enjoyed for its sensual qualities. The introduction of radio strongly influenced the ways in which people experienced music, and phonographs, tape recorders, videotape players, iPods, streaming on smartphones, and other technologies have made the change revolutionary. People once had to either make their music themselves or go to a place such as a concert hall, marketplace, or tavern, where others were making music. Music could not be experienced apart from the musicians.

Music and Healing

An old saying goes, 'Music alone with sudden charms can bind the wand'ring sense, and calm the troubled mind'. Music has a very important healing task to balance the impact of technology and the frenetic pace in our lives.

Parents should learn to listen to the music which their early adolescents are hearing and distinguish the various forms, groups and styles. Some groups are trying to be socially responsible, while others try to exploit and poison youngsters. By listening to the music and lyrics together, they can build a bridge by discussing the pros and cons of a song or group. It is not sensible to say that all rock music is bad and forbid a teenager from listening. It is also misguided to let the youngster play anything they want on the principle that 'every generation's music is obnoxious to the preceding generation'.

Parents should regulate the amount and kind of rock music an early adolescent listens to, and they should introduce other musical experiences as a balance. If the parent attempts to appreciate some of the teenager's music, the teenager may be more open to the parents' tastes. It won't be possible to do so in another year or so.

Parents have to stand on the thin line between being open-minded and being concerned for the young adolescent's well-being. The parent, not the young adolescent, is responsible for deciding whether they should attend a rock concert (or an R-rated movie). There is still an opportunity during the middle-school years for parental authority, and it won't come again.

Conclusion

Art is the perfect integration of form and freedom. Each art form has its own structure and rules which need to be mastered before the moment of freedom arises. I had the good fortune to teach a class for six years, beginning in seventh grade through their high-school graduation. Most students had already been immersed in the arts from kindergarten through sixth grade. Five boys joined the seventh grade with little or no previous experience in art. While studying Renaissance history, two of them began to copy works of Leonardo, Michelangelo, or Raphael. Their work was stunning. Paul said that when he closed his eyes, his hands knew what to do. Peter took to all of the crafts with gusto. I observed how they developed the skills and began to create original work. Today, Paul is an architect, and Peter is a significant sculptor creating very large metal pieces.

Ray played the guitar as we sat in handwork classes or sat around the fire on a camping trip. Thanks to him, we got to know the Beatles' songs. Today, he is a professor and a musician, performing concerts on his classical guitar. Virginia loved drama, and today she is a scientist, but is still involved with community theater. Noel manages a large laundry business, but she also spent years as an interior designer. The school didn't teach them to be artists, but it gave them the opportunity to discover it within themselves and make it a part of their lives.

Another class was very connected to literature. In seventh grade they loved puns, reading, writing, and expressing themselves. In high school they gravitated to drama, poetry, and creative writing. A number of them went into careers in publishing, writing, drama, and journalism. Heidi became a pioneer in home death (Her film *Into the Parlor* was included in the *New York Times* magazine, December 2019), as well as the head designer for the Dickens Faire in San Francisco.

Not every teenager has such richness in their education. However, an introduction goes a long way. In my own twelve years of schooling I had only one semester of art. In that seventh-grade class, we painted a hibiscus in water colors, shaped and glazed a clay ashtray, and drew blue prints for a house. That started me in my love of art in all its forms.

The arts are healing and transformative, no matter whether the teenagers pursue art professionally in their lives or enter into the sciences, mathematics, teaching, medicine, law, building, business, or become stay-at-home parents: the arts continue to nurture their sense of self.

At the beginning of this chapter I described art and the ways it ennobles and transforms teenagers. These are not just flowery words; they are realities. Though we live in a splintered world, art is a bridge which heals the soul by uniting our spirits with the outer world and which heals young people. By sharing with them the Truth, Beauty, and Goodness which true art conveys, we give adolescents art's greatest blessing: hope.

In a Nutshell

Teenagers and the arts

- Arts are an important part of the high-school experience, offering opportunities for creativity and judgement.
- Students participate in many different art forms, each awakening a new capacity.
- Adolescents experience enlivening feelings through the arts as they explore ideas in a non-verbal, non-linear way.
- The artistic process awakens the intellect and activates the will, with the feelings mediating the meeting of the two.
- Rudolf Steiner introduced an Aesthetic Course Curriculum from ninth to twelfth grade that is unique to Waldorf high schools.
- Crafts are also significant in the high-school curriculum offering students an opportunity to be creative, practical, and appreciative of what they can do with their hands.
- Adolescents connect with their peers through different styles of music.
- Music uplifts the soul and is important for individual development as well as learning about music throughout history and in different cultures.
- The arts are healing and transformative for adolescents, regardless of what they choose to do in the future.

Chapter 16

Power and loyalty

Before I built a wall I'd ask to know
What I was walling in or walling out,
And to whom I was like to give offense.
Something there is that doesn't love a wall,
That wants it down.

Robert Frost, *Mending Walls*

As children become self-conscious, they experience themselves as one person among many. They feel the effects of other people's actions, and they see the effects of their own. They learn early that a temper tantrum may get them what they want. They feel inner turmoil when two people they love are on opposite sides of an issue. In brief, they awaken to the fact that human beings live in groups, and this means there are times of stress as well as times of joy.

Social skills allow children to find their way into the whirlwind of human affairs. Inconsistency, mixed messages, and hidden expectations are among the obstacles that confuse them as they try to understand what is coming to them from the environment. They gradually become familiar with their family and their culture's way of interacting. Whatever is around them they assume is normal, the way it's supposed to be.

As they become teenagers, they must reckon with two powerful expressions of individuality: power and loyalty. Within bounds, these are valid means of identifying with the group and strengthening their sense of self. However, getting stuck in the urge to power or in loyalty-at-all-costs is very limiting. Working through these issues helps adolescents move beyond personal satisfaction and thus gain a wider relationship to society.

The Need for Power: Proving Oneself

The adult and the adolescent have similar needs — to communicate with other people and to experience some degree of control over their own lives. In our society, these needs are often expressed in terms of power, which is even conveyed through body-language, by the walk and the gesture of hands. A carefully studied strut, for instance, is supposed to show confidence and strength. It says, 'Look out! Someone powerful is coming.' A studied look may also convey power, especially a look that challenges and tests. A tall boy may saunter over to a short one and say, 'Carry this, Shorty'. Shorty is already self-conscious about their height, and the last thing they need is to be bullied. The more fear they show, the more the bully lords power over them.

Power is an issue in arguments with parents. When teenagers realize that their logic is as good as the adult's, the chin juts out, eyes glisten, and they exploit the advantage they sense in the moment. Their sense of power merges with their sense of identity. Adolescents become what their point of view is. If the adult disagrees, they take this as rejection of themselves, and the confrontation ends up bigger than at first it seemed.

Girls tend to use power more subtly than do boys. The girl wins over adults, especially men, through coquettishness. They twist them around their finger. In addition to being flirtatious, they can be very aggressive. All obstacles fall before the onslaught of a teenage girl's expression of self-righteousness.

When adolescents sense their strength, they are capable of consciously manipulating adults. In this situation, they assess the adult's weakness, and attack. Teenagers are also capable of being rude and defiant one moment, and sweet and gentle the next. Is it any wonder that adults become suspicious of their shifting approach, and wonder what the youngsters' real motivations might be. Teenagers use their power to drive an adult into a corner to get the decision they want. Their energy is intense, especially when they gang up, and adults sometimes cannot withstand the intensity of the confrontation and back off, saying 'OK, alright'.

During a ninth-grade trip to Yosemite Valley, several students planned to sneak out and go drinking. When one boy asked if he and others could ride the shuttle bus that evening, I responded on a hunch and replied, 'No'. The conversation that followed went something like this:

You don't trust us.
I'm not discussing it further. The answer is simply 'no'.
You're on a power trip.
If that's what you want to call it, fine.

We stormed away from each other. They were over their anger in a few minutes, but my evening was ruined. I brooded over the unpleasant exchange late into the evening and again the next morning. I was annoyed at the way I had responded, yet I trusted my intuition. Years later, the students confirmed my hunch and sheepishly apologized.

Emotional scenes such as this one occur in many homes each evening. Often, the apparent issue is quite unimportant, but the real issue is over who is stronger. Problems are bound to occur if parents feel that they must defend the position of authority above all else. The parent must sort out the issues and decide which ones allow room for compromise, and which do not. The self-esteem of each individual is at stake, so once the battle begins, it is difficult for either to back off without losing face.

Parents often do not realize in the moment that they are over-reacting. Parents, also are sensitive about self-esteem and acceptance by friends, neighbors, relatives, or colleagues. The threat of losing acceptance because of a son's or daughter's behavior produces anxiety, and causes parents to become angrier than they otherwise would be. This occurs especially when teenagers confront or defy parents in public. Instead of saying, 'I don't want the neighbors or friends to see you like this because they won't respect me', they usually say something like, 'It's for your own good', or 'You're ruining the family's reputation', or 'What you're doing is not decent or right'. Underneath it all, the parents feel humiliated and helpless.

They feel frustrated at the shortcomings of the adolescent, and fear that these shortcomings are being projected on to them by others. They may even feel they have failed as parents. One father expressed his frustration because his son was withdrawn. He didn't feel that he could take his son where other fathers took their sons. His frustration was so strong

Chapter 16 — Power and loyalty

that he lashed out and blamed everyone else for it. Finally, he broke down and wept: 'I just want to shake him into talking to me. What have I done wrong?'

The Dynamics of Power Struggles

Having arguments with teenagers sometimes resembles a duel; the teenager's thrust can wound as deeply as a sharp sword. The adult can hardly match the directness and concentration of the attack. I have had this feeling many times in my years of teaching adolescents, and have learned not to take it personally — but that doesn't mean it isn't hurtful. A student once accused me of ruining his life by giving him a lower grade than he deserved. In his tantrum, he kicked the door and raised quite a ruckus. There was no point in my becoming outwardly upset also, although my stomach was turning. Two years later, he was much mellowed, matured, and humbled by life.

Sometimes a power struggle is triggered by a misunderstanding or an unrealistic expectation on either side. Teenagers do not yet realize that the world is composed mostly of shades of grey. Instead, they see everything in black or white, good or bad, winners or losers. This renders them impatient, and causes them to label many adult actions as hypocrisy. When teenagers come into their 17th or 18th year, greater tolerance and understanding occur. It is then possible to have productive discussions, with compromise and benefit to all involved.

Many power struggles occur because one side or the other assumes that one view is right and the other is wrong. A helpful way to avoid this is to present the problem and ask the teenager to offer solutions for the parents' consideration. Problems with chores, curfews, and expectations, for example, usually offer room for many approaches. The teenager's attitude changes when they are able to think things through from several points of view and come up with a reasonable solution. Parents are generally surprised by the reasonableness of teenagers' proposals.

As defensiveness is reduced on both sides, trust increases. Adolescents need opportunities to develop responsibility as well as to test their ideas.

In these situations they will generally accept fair punishment for serious mistakes in judgement. Self-evaluation is far more effective than grounding or loss of privileges. However, it is not easy for parents to switch into this new mode. All too often, adults feel they need to prove that they still have power over the adolescents, and the battle lines are drawn again.

If we can remember that the soul of the individual is struggling for freedom, perhaps we can be more sympathetic with our youngsters. We can understand this if we can understand that they want freedom *from* rather than freedom *to*. Any limitation is at first seen as authoritarian or dogmatic, as a denial of their freedom. As long as adults issue final decisions without sharing the process of decision-making, teenagers will react, and their reactions are seldom gentle. To protect their need for independence, they protest, sometimes viciously. Later, they may apologize. 'I didn't mean that. I just felt I had to gripe. It wouldn't be any fun otherwise.'

Many power-struggle scenarios are played out daily. Here are a couple of typical ones.

- After evaluating an unpopular decision, parents decide that they cannot give an acceptable or logical explanation because they have arrived at the decision intuitively. They feel that what the teenager wants is inappropriate, and — as unreasonable as the decision may seem — they must stick by their position. No amount of crying or pleading, badgering or pressurizing will change it, but the teenager tries anyway. Eventually, both sides sense when enough is enough, and the contest ends. The next morning, however, the teenager tries again, just to be sure there hasn't been a change overnight.
- A 16-year-old girl relentlessly argues to do something her mother is not comfortable with. Finally, the mother wears down and gives in. The girl tosses their mother a triumphant look and breezes out of the room, but that night the girl is moody. When their mother asks what is wrong, the daughter replies, 'It was terrible this morning when you gave in. It was as if you had died.'

If parents walk the narrow line between acting unreasonably and acting responsibly, they must be able to tell when they are simply protecting their own power and when they are acting out of conviction. If adults give in whenever they are challenged by their teenagers, the adolescents never have a strong foil against which to test their own convictions. It is like pushing against marshmallow fluff, and nothing pushes back. Teenagers may be momentarily pleased, but in the long run they experience the lack of resistance as a lack of caring. The parents did not feel strongly enough either about the issue or about the adolescent to take a stand and hold it. Teenagers do not admire weakness, and will feel disdain as well as disappointment.

Parents are challenged most often over such issues as the choice of schools, responsibilities in the home, summer activities, curfews, the car, friends, behaviors, and punishments. Some parents make it clear that certain areas are non-negotiable, such as health, education through high school, and behavior within the family. This may mean, for example, that rudeness to parents, siblings, and grandparents will not be tolerated, that the youngster's diet must be healthy, that they will not be allowed to play interscholastic football because of the danger of injury, or that they are expected to maintain a specific grade average in school.

Teenagers do have some influence, however, in such negotiable areas as choice of friends, dates, interests, entertainment, clothes, and decoration of their bedroom. Some parents would choose the reverse, and would be uncompromising in the choice of clothes, friends, and dates. This is an individual matter. Whatever, the situation is, teenagers should be clear about which decisions are left to them and which not, and when it will change based on their age and responsibility. This enables them to know where their input is expected and even welcomed, and in which areas they must accept decisions, even when they disagree.

During the early teenage years, through age 16, it is especially critical for parents to stand firm. If they give in too much to 13- and 14-year-olds, it is very difficult to hold back later. Yet even then, there must be some wiggle room for compromise. Young adolescents often disagree with their parents for the sake of disagreement, and they don't really know what they want. As one 15-year-old boy remarked, 'Isn't arguing just part of being a teenager?'. Disagreements with 16- or 17-year-olds are different, however, and parents should take seriously the adolescents' reasoning.

What seems to be a power struggle is sometimes really triggered by the parents' fear of letting the child grow up. The fear is understandable as there is much to fear. But when parents take an entrenched position, they may not recognize the capacity of the teenager to cope with the situation. They fear letting go of the child, and they fear being left alone. The growing independence of their child reminds them that they, too, are growing older. This is particularly true of the millennial generation and beyond where families tend to be closer and their children less often rush to leave home.

All adolescents go through a period of testing their power against parents, siblings, teachers, and friends. This normal step in development of the self becomes difficult when the parents cannot handle the challenge, and either withdraw or react too aggressively. Both reactions end up cutting off communication.

In American culture, it is accepted that a young man shows power through competition, either on the athletic field or in academics. Teenagers are raised to be success-oriented and are taught to win. Pressure builds up, promoting a value system based on the Roman principle of 'Might makes right'. Other slogans in this value system include, 'Push 'em again. Harder! Harder!', and 'Win at any cost'. This attitude is especially seen in competitive sports, when parents confuse their children's win–loss record with their own egos. In other cultures they are taught to share. When American teenagers come into contact with people sharing those other values, they have a major adjustment to make. It is one of the reason why travel and exchange to other countries are valuable so they can gain new perspectives.

Other Ways of Expressing Power

Sportsmanship and cooperation are also dynamics of the competitive scene. If parents, coaches, or schools emphasize sportsmanship and cooperation, teenagers develop both appropriate pride and appropriate modesty. Youth sports then become the vehicle for character-building that they often proclaim to be. Teenagers can enjoy winning, but their sense of self is not identified with being on top. They appreciate a good game if the team plays well, regardless of who wins. They share the joy of a team mate's achievement without feeling put down themselves, without feeling 'I hate him. He beat me.'

When too much pressure is riding on a teenager's performance, whether in athletics or in a classroom, they will develop a win-at-all-costs attitude that justifies cheating, giving someone misinformation, or other devious means. Sometimes they fail because they are too tense to function well. In that case, they need to know that they are loved and accepted for themselves, regardless of their prizes.

This issue leads us once again to the parents' needs. How much are they living through the achievements of their children? In 2019 the case of cheating on college applications became a major scandal in the USA. In some cases the students were not aware that their parents had arranged illegal means to get them into top schools, and in some cases there was collusion with staff members at the school. One of the students commented that they felt their parents didn't think they could do it on their own and had to cheat for them to be accepted. This was not confidence-boosting, to be sure.

Adolescents need ways of expressing and testing their powers because these experiences give them a sense of their limits. They need to set goals — and go beyond them. They need to feel the joy of accomplishment, of self-satisfaction. There are many ways this can be achieved without doing it at the expense of others, such as survival trips, backpacking, bicycle trips, orienteering, hiking, swimming, Outward Bound programs, volunteering in a hospital, becoming a camp counselor, taking first aid, being a lifeguard — in short, giving service where their strength and power will be helpful to others and will add to their own healthy development. Then their power and strength are put to the service of humanity. I have seen rumbustious teenagers transformed by the responsibility (and hero worship) that came with being a camp counselor.

The Question of Loyalty: Where Do I Belong?

Another serious issue between adolescents and parents is that of loyalty. Parents generally assume that their children will feel loyal to family values, family friends, and to the social customs of their family and society. But adolescents' first loyalties are shifting to the peer group and often to the youth culture too. A teenager's growing identification with the peer group and a growing-away from the family can shake up the family structure. However, this may be only a temporary shift, long enough to establish them in their contemporary world, but also long enough to cause confusion.

Parents may not like the friends their adolescent chooses, but teenagers often experiment, trying on new friends as they might try on new clothes. Sometimes they choose friends their parents don't approve of simply to shock them or show their independence. They may be trying to understand different kinds of people; they may be exploring values different from their own family. Parents become nervous that the friend may be a bad influence on their sons or daughters or that they may reject the parental values. They are concerned that the young person may shame them, or make poor judgements concerning money or time.

Another aspect of loyalty is the teenager's commitment to the contemporary culture. Parents are usually still carrying the value and dreams of their own youth culture. The music, styles, and heroes of their youth felt right to them when they were young, but they do not feel comfortable in the new youth culture. Usually, they don't like the way the heroes look or sound. They are not familiar with the language or jokes.

Some parents dive into the new youth culture as a way of communicating with their children. If this is overdone, it looks rather silly, but at least the parents are making an effort to be informed. This is valuable as long as the adult doesn't attempt to become one of the gang. That is embarrassing to adolescents who are trying to maintain a sense of distance from their parents.

Each generation produces some who stand apart to make a point. They may have a passion that separates them from the group, and they are willing to sacrifice everything to feed the passion. Others lead by example, not really knowing if anyone will follow. They are committed to social change and stride out in front.

Teenagers struggle to identify what they are actually being loyal to — a fad, a group, or a particular person within a group. There are subgroups within the larger teen culture. Teenagers know the characteristics of each subgroup, but sometimes they get into one without much thought. Just because of a dare, for example, they may join a gang or clique. It can seem important not to appear 'chicken'. Other times, this may happen because the teenager is friends with a member of the group.

Each group has its own brand of elitism, and teenagers are soon introduced into a hierarchy. Some would like to explore a number of groups, but this is difficult in a large school as the groups tend to get fixed. During the summer, however, teenagers can often explore new identities at camp, in a drama group, working at a ranch or farm, or at a job. They have an opportunity to try on roles, see what it's like to be a 'jock' or a 'brain' without committing themselves for all of high school.

If teenagers give signs of wanting to change groups, they may be accused of disloyalty. Once they join a group, their identities are fixed and their social interaction limited. A teenager who is unhappy in a group suffers heartache. This is one of the tragedies of adolescence, and sometimes a change in school or neighborhood or activities is needed to give them a new start.

It is far healthier when teenagers can express their talents and interests without being locked into groups. For instance, they can show several aspects of their personality and abilities in such places as camps, church groups, and small schools. They are less likely to simply be labeled as a member of some group. Small size alone, however, does not insure open-mindedness, as cliques can exist anywhere.

Teenagers Relate to Parents in Different Ways

Some teenagers identify so closely with their parents' values that they are uncomfortable with aspects of the youth culture. This can narrow their social options and prevent them from identifying with their own generation. Their need to break away from their parents will have to find a different form or wait until later. If the peer environment is too one-sided — either too loose or too tight — or if the adolescents are uncomfortable with the behavior or social attitude of peers, they may be left with the alternative of standing alone and relating mostly with adults, or looking further afield for contemporaries they prefer. They are fortunate when they find such friends because it allows them to continue being connected with their generation without placing them in conflict.

This is not always possible, however, and some teenagers shy away from the youth culture so much that they are seen as 'goody-goodies'. They take no risks and never misbehave. Outwardly they are model teenagers, but secretly they yearn for excitement. They may fantasize escapades or actually carry them out surreptitiously. By choosing a safe and narrow path because they are afraid of risks or of their parents' disapproval, these youngsters may be missing their youth. For this reason, parents should be alert to their children's needs for new interests and new groups.

A teenager sometimes has to be caught doing something wrong in order to wake up the parents. Parent should appreciate the opportunity to open up communications and not be too involved with punishment. Very often, the embarrassment itself is punishment enough. It is important for parents to separate their anger or annoyance with the act from support and love for the teenager. If this can be done, there is a good possibility for increased growth and communication. Most adolescents appreciate the opportunity to tell their parents that they are in trouble before it comes from outside authorities. Giving teenagers a chance to do this helps them take responsibility for themselves, and gives them a better opportunity to benefit from their mistakes.

Some teenagers have open communication with their parents and tell them about things they have done, even if they haven't been caught. They are open to their parents' advice and gain maximum benefit from parental support.

Many adolescents will speak to one parent and not the other. This burdens the parent who is receiving the information. How should the parent handle this? Keeping it a secret from a spouse often backfires.

Chapter 16 — Power and loyalty

A 16-year-old girl was caught smoking marijuana. She asked that her father not be told. The mother agreed with her daughter and the punishment was given without sharing it with him. When he found out, he was furious, which left him resentful as well as angry.

Adolescents feel divided loyalties, but when they are forced to choose, some will be loyal to their friends rather than to the adult. When asked to give information about a peer, they want to tell the adult, but they are loyal to their friends. Teenagers have to live more closely with their friends than with their adults. We can make their lives miserable by turning them against their peers, and we have to respect the delicacy of such situations. Parents and teachers should be sensitive to the inner conflict of the young person. When confronted later with the lie they told the adult, teenager's response is plaintive: 'You wouldn't have expected me to tell on her, would you? Would you tell on your friend?' Others, when forced to choose, will stay loyal to their parents and risk disapproval from their peers. Each response creates tension and a fear of losing support.

A 17-year-old boy was in agony because his twin brother's life was threatened with heavy drug use. He was concerned about his brother and needed his parents' help, yet he didn't want to lose his brother's confidence. We decided to call his parents, and the four of us sat down and talked. His parents responded very well, appreciating the possible repercussions and grateful for their son's concern and courage. They found a way to help their troubled son without implicating his brother.

Being able to confide in a family member can ease the teenager's pressures. Older siblings may help by guiding the parents in the way they deal with their teenager. Often, the siblings see what the parent cannot, or they can offer help and support because they are less threatened by the youth culture. It is a lucky adolescent who has such an older brother or sister. Sometimes it works the other way. One sibling may side with another against the parent in order to get a decision changed. This is a difficult situation for the parent, and parents feel stressed when they have to deal with a double onslaught.

To Whom Am I Most Loyal?

Adolescents do need a way to evaluate their loyalties. Parental understanding is a good first step. Loyalty to the peer group is likely to be a pro-peer stand rather than an anti-adult one. Adolescents themselves have to judge the importance of the immediate social group, their peers, and decide whether, in the particular situation, the peer group is the more important one in their life.

Power and loyalty are outer manifestations of inner attitudes. If teenagers feel secure in themselves they will not feel a need for exorbitant power over their environment. If they feel appreciated in their homes and schools, they will be loyal without being slavish. Their identity in the group is important, but not critical.

Robert Frost's poem, *Mending Walls*, began this chapter. When we build walls, we wall ourselves in and others out. An insecure adolescent divides the world into friends and enemies, feeling secure within a confined group of like-minded peers. People who are different are considered enemies and need to be walled out. They are labeled as weird and strange; they are put down, kept away, or intimidated. Because these teenagers feel powerless, they seek ways to be more powerful than their adversaries. In showing their power, they feel big, but they shut out possibilities of growth. When Frost says, 'Something there is that doesn't love a wall, that wants it down', we have a picture of maturing adolescents who have reached the point where they enjoy camaraderie, but not at the expense of others; they are able to transform power and loyalty into capacities for courage and compassion.

Behind the struggle for power and loyalty lies a much deeper issue — namely, meeting another human being. When teenagers learn to accept themselves, respect themselves, and like themselves, if they do not have to prove that they are bigger, better, faster, or tougher, they can begin to glimpse the ego that lives within.

Respect for and acceptance of the other person, whether the adult or peer, is the first step in 'seeing the other'. When teenagers develop emotional maturity, they are making progress specifically in this area of human relationships. On the other hand, if this maturity does not develop, and they relate to others in a highly competitive and overly aggressive manner, the scene is set for a chaotic and painful adulthood. In its essence, the question of power and loyalty is the social issue lying at the basis of relationships between people, as well as between groups such as nations. Many adults walk around with unresolved attitudes having to do with power and loyalty. These attitudes give rise to unworthy impulses, especially when the individual's higher self has been worn down by fatigue or stress. Because these attitudes are unresolved, unconscious and powerful influences are ready to jump out whenever the lower nature or 'the double' rears its head. This occurs especially at times of stress. The biting, searing, cutting statements that flash out in an argument are the residue of unresolved power–loyalty conflicts which go on to haunt personal and professional relationships.

It is good to remember that the development of executive function, or higher-level brain development, which begins around age 16–17, is not completed until their 20s. There is still time for mature development to occur in this area.

What began as an examination of issues between parents and their adolescent moves naturally into the greater issue of living in harmony with other human beings. This subject includes a variety of communication skills such as admitting their mistakes, assessing their needs and communicating them objectively, expressing hurts and disappointments when they occur instead of waiting for them to build up and explode, developing tact and honesty, and realizing that we do not have the right answers for every situation.

Dealing with the conflicts of everyday life teaches us that one person is rarely right and the other consistently wrong, and there does not always have to be a winner and a loser. Both sides can win by discussing the problem and finding a new solution that they may not have considered earlier, and finding ways to collaborate. Learning to deal with conflict enables teenagers to develop necessary skills.

The highest expression of human interactions is the I–Thou relationship. In this special relationship, they acknowledge the spiritual essence living in the other and respect the importance of the other's concerns as equal to their own. Resolving the issues of power and loyalty enables teenagers to build a firm foundation for deep relationships in their adult lives.

In a Nutshell

Power and loyalty

- Adolescents need to experience some control over their own lives in their relationships with adults and peers. Parents also struggle with their need to exert control over teenagers. Such struggles are common issues in parent–child relationships.
- Parents need to be clear about on which issues they will have the final word, and which are negotiable.
- Disagreements with young teens up to age 16 have a different quality from older teens from 16–17 and require parents to adapt to the different ages.
- Adolescents need to find ways of testing their power, whether it be on the athletic field, challenging hikes, taking jobs, or giving service.
- Adolescents struggle with their loyalty to parents, friends, and contemporary culture.
- Parents also have a hard time figuring out how to deal with their children's loyalties that are different from what they would choose.
- Resolving issues of power and loyalty enables teenagers to build a firm foundation for deep relationships later in their lives.

Chapter 17

Love, relationships, and sex

For one human being to love another human being: that is perhaps the most difficult task that has been entrusted to us, the ultimate task, the final test and proof, the work for which all other work is merely preparation. That is why young people, who are beginners in everything, are not yet capable of love: it is something they must learn. With their whole being, with all their forces, gathered around their solitary, anxious, upward-beating heart, they must learn to love.[28]

> What are we doing in love?
> What are we doing in love?
> I'm too young.
> I am scared.
> What am I doing in love?
> The flowers are still blooming.
> The grass is fresh and green.
> What am I doing?
> What am I doing?
> 9th-grade girl

Love

Love — is there any other word in our language with such a wide range of meanings? Is there another word with such power? Is any other word the subject of so many poems, letters, or songs? And does any other word have so many interpretations and misunderstandings? Love is the greatest creative force in the world. It is the ideal of human relationships, and the basis of sacrifice between parents and children, husband and wife, friend and friend, person and God. Yet it is also trivialized, cheapened, and denied its deeper meaning.

When children come into the world, they are an expression of pure love. They give total trust to those who care for them. As they grow and slowly separate themselves emotionally from parents, their love is extended to neighbors, friends, teachers, and grandparents. And, of course, they have a special love for animals.

When children reach adolescence, a new experience of love is possible. From deep within the soul comes a new awakening on two levels — ideal love and sexual love.

Ideal love carries with it the qualities of pure spiritual love, total union, sacrifice, and joy. The light of the higher self illuminates the journey of the soul. It is all-giving and all-forgiving, and its radiance is wide enough to include all of humanity.

The impulse of sexual love comes from the newly freed soul life, referred to earlier as the soul body. Feelings are kindled and warmed for another of the opposite sex or of the same one. In everyday life these feelings are connected with instincts and desires, and they lead to an awareness of personal sexuality. Youngsters become especially conscious of their sexuality as they enter puberty — girls through awareness of menstruation, boys through erections and wet dreams. They are both fascinated and embarrassed by the functioning of their bodies.

Ideal love lives in the mind and fills the soul. Teenagers form thoughts about the inner being of the other person, and idealize them.

Changes in Puberty

As youngsters come into puberty, their emotional life as well as their physical body undergoes change. Power struggles increase, mood swings erupt, new desires awaken. Young teenagers are vulnerable to what the world pours in on them. Physiological changes, especially hormone changes and changes in their brain, significantly influence behavior.

Views on gender have gone through many changes over the centuries, and we are going through a transition in this time. People, and especially young people, are demanding that we look at gender differently; define gender, sexual orientation, and identity in a more fluid way.

For example, even those young people who are comfortable with the sex they were born into identify themselves as *cisgender*. ('Cis' in Latin means 'on the side of', in contrast to *transgender*, which means 'on the other side of'). They do this in order to separate themselves from those who identify differently.[29]

This generation is open and supportive of the number of ways people identify themselves, to those who are transgender or asexual, and they recognize the courage it takes to step out of traditional roles. Over time, both younger and older people are getting used to this, and honoring the intentions of the individual.

As I describe girls and boys in this chapter, I hope the reader will understand that I recognize and embrace a whole spectrum of male and female, masculine and feminine, when I use these terms.

Because girls come into puberty earlier, they become more sexually aware before the boys do. Girls talk about who likes who, and what they will do about it. Some of it is just talk, but in other cases they reach out to boys in their class. Parents of middle-school boys may be surprised by the way girls speak to or text their sons, suggesting sexual behaviors, when the boys hardly understand what the girls are talking about. I was speaking with a 13-year-old boy about his class, and when we spoke about some of the girls, he said in a forlorn way, 'I'd never have a chance'. I think if he had a chance, he wouldn't know what to do.

Boys are very insecure about changes in puberty and seldom talk about it. They are watching their bodies change, feeling confused about ejaculation, spontaneous erections, masturbation, and wet dreams. They have many fears based on labels (nerd, macho, fag) and fears about their abilities. They can be sharp with words as they tell sick jokes or cut each other down. At the same time they are very sensitive to criticism. They

Chapter 17 — Love, relationships, and sex

are clumsy and awkward, sensitive to comments about their growth and about whether they are strong.

Although boys go through this stage later than girls do, the quality of the change is similar in terms of vulnerability, confusion, and struggle to understand what is happening. Their thinking is still concrete, and they have difficulty thinking through the possibilities that will result from their decisions. This is especially true in relation to sexual activity. They may have sexual feelings, but they aren't sure what to do about them. If they find themselves in a situation where they can be sexually active, they haven't planned for it, they don't anticipate the consequences, and lack the intellectual ability to set limits. Because of their concrete thinking, they have problems making sound judgements about their sexual behavior. They are sensitive about being seen as babyish, and may get involved in sexual activity to show they're not afraid.

Early adolescent boys build up their feeling for intimacy not by coupling, but by having relationships with best friends, social groups, connections with parents and other family members, or with mentors or coaches.

Before 16, boys have not gone through the body and brain changes that will help them understand what a relationship is. They have significant developmental steps to experience first. Michael Gurian in his book *A Fine Young Man* points out that early adolescent boys still do not understand what intimacy is.

> A good rule of thumb for American culture is: No dating till sixteen. If we all shoot for it with our adolescent boys, we'll be allowing their body and brain changes to reach positions of advancement that make the building of romantic love a help rather than a hindrance to core-self-development. In other words, if we help them to mature the core self through other intimacies first, they will be more likely to love a mate without becoming emotionally dependent on that one mate for their core self-development. [30]

One child psychiatrist commented that to ask an early adolescent boy to connect with the idea of relationship with sexual experience is to miss the point. He is not there yet. His problem is what to do with his penis, not what to do with a girl's feelings.

After boys come into middle adolescence, after 16, they begin to explore intimacy in conversations and their feelings about sex, but they are trying to figure things out and are sensitive to any sign of rejection. Boys are far less sexually active at this age than you might expect based on what is shown through the media.

What about girls? Girls struggle to hold on to their assertive, confident selves as they enter the middle-school scene. They often split into two at this time: wanting to be smart, wanting to be sexy. They want to be treated with kindness, but they can be mean to their peers. They try on new roles, think their families are boring, don't want to be embarrassed by their parents, fantasize about having freedom, test limits, are obsessed with their bodies, want to grow up, want to stay young. Appearance strongly defines social acceptability. They talk a lot with friends, and become secretive with adults. The big question, is, 'Am I normal?'. They constantly compare themselves with others.

Some girls have no interest in boys until a few years later, and some, not even in later adolescence. It can be hard for them to find their place in the social scene unless they can connect with another girl with similar feelings, or develop a platonic relationship with one of the boys. Children mature at different rates, and some girls come into their own after they leave high school. Some may be nervous, insecure and immature, and others decide they are gay, or asexual.

It is especially difficult when young teenage girls hang around with older boys. The girls may feel special by being invited to be with them, but they need to know that they do not have to do whatever the boys ask. Out of their insecurity, girls succumb to older boys' requests, using their body particularly to service older boys. A girl who may not have been clear in her feelings, after doing what the boys asked, described that it wasn't what it was cracked up to be.

The combination of sexually stimulating movies, videos, and music puts tremendous pressure on young adolescents who are not emotionally or intellectually capable of dealing with them. They have a difficult enough time understanding their own needs, and they have an even more difficult time perceiving a situation from another person's perspective. Once early adolescents' feelings are aroused, they feel pressure to act, and everything can get out of control.

Girls are less protected by the society, yet the imagery in popular culture encourages them to become sexually active. They are encouraged to dress in a sexually provocative way, and to project themselves as sex objects. 'Girls today are bombarded with the notion that revealing your body is a valid means of self-expression, even a manifestation of girl power.' [31]

When I was in eighth grade and high school, it was very clear which girls were good and which were bad, which hangouts were trouble and which were safe, and which things you would do sexually and which ones you wouldn't. Our information was limited to one book which we could read in the back of the public library shelves. How exciting that was!

Girls today have more freedom, more choices, more ways to get information, and more pressures, but what they don't necessarily have is guidance from parents or other adults. It is a big world out there, and it is hard to navigate.

Sex education is different in different schools and in different communities. Some parents try to protect their children from knowing about sex, but social media, their peers, and images in movies and magazines get there first. Even if they are uncomfortable, parents need to speak with their children about sex in a way that seems appropriate at the time. If they leave it to street talk, the youngsters will have misinformation and may make bad decisions. Leaving the information to the school is also not enough because children may not feel comfortable asking questions. Parents' attitudes actually make a big difference in the way young teens regard sex. However, parents should not be naïve about what is happening today among both young and older adolescents.

It is important for adolescents to understand the consequences of being sexually active and to take precautions. Power to Decide is an organization in Washington, D.C. to prevent unplanned pregnancy. It believes 'all young people deserve the opportunity to decide if, when, and under what circumstances to get pregnant and have a child. And that means knowing all there is to know about birth control.' They can also be accessed through You Tube.

Sexuality and Sexualization

Dr Leonard Sax makes a distinction when he says:

> Sexuality is good, but sexualization is bad. Sexuality is about identity as a woman or a man, or about feeling sexual. That's a healthy part of becoming an adult. But sexualization is about being an object for the pleasure of others, about being on display for others. Sexuality is about who you are. Sexualization is about how you look. [32]
>
> For boys and young men, sexualization is often the driving force behind a relationship. But for most girls and young women, it's usually the other way around: the relationship has to drive the sex — otherwise the sex won't be any good. The most fulfilling sexual experience for most teenage girls, and for most young women, is physical intimacy with someone with whom they have a meaningful and ongoing relationship.[33]

Teenagers exploring sex and love

Over the next few years, the relationship to sex changes. As adolescents are maturing, their early feelings of attraction to others results either in hero worship or sexual desire, as expressed in the form of the crush, which I spoke of earlier in Chapter 2. Many of us can remember back to our first crush — the unattainable love. We might remember the first time we spoke to that special person, or the moment when we realized the object of our crush was falling down from the pedestal into being an ordinary person. Holding the hero on a pedestal gives the teen time to mature before engaging in complex romantic, sexual relationships. However, with the advent of internet pornography and social media, the time of the crush is often cut short, and sexual activity among young adolescents has become more common.

In spite of all the media impressions of how much fun sex is, how 'everyone is doing it', many teenage girls feel a sense of loss. A 16-year-old described her feelings when she lost her virginity.

> After I had sex for the first time, I went for a walk and sat on the shore of the lake and stared into space. I felt grey and empty. I loved my boyfriend, and my unhappy feelings did not have anything to do with him. I just felt different. I felt older and alone. I knew my childhood had passed and I could never be innocent again. I spent hours sitting and staring. It was one of the saddest days of my life.

However, girls and boys are changing, and there is a wide range of sexual activity going on, whether it is in a group or in pairs. Some are getting involved sexually because they are attracted to someone and want to engage, knowing the relationship may not last. This doesn't mean that they are especially promiscuous, but they have made this decision consciously, at least they think so. Some girls feel insecure and allow themselves to be taken advantage of by boys in a way that shows a lack of self-control. Unfortunately, reputations are often ruined, and harm can take years to be undone.

It is especially helpful to have conversations with girls to discuss boundaries so they have a way of working through these issues. Despite all the hype about being sexually active, there are also adolescent girls who refrain, and want to develop long-term relationships first.

Girls often become sexually active with boys, particularly oral sex, without being in a relationship. Because sex is so available, boys don't need to invest themselves in being with a girl before engaging sexually. The message is that sex does not have to be part of romance. Because porn culture has become easily accessed, sex has become separated from relationships. This is particularly difficult for boys, who may find it more satisfying to masturbate to a porn video than invest in a relationship where more is required of them emotionally.

Relationships

As adolescence progresses, the ideal of love intensifies, and romantic love blossoms. Ideal love is cultivated as the teenager forms thoughts about the higher and finer nature of the other person. The feelings that emerge out of ideal or romantic love arise from such nurturing thoughts, whereas sexual love arises from instincts and desires of the person. This is different from sexual experimentation arising out of curiosity. Of course, ideal love and sexual love together are part of the love experience.

Healthy relationships exist among teenagers in which there is respect and affection. Some youngsters experience sweet relationships around the age of 12, when they participate in the ritual of 'going steady'. The ritual changes over time and in different places. Every generation has its own version. 'Going steady' involves careful preparation, usually a short-term relationship and a speedy dissolution. For the 11- or 12-year-old, going steady has a completely different quality from the going steady of 16- and 17-year-olds. The following sequence is one possibility.

Step 1: Thinking about it, planning with friends, asking others to find out if the feelings are mutual;

Step 2: Asking the question, usually in an offhand, awkward manner, probably by telephone or text rather than in person;

Step 3: Going steady. This could include sitting together, occasional hand-holding, possibly sneaking kisses and endless telephone or text conversations;

Step 4: Breaking up;

Step 5: Gossiping about what did or didn't happen. In going steady, young teens are more in love with the idea of love than with each other. There isn't very much *going*, and even less *steady*.

Steps 1, 2, and 3 can be very tender. Step 4 is never easy. Step 5, the gossiping stage, is where danger lurks, as others exaggerate or fabricate what happened.

Going steady among adolescents around 16 has a different character, and they may not even use that term. As with earlier relationships, these also have their share of joy and pain, but they are usually more complex than what their younger friends experience.

Relationships come in many forms — best friends, platonic cross-gender, older and younger teens. Best friends can be of either gender. They are powerful magnets that draw two teenagers together, sharing interests,

Chapter 17 — Love, relationships, and sex

activities, explorations, and their own coded language. Best friends for ever (BFFs) are mainly active in middle school, where friendships come and go, and young teens have to learn to start again without trashing the other.

In high school, relationships become more complex, and often have room for different kinds of best friends. They may be school relationships only, or ones that exist beyond school and even further. They may develop on a sports team, in a drama club, on a debate team, or in a service project. They may include socializing on the weekends, spending summer vacation together, or exploring new places. What they all generally include is trust. If that is broken, the relationship can break apart in a disheartening way.

It is normal in high school for boys and girls to develop new interests. This is part of expanding their horizons, and it doesn't always have room for a former close friend. As teenagers begin to form a more complex understanding of themselves, they may realize that the old friendship doesn't fit any more. Unfortunately, such break-ups affect the friends around them as well, and one of the heartaches of adolescence is the recognition that the familiar may not last. It is natural that feelings such as betrayal, anger, and jealousy erupt at this time, and there is much room for everyone involved to be hurt. Having an older person to speak to about this can be very helpful.

Learning new skills of communication includes being honest while being sensitive, stating each one's needs in a relationship, and even being able to speak about how they would handle it if their friendship broke up. Teenagers are watching relationships all around them — their teachers, their parents, their friend's parents, and even people they don't know such as sports stars and actors. They speak about them as if they knew them intimately. They project on to these people romantic ideas, and live in a fantasy-rich aura. While watching, they are learning.

Young Couples Explore Love

These first experiences with love become the foundation upon which other relationships are based. While each positive experience gives confidence for the next one, painful experiences occur too, and the adolescent must overcome these in order to develop security and trust in a new relationship.

However, growth is often born of pain, and emotional maturity is a blessing, even if it has a bittersweet quality. The ending of teenage relationships can be painful, yet how often we adults look back with gratitude that intense relationships which seemed so perfect at that time did not lead to marriage! How thankful we are that the popular heart-throb of our senior year of high school or freshman year of college did not become our life's companion and the parent of our children. We had so much learning to experience.

For teenagers, love offers the same challenge it does for lovers of all ages — how to transform the intense and exclusive love for one's partner into love for humanity? As long as love is reserved for the loved one only, it is egoistic and possessive. 'I want this for *us*' is only a slight variation on 'I want this for *me*'. In teenage love, egoism is intensified by the adolescents' need to separate themselves from their parents and to find independent identities. Exclusivity is experienced as independence from authority, as two against the world. How often the drive to stay out late or sneak off to forbidden places stems as much from a need to rebel as from a need to be with the boyfriend or girlfriend.

The couple often feels singled out. On the one hand, they feel that the world revolves around them. On the other, they feel that life's restrictions are aimed directly at them. They became a fortress, protecting their love from the world. They become so closely identified with each other that they find it difficult to function separately within a group.

A couple may enjoy these intense feelings for each other, but an antisocial element develops when they are with friends or at school. They find it difficult to participate in a group because they have eyes only for each other. Resentment builds as friends feel rejected and frustrated by the couple's lack of interest in the group. Parents or teachers who try to penetrate the fortress must do so with tact. The couple is often so insecure and, thereby, defensive that any word from the voice of authority is reacted against rather than listened to. They do not see the inappropriateness of their behavior, and accuse the adults of meddling, lacking understanding, of disliking them, or even of jealousy. Their resentment may come out in such comments as, 'What's your problem?' or 'Why are you always on our case?'.

Yet the fortress must be penetrated, and the young couple needs to wake up to what is fitting in each situation. Such a discussion, when successful, helps them strengthen their individual identities as well as their identity as a couple. Indeed, deep in their souls they know what is appropriate, and they even appreciate the adults' nudging them out of their excessive dependence on each other. It the teenagers accept the advice of the adult and move back into the larger group, it very often helps their relationship move to a more mature level, allowing them as individuals to pursue their separate interests while nurturing their mutual feelings.

When adolescents experience love they are setting out on one of life's most transforming experiences. If it is allowed to do its work, the teenager's narrow, indulgent love will blossom into love which is the basis for human social progress. Love that is rooted in wisdom and understanding celebrates the spiritual in the other human being. Thus, the love of humanity that is needed for social renewal is a transformation of the sexual love prevalent in adolescence.

Sexual love, usually characterized by possessiveness and self-love, must be transformed so that it is freed from the body and becomes love of the other. This love for the other is usually expressed in the form of family love, for one's companion, spouse, child, or grandparent. It is a higher form of love than mere sexual love, but family love can still be too egoistic to develop into a true social impulse.

The crowning experience is the love of the higher Self of another person, regardless of sex or family relationship. A friend quoted one of their mentors who said, 'Love is not blind. It's visionary.' The person in love sees the highest aspect of the beloved.

When two people meet ego to ego, a spiritual communion takes place, and love arising from such a meeting nourishes not only the two individuals, but also the social life of the community. At this stage of development, each works to rid their selves of egoism. The person becomes involved in the needs of others. When this occurs, people may experience a spiritual presence in the physical world, enhancing their own ability to experience love and sympathy. Such a deep soul-experience leads not only to understanding, but to feeling the needs of others as one's own. The task of modern times in the spiritual evolution of humanity, according to Rudolf Steiner, is to develop the capacity for such love.

The capacity of love is with us at birth and never leaves us. Although sexual love comes early in human development, ideal love is placed side by side with it. Although sexual love is compelling in its demands on the present moment, if it is appropriately awakened it becomes a gateway to the transformation of the individual's feeling life.

Ideal love points to the future. It lights the way. Sexual love is necessary for the continuation of the human race and as a vehicle of tenderness and intimacy. It is the seed for meaningful social relationships for the renewal of society, but it is only a seed. Beginning by fostering respect and caring for the relationship, the two people need to extend their concerns over an ever-larger community until they love all of humanity. In this broad perspective, we can appreciate why adolescents need to understand love, sex, and relationship. To cultivate respect and learn to listen, and to nurture support and understanding, are to pave the way for developing new capacities of love.

In a Nutshell

Love, relationships, and sex

- Ideal love and sexual love together are part of the love experience in adolescence.
- Understanding the difference between sexualization and sexuality is helpful as adolescents learn how to handle their emotions.
- Popular culture with sexually stimulating movies, videos, and music pressures adolescents who are not emotionally ready to deal with this part of life.
- Developing healthy relationships is an important part of maturing.
- Early experiences with love become a foundation upon which other relationships are based, including feeling the needs of the other as one's own.
- Teenage love is part of adolescents' search for their own identities separate from the adults around them.

Chapter 18

Self-esteem

Despair is the price one pays for setting oneself an impossible aim.

Graham Greene, *The Heart of the Matter*

I recently attended a gathering of teenagers who were discussing alcoholism. A few weeks later, I attended another discussion, and the topic this time was teenage sexuality. During both evenings, the recurring concern was self-esteem. It didn't seem to matter what gender the person was, the most popular teenager in the school, an academically outstanding student, a sports hero, or a shy teen who had difficulty speaking out in class.

Lack of self-esteem causes youngsters to demean themselves, to make dangerous decisions they do not want to make, and to walk around feeling, 'I'm not good enough'. Teenagers handle this feeling in diverse ways. Some become compulsive super-achievers; some withdraw; some take severe risks. Most teenagers experience depression that rises and falls according to their maturity, the strength of their self-image, or the affirmation they experience — or don't experience — in their relationships at school, at home, and elsewhere.

What is Self-esteem?

Self-esteem has to do with whether people regard themselves favorably, whether they feel good about themselves. Already in early childhood, children form self-images based on how their family treats them. Children always try to win their parents' approval. An unspoken question is, 'How do my parents want me to be?'.

During the 7 to 12-year phase, the teacher becomes a powerful influence on the child's self-image. Whether the child feels competent, stupid, brilliant, or mediocre is a reflection of the teacher's attitude. Now the child also asks, 'How does my teacher want me to be?'.

As the soul develops, individual identity becomes a major issue. Teenagers are fascinated with how they appear to others. They develop what David Elkind refers to in his book, *All Grown Up and No Place to Go*, as 'the imaginary audience'. Elkind writes:

> Because teenagers are caught up/with the transformations they are undergoing — in their bodies, in their facial structure, in their feelings and emotions, and in their thinking powers — they become self-centered. They assume that everyone around them is concerned with the same thing they are concerned with, namely themselves. I call this assumption the 'imaginary audience'. It is the imaginary audience that accounts for the teenager's extreme self-consciousness. Teenagers feel that they are always on stage and that everyone around them is aware and as concerned about their appearance as they themselves are.[34]

They feel that they have to impress those around them, but they are not sure who *they* are. To find out, young teenagers put on many different masks. The response to each mask gives the teenager clues to the acceptability of one personality type and another. Thus, the teenager decides whether to adopt a particular way of behaving.

The teenager turns to peers to define behavior. The unspoken question to the peers is, 'Tell me who I am', or 'What do you want me to be?'. Of course, advertisements, teen magazines, movies, and songs have a significant influence on the way the peers form their evaluation. The greatest contemporary influence is social media, whether it is texting, Instagram, or any new form of technology in which others, even those whom the teenager has never met, comment on their appearance.

As the teenager passes through the 16th-year change, the mask becomes less important, although it is still there in the background. The teenager gradually gains greater control over their sense of person. Comments such as 'I've been thinking…' or 'I'd like to be …' become fairly common. It is easy to become stereotyped in adolescence, and some teenagers have to leave home or change schools to start over again with a new image. What they will wear or how they will act on the first day in a new school will invite a particular image.

An 18-year-old who has been extremely withdrawn came to life in their senior year. She told her class, 'I'm not sitting here quietly any more. I've got a lot to say, and you're going to hear me say it. I'm bursting out of the shell I've had around me for years.'

Another girl, who had a traumatic relationship with her mother, could not feel good about herself. She said, 'I can't figure out what I think of me until my mother accepts me. How can I accept myself if she doesn't accept me?'

For healthy emotional development, adolescents need a protective circle of support. This circle should include their family, their school, their religious leaders, and their community. However, with the breakdown of the family, de-personalization of the school, weakening of religious ties and instability of the community, teenagers do not have a protective circle. Instead, they live in a world that limits and defines their acceptance according to narrow standards set by someone working in Madison Avenue, Hollywood, or in You Tube videos.

The expectations placed on teenagers cause stress and frustration. The youngster unconsciously asks, 'What does society want me to be?'. Advertisements, magazines, videos, and movies create an image of the acceptable look, how teenagers should socialize, what they should drink, what soaps they should use, etc. They define acceptable behavior, and they set standards for beauty and style.

As 16-year-olds, my friend Debbi and I pored over an issue of *Seventeen* magazine, reading a quiz which told us our type. I never could figure out whether I was a gamin or a realist, but whichever I decided I was would determine the clothes I would wear and the way I would approach boys and school life, so some days I tried to look like Audrey Hepburn, and other days I tried to resemble Lauren Bacall.

Teenagers never feel good enough compared to the models in adverts or to movie stars. Because they cannot measure up to these idealized figures, they are left with the feeling, 'I'm not good enough. I'm either too fat, too skinny, too tall, too short, too flat-chested, too large-busted, too full-hipped, too lean. My hair is too straight, too curly, too long, too short, too fine, too thick.'

They fantasize that other teens are confident, look better, have an easier life, know what they want, feel OK about themselves. They are always shocked to find out that others also feel insecure. Developing a sense of humor about oneself during this time is one of the greatest aids a teenager can have.

The adolescent is in the process of becoming a person. In their mind, questions nag. 'Do you like me?' 'Does he like me?' 'Does she like me?' At the deepest level, these questions might be seen as, 'Do I like myself?' and 'Does God like me?' The biggest question is, 'Who am I?'.

The teenager's inner life is a great mystery. We never really have access to it, even though we may see them every day. They are not even sure who they are from one day to the next. They can be impulsive, they can be reliable, they can be open, they can be closed. They are unpredictable, and they are predictable. We may think we understand them, but we don't.

When teenagers ask, 'What do I have to do to be liked?', they do not hear the same answers that a helpful adult might suggest, such as 'Be kinder, more considerate, more understanding, give more time to other people, be more helpful, get to know more people, be interested in their interests and see if you can make someone feel more comfortable'.

When the teenager looks to society for answers, the messages that come back are, 'Wear your hair in the latest fashion, buy certain brands of clothes or shoes, walk in a certain way, flirt in a certain way, pose in a certain way, put on a mask, hang around with certain people, avoid other people, count the time you are liked or that other teens say "hello" to you, identify the groups you want to stay clear of and which ones you want to be part of, don't put yourself out too much, don't be too smart, don't be a goody-goody, listen to the right music — and then you'll be OK'.

The dreams that teenagers carry in their hearts don't seem greatly valued by their community. They soon learn what is acceptable and what isn't. The teenager's place in society has become tenuous. Instead of being needed, instead of feeling they have a place in the community, they don't know where they fit. They are not children and not adults either. Most of what they want to do when they are 14, 15, or 16 is illegal or unadvisable, yet they are being urged to do it anyway.

They find out that their dreams are not as attainable as they thought. During the senior year of high school, many teenagers are naïve about what they'll be able to do in life. One idealistic young woman in October of her senior year referred to life as a candy store with so many things she could have or do. By April, after college acceptances and rejections the candy store had narrowed its offerings. Six months later, after being exposed to the world of employment and to college, her choices were even fewer. She was more realistic and more disappointed than the way she had felt 12 months earlier.

Adolescents find out that the road to their dreams takes longer and requires more preparation than they had expected, and that there are more and more limitations along the way. While they are students, their identities become merged with the school's. How often does a young person feel, 'I've got it made because I got into this school', or 'My life is finished — I didn't get in'. Or someone thinks that a teenager is special because they're accepted or attend a prestigious school. When a teenager is rejected by a college because of stiff competition, they often interpret that as, 'I'm not good enough. They didn't want me.'

As a high-school teacher, I came to resent April — that dreaded, yet exciting month of acceptances or rejections. It used to be that the mail would bring thick envelopes for acceptance and thin ones for rejections. Now, the notices are on line, but the results are the same. The teenager may still feel they have failed, haven't lived up to their parents' or teachers' expectations. Depression sets in.

A similar series of disappointments occurs in the job world. The teenager lands a job and is treated in an impersonal way. Schedules are changed around, the interests, sensitivities, or their values are of no concern to the employer. The teenagers soon see themselves as another anonymous body in the job market. A sensitive vegetarian finds himself pounding meat in a hamburger joint. If he doesn't want to do it, he loses the job. A young woman is told to set up the salad bar in a particular way. Out of interest she asks 'Why?', and is fired for having a bad attitude. Teenagers are promised 30 hours a week, and are given 15. Their lives are messed up because they had one expectation, and the reality is something else. They find themselves running between jobs. They cannot question or they lose their jobs, and there are many more teenagers waiting to take their jobs if they become available.

Most teenagers' dreams of ideal family life have already been dashed, either by dissolution of their own family or by that of a friend's family. Insecurity in relationships combines with the tentativeness of the youngster's sense of belonging to leave them feeling alone. Panicked by the sense of isolation, teenagers join groups, become part of a pack, become 'we' and 'us' in order to feel safe. Paradoxically, they worry about finding friends, they find them, and then they're afraid of losing them. They worry about being rejected. If they don't have the friends they want, or if they lose their friends or are rejected by them, they become depressed.

Adolescence with strong self-esteem know who they are and what they want; they are not easily influenced by peer pressure. Self-esteem, of course, offers no protection against misguided experiments and other forms of poor judgement.

However, the lack of self-esteem exposes the adolescent to additional hazards. Over and over again I hear teenagers speak of getting drunk, getting stoned, playing chicken with cars, or getting pregnant because they want to feel accepted, because they don't want to look like a 'jerk', or because they want to show they know their way around. Had they strong self-esteem at a particular moment, they might have said 'No'.

With strong self-esteem, a teenager may choose to avoid a bad situation, but to do it in a way that does not isolate them from the group. A 16-year-old knew that her friends were planning a Saturday-night bash, and she didn't want to be part of it. She created an excuse that her parents had something else planned. She didn't confront her friends, but she also didn't want to lose their friendship. Other youngsters just don't show up and simply make an excuse.

Excuses can't be used often, however, without causing resentment. At some point, the teenager who has grown uncomfortable with the crowd's behavior will have to take a stand, or else leave the group. Surprisingly often, if the teenager is well liked by the group, taking a stand can awaken their consciousness, as well as turn the group around.

Most groups will accept a teenager who makes their limits clear, as long as they have a secure position in the group to start with and don't preach to the rest of the peers. 'Whatever turns you on' seems to be a motto among many teenage groups. 'If you want to do it, cool. If you don't, cool.' The typical teenager assiduously avoids judging their group friends with the implicit attitude, 'I'm not taking a stand, and I won't be influenced by anyone else'.

Depression

Depression, disappointment, and despair are a normal part of human life, but problems arise when a teenager suffers such prolonged depression that it affects their ability to respond to challenges, especially when they feel that there's no way out of the problem.

Depression may result from feelings of rejection, loneliness, loss, isolation, or from a change in family life, or a move. The cause can also be something as vague as a lack of direction or simply being overwhelmed by the experience of being an adolescent in today's world. The reason can be something as seemingly simple as a loss of a stuffed animal or a cancelled appointment. Sometimes a combination of things triggers depression — a friend moves away, a pet dies, a parent is hurt — and the youngster feels overwhelmed and helpless. As such times, it's especially easy for the adolescent to turn to alcohol or drugs.

How to recognize depression
It is difficult for most of us to tell whether teenagers are deeply depressed, or whether they're simply moody. The everyday frustrations of a sensitive adolescent may look very much like depression, yet they are completely healthy and have normal feelings.

It seems strange to be on the alert for adolescent depression. We can understand a 45-year-old being depressed, but don't teenagers have everything in front of them? What can be so bad to be discouraging them at this young age? Psychiatry once claimed that true depression could not exist before the age of 18, but now we know better. Children and even infants can become depressed when they experience separation. Youngsters of all ages, and from all classes of society, can experience deep depression.

Symptoms of depression are usually not directly related to the problem. They may be psychosomatic — headaches, stomach aches, or chest pains — or the teenager may stop doing homework, fail school, become truant, or become listless and generally torpid. Because they feel lonely and isolated, they may seek escape in video games, sex, pregnancy, truancy, running away, or suicide. Other symptoms of depression may be trouble at school, drug or alcohol abuse, repeated abortions, or violence.

It is always better to be concerned than to ignore symptoms of depression. If teenagers have the symptoms mentioned here, especially after a significant loss, the situation should not be ignored. Parents should speak with the adolescent, with a doctor, a counselor, a religious leader, a teacher, a psychologist — anyone in whom they have confidence to help determine the extent of the problem.

Depression often arises from a stress, or a combination of stresses. Common stresses are change, loss, and high expectations. The adolescent responds to them by feeling grief, guilt, and/or anger.

Change and loss
Change means leaving something behind and moving on to something new. Inwardly, the teenager experiences the leaving as a loss, as a death, and goes through a period of mourning or grief.

Growing up means leaving childhood behind. Children must adapt to new feelings and new ways in which their body behaves, such as the awkwardness of their legs and arms or the changes in their voice. Losing confidence in their physical body can generate tension, frustration, and melancholy. The onset of menstruation is a significant cause of depression in adolescent girls. The adolescent grows moody. What am I supposed to do? How am I supposed to act? I'm not ready to grow up! Why does it have to happen to me?

Growing up also means losing childhood innocence. Youngsters hear and see things of the seedy side of life, destroying the purity they once felt. The grapevine of information from peers, and the overwhelming amount of information on internet, bring them all kinds of information and mis-information. As they 'fall into matter' they may become fascinated with the grotesque, the sick, the gross. Lust, violence, or perversions may flood their imagination, while part of them longs for the time before they knew what life was like.

Growing up means losing dependence upon parents. New freedoms and privileges cause stress for teenagers. They are concerned with knowing how to behave in new situations, how to do the right thing, how to know what the right thing is. They fear making fools of themselves, or giving the wrong impression.

Along with the general loss of childhood come specific losses, and the adolescent is more vulnerable to them than parents imagine. At a more stable time, loss would not cause the same stress. For example, if the family moves, the youngster's familiar boundaries are lost, and everything changes at once — friends, home, social rules, and lifestyle. My family moved from a Bronx neighborhood in New York City to a small Florida town when I was beginning seventh grade. Each new experience produced anxiety — riding my first bike to the new school, getting lost, registering for classes, trying to understand the Southern accent. My dress was wrong, and my speech was wrong. I didn't know anyone, and in addition we were in the middle of hurricane season. How could life be so miserable? Instead of experiencing adventure, I experienced stress. Once I was registered and classes began, the stress was reduced, and I was busy trying to understand the teachers and find a friend. Happily, joining Girl Scouts was a perfect solution.

Changing schools or neighborhoods, even within the same city or town, causes stress as expressed by the following questions: Who do I talk to? Will I be accepted? Which group should I try to get into? Will they like me? What if I eat lunch alone? What are the teachers' expectations? Where is the rest room? Where are my classes? Will I get pushed around? How do I impress people?'

Adults who make changes experience stress, and adult stress is common, yet we don't take adolescent stress seriously. I remember attending a week-long conference at a prestigious university. Having come from a struggling immigrant family, I do not have a prestigious educational background. I

Chapter 18 — Self-esteem

felt anxiety building in my stomach. I didn't know if I was wearing the right outfit. I didn't know who to sit with. I abhor cocktail hours, but each meal began with one. As an adult, however, I have learned to deal with new and threatening situations. The new situation was uncomfortable, but because I am older and have a better sense of who I am, it is not as threatening. To an inexperienced and insecure adolescent, however, such stress can be overwhelming. Helping them understand the difference between discomfort and threat is a good start in bringing self-awareness.

The pain of separation which accompanies loss is like a death experience and can cause deep grief. The loss of a best friend, the loss of a romantic relationship, divorce, or the death of a pet, a friend, a parent, or grandparent — all may be a major turning point in the teenager's life. The combination of several losses can cause an adolescent to withdraw into seclusion, or strike out with hostility. The teenager feels helpless and abandoned.

In the case of divorce, the teenager not only feels the loss of the parent who is no longer living at home, but the loss of a family-centered life. Even though some stress is reduced by diminishing the tension between two parents, the change is resented. New stress comes to take its place, and the loss of familiar routines and expectations shakes the adolescent's feeling of security.

Expectations

One of the major stresses in a teenager's life is the inability to live up to high parental or teachers' expectations. Adolescents are caught in the tension between hyper-sensitivity and hyper-criticism. Parent criticism leaves them feeling vulnerable and rejected. They feel unappreciated, unnoticed, and unloved. Yet at the same time they are insensitive to the fact that they trample on their parents' feelings, criticizing and rejecting as they please. They are quick to point out hypocrisy in others, but they can't see it in themselves. It doesn't help to point this out because it only aggravates the situation. What helps most is to have conversations in which the adult expresses appreciation and understanding for them.

Parents are seldom conscious of how many goals and expectations they set for their children. When these goals cannot be met, the teenagers feel insecure and unworthy. If the expectations were unrealistic in the first place and cannot be met, the teenager does not recognize that they were unrealistic, but instead experiences failure. Here there is much the parent can do. Expectations should be discussed and arrived at together. The teenager should have an opportunity to question the expectations before they're set. If teenagers can agree that the expectations are fair, or if they can come up with their own which the parent approves, they have not only established a working relationship with the adult but they gain some control over their own lives. The older the teenager, the more expectations should be established out of joint agreement, and less from parents' wishes.

A temporary form of let-down after high expectations comes during the senior year of high school. Successful students have achieved their goals, done very well in high school, and have been accepted at the college of their choice. What is next? What about the reactions of other people? A best friend did not do as well. Another friend is jealous of the teenager's accomplishments. The successful students may feel isolated from friends. The honor has distinguished them, but it has also separated them from others.

Other students who have done as well, and were not accepted at a school of their choice, often deal with the feeling that they were not good enough. They don't understand how complicated the acceptance to universities is, and that being turned down is not a reflection of their worth. Or teenagers may have plans for a job after graduation. Or they have plans to travel. They feel they are ready to go out and meet the world. But are they really ready? They may feel unsure. They're itching to get out of high school and challenge the world. How can they get through the daily routine for the next five months? They become moody, restless, bored, irritable. But *Senioritis* will pass, and it does not give most parents and teachers concern.

When I was not able to give a top grade to a young man who felt under pressure to succeed, he lost his self-control and told me I had ruined his life. When some didn't get into schools of their choice, they became depressed. It takes time until they mature and realize it wasn't a reflection of their worth.

Chapter 18 — Self-esteem

Similar experiences of feeling let-down after success is also felt by athletes and actors. After so much attention has been focused on them, after they have been cheered, what comes next? What can compete with the sense of exhilaration? It is not unusual for depression to follow, but it is usually temporary.

Many youngsters do not understand how natural this pattern is in life. They try to keep the high and avoid the let-down through drugs and alcohol. Adults can help teenagers by discussing this pattern with them, by preparing them for this experience, by lending them support and not just praising them when they're succeeding.

Teenagers can see the future hanging on one small event. When that event does not turn out as expected, they sense that tragedy is just around the corner. Most of them can absorb temporary depression as part of life. Dealing with disappointment helps them come to terms with reality. What is the fine line between temporary depression and a serious depressive state? This depends on the individual teenager and the situation.

Lack of trust

Another weakening of self-esteem comes when adults send out a clear signal — I don't trust you. I have sat through parent conferences in which a parent dominates the discussion. Whenever the teenager tries to speak, the parent interrupts and fields the question, explaining how the adolescent feels, what their hobbies are, what school activities are preferred, and so on. Is it any wonder the teenager feels intimidated? When the parent interrupts to explain what the youngster is trying to say, such an experience is a blow to their shaky self-esteem.

Teenagers are more receptive to criticism if it is given in small doses rather than as direct confrontation, which is experienced as a personal attack. Then they feel they must defend themselves. Teenagers want to be respected and listened to the way anyone does. When adults hold back this respect, when teenagers feel that what they say is not important, their self-esteem suffers.

When adolescents feel their parents do not trust them to make decisions, they feel suffocated, and crisis builds. When they feel every decision is being made for them, they feel powerless over their own lives, and this sense of helplessness can lead to depression.

Parents are busy, working, trying to keep their lives together. Teenagers feel the loss of time available as a loss of caring. The adolescent internalizes this as rejection. Because teenagers need their parents so much, even though they may not admit it, they may interpret the lack of time as lack of love. They are left feeling unloved and unwanted.

Specific family problems can also cause depression. Arguments and physical fighting, alcoholism, drug abuse of parents or siblings can also cause the teenager to feel helpless and unable to do anything to improve the situation. If parents do not communicate well with each other or with their children, the home feels empty and cold. Feelings are suppressed, and everyone goes through the motions of daily life, but there is no joy.

Examples of teenage depression
In the following examples, I have gone back to using conventional pronouns for clarity.

- A 16-year-old girl desperately wanted friends as well as a special boyfriend. She attracted friends quickly and lost them quickly. She drained her energies, and was exhausted. Insecure in her family and jealous of a very talented sibling, she would fall into dark moods and then further alienate those who reached out to her. At the core of the problem was a lack of self-esteem. On the one hand, she didn't feel worthy; on the other, she was furious when rejected.
- A 17-year-old boy was preoccupied by his lack of growth. Concerned about both parents, who were alcoholics, he felt rejected and a failure. It was easier not to try in school in case he might fail there also.
- A 15-year-old girl went into depression because she didn't feel accepted by the 'in group'. She tried everything, yet whatever attention the group gave her, it wasn't enough. She was jealous of the other teenagers' homes, families, clothes, the 'right' way they dressed, and their social confidence. The girl finally left that school because she could not overcome the depression.

- A 17-year-old boy felt rejected by his girlfriend's parents. Under pressure from them, the girl wanted more space in the relationship. The girl asked the boyfriend to relax his intensity. The boy wanted her. He said his life would never be the way he pictured it in the future. He had to have her. No matter what was said to him, he stared at the ground and repeated, 'But I want her'.
- A 13-year-old girl became ill, yet no symptoms could be found. She couldn't (or wouldn't) get out of bed. She felt sad all the time. She was part of a triangle of girls and felt left out most of the time. She wanted the other two girls to reach out to her more often. She felt sorry for herself and wanted them to feel sorry for her also. So she stayed in bed, unable to face the day.
- A 14-year-old boy felt unlike the rest of his family. Convinced they didn't understand him, he asked, 'Why was I born?'. He retired to his room, ate by himself, ran away, and fantasized about being adopted by a family that would understand him. His depression confused his family but they didn't know what to do about it. His minister told him he must respect his mother's wishes. His mother told him he had to be part of the family, and he cannot spend so much time alone. He felt trapped.

Why do some teenagers get depressed while others who have reasons to do so, don't? Many depressed teenagers have one or both parents who are themselves depressed. When the teenager needs support, the parents are lost in their own problems and not available to help. Adults usually show signs of depression by withdrawing. But teenagers often show their depression by getting angry, by being rebellious. They don't know how to handle the frustration and rejection, so they strike out and attack.

Because teenagers lack knowledge or experience, they see the world in black and white; it's terrible, it's wonderful. Even though adults often feel depressed, they mainly know that time heals. They know they will wake up one morning, and the world will look better. But teenagers feel hopeless when they experience loss or frustration. The epidemic spread of suicide attempts is related in part to teenage depression.

Many of the situations described in this chapter would not in themselves cause depression. Usually there is one situation that sets off the depression as a reaction. The symptoms that may alert adults to depression in the teenager are:

- lack of interest in food
- unexpected weigh gain or loss
- the inability to sleep
- sleeping too much
- difficulty in waking up
- sadness, listlessness
- boredom
- little interest in past enjoyments
- no friends
- sudden change in behavior
- conflicts
- running away
- becoming sexually promiscuous
- shopliftings
- truancy
- extreme self-esteem
- feeling ugly
- feeling a failure
- feeling unpopular
- having a feeling of incompetence
- risky behavior including drugs, alcohol, reckless driving
- video-game addiction
- suicide talk or behavior
- self-harm

When parents or teachers see these signs, they should seek professional help for the teenager.

Suicide

According to the World Health Organization (WHO),[35] even though there are countries that do not keep good records of suicide attempts or completions, suicide continues to be a leading cause of mortality world-wide, and a major public health concern.

Within the Native and indigenous ethnic minority populations, teenagers are at significantly increased risk of suicide. Female teenagers are more likely to think about attempting suicide (termed 'suicidal ideation'), while males with higher presence of alcohol abuse, availability of more lethal methods such as guns, and higher levels of aggression and violence, complete the suicide attempt.

Suicide risk factors include a family history of suicide, access to firearms, and stressful life events. However, the greatest risk factor is a prior attempt, with 17-year-olds having the highest rate of completion due to depression and substance abuse. Mental illness elevates risk for suicide and suicidal behavior.

From a world-wide perspective, the population most at risk are those living in poverty in rural areas, and those in intergenerational conflicts, particularly in the treatment of females who feel helpless with low social status. In Eastern countries, self-poisoning through toxic pesticides and severe economic crises have also been significant factors, although these are not often reported

A large contribution to teenage suicide has to do with the developmental stage of adolescence, including impulsivity and sensation-seeking, inability to recognize the results of action, and alcohol and drug use, and especially heavy use while feeling down or depressed.

At this time, when feeling accepted is so important, to be victimized or bullied can be devastating. Cyberbullying is problematic because it is faceless and is present and ongoing on social media. Another factor is 'social contagion' which refers to the effect of suicide being reported either in groups of teenagers, or by social media and articles in newspapers or television. They act as suggestions to the vulnerable youngsters.

The warning signs of suicide include most of the same signs as depression. If a youngster comes to an adult to speak about suicide, the adult should always give this serious attention. Talking about problems often helps to make the problems become less important. However, suicide is a mystery. Not all teenagers who commit suicide exhibit signs of depression. Not all leave a suicide note or give clues. What is left in such cases is a big question mark that the survivors live with for the rest of their lives.

Perhaps the central message that needs to be communicated to teenagers is that committing suicide is no solution for the problems. Although pain can seem so intense that at the time the only way out seems self-destruction, it is not a way out at all. All the options are removed to resolve the problem. It is a solution that is no solution at all. The people who care about the teenagers have no way of helping them, and the teenagers lose the opportunity of maturing beyond the problem, and the precious experience of life is foregone. As one young friend of a boy who committed suicide said, 'He had so much to live for. Look at all he'll miss.' Another friend of the same boy said, 'I am so angry that he could feel so alone that he could not have reached out to someone to share the problem'.

Two examples of suicide situations at the Golden Gate Bridge in San Francisco follow:

Kevin Hines, a 19-year-old struggling with mental illness and depression, and diagnosed with bipolar disorder, said, 'Emotional pain is 300,000 times worse than physical pain. It's the enemy within that you cannot defy. When I was on that bridge, the voices in my head were screaming that I had to die.'

He leapt over the railing with the idea that it would be the easiest way to die. As soon as he cleared the railing, he felt regret and was able to maneuver his position so that his legs rather than his head would hit the water first. The contact from a fall like this is similar to hitting concrete. He was only millimeters away from severing his spine.

A beautiful image out of this catastrophic attempt was that as he was struggling to the surface, he felt a creature nudging at him, and he thought it was a shark coming to eat him. Later, a witness told him that it was a sea lion that helped him stay afloat until the Coast Guard came.

Chapter 18 — Self-esteem

Before attempting suicide, he made a pact with himself: If anyone asked whether he was OK, he would not have jumped. Hines survived, and with his wife, Margaret, started a foundation that seeks to educate and train communities across the USA on mental wellness and suicide prevention. Along with families of victims, he has fought to have the bridge net constructed as a suicide deterrent. When he saw the segments of the net for the first time, moved to tears he said, 'This is one of the most special days of my life'. (It is due to be completed January 2021.)[36]

Suicide, when completed, leaves no possibility for changing one's mind.

Another family affected by suicide and who have worked to secure the bridge net are the Gamboas. Kyle Gamboa, senior, captain of the basketball team, a successful athlete who excelled at many sports, a person with a zest for life, with no apparent reason to do so, drove to San Francisco in September 2013, climbed over the railing and leaned over the side of the bridge. The impact was so hard that the coroner said that his heart, liver, and lungs essentially exploded on impact. A couple sailing on the bay lassoed him with rope so the tide wouldn't drag him out to sea. In this case the teenager did leave a note. 'I think this is a good place to end it. I'm sorry for the pain this might give you, but please be happy knowing this is what I want. The world isn't ready for Kyle Gamboa.'

His mother, Kimberlyrenee with an engineering degree, had worked in construction management for Sacramento County for 16 years, and knew the impact of public comment on government officials. Either Kyle's parents or his brother, Manual III, attended almost every board meeting of the Golden Gate Bridge, Highway and Transportation District board meeting since that terrible event, fighting along with others for the bridge net. Because people had the misperception that suicide was a choice rather than a treatable mental-health issue, it is hard to understand that suicide is often an impulsive decision.

In 2008, the district finally approved a suicide net, but there was no funding. Finally, in 2013, a measure to fund the net was put before the board members. In the months before the 2014 vote, Kymberlyrenee started an online petition in support of the net, gathering 158,000 signatures from around the world. The full budget for the project was brought together through a variety of agencies and commissions, as well as state funding in 2017.

The Gamboa family's experience has so much to teach us about suicide. His mother comments that her son was a daredevil, always pushing boundaries. 'Maybe this was a stunt — or maybe it wasn't.'

There is no way to avoid stress and loneliness in the process of growing up. Everyone has problems. Some youngsters experience their problems more intensely, more painfully than those of others, especially if they are already dealing with mental-health issues. They cannot bear to go on. Whether they actually contemplate the repercussions of their deed or whether they are acting out of the moment or are asking for help, this is a question we will never be able to answer.

We must reach out to support teenagers during this sensitive time. We must take their concerns seriously, but we cannot insulate them from feelings of inadequacy, frustration, or loneliness. We can hope they have the strength to bear what comes to them in life, and we can tell them and try to show them how much we love them. Sometimes, even that is not enough.

In a Nutshell

Self-esteem

- Self-esteem, whether adolescents feel good about themselves or not, is at the heart of many issues.
- Young teenagers often turn to others to define acceptable behavior, but when they move past the 16–17th-year change, they gain a clearer sense of themselves.
- Social media, advertising, movies, and magazines often set standards for teenagers to adapt in order to feel confident about themselves.
- Disappointments in high-school experiences can challenge the adolescent's sense of self-esteem, and they need to over-come them as a part of life. Support from adults can help them adjust.
- While depression, disappointment, and despair are a normal part of human life, some adolescents need professional help to work through these experiences.
- Growing up, just by itself, is challenging to the loss of child-hood and the sense of feeling helpless and alone.
- Parental expectations and criticism can affect a teenager's self-esteem and sense of belonging.
- With increasing numbers of teenage suicide, adults need to take seriously any indication of such an intention.

Part III

The Challenges of Adolescence

Chapter 19

Teenagers and alcohol

It's OK not to drink.
> Bumper sticker

When Noah planted grapevines, Satan revealed to him the possible effects of alcohol. He slaughtered a lamb, a lion, an ape and a pig. He explained: 'The first cup of wine will make you mild like a lamb; the second will make you feel brave like a lion; the third will make you act like an ape; and the fourth will make you wallow in mud like a pig.'[37]

I recently attended a meeting with teenaged alcoholics, and some of the statements they made are still buzzing in my mind.

'I was afraid of everything. When I drank, I wasn't afraid.'
'I don't know how I drove home. I was drunk, but somehow I got the car into the garage.'
'I got really scared when I realized I was losing my short-term memory.'
'When the teacher asked me if I was on something, of course I said I wasn't. At that particular moment, I wasn't. I thought I was so smart.'
'I got to the point where I felt I was dying, and I begged for help.'
'What really bothered me was when one of my high-school drinking friends said, "I'm worried about you".'

Alcohol and its Effects

Alcohol is made from fruit or grain. There are two types of alcoholic beverages. One kind includes wine and beer and is made by fermentation, in which yeast is used to change sugar in the fruit or grain into alcohol. The second type includes various hard liquors, made by distilling the alcohol from a fermented liquid and aging the distillate. This produces a more alcoholic beverage than wine or beer. Beers range between 2 per cent and 8 per cent alcohol. Wines range from 8 per cent to 21 per cent alcohol, with the so-called 'dry' wines having the lower alcohol content. Vodka, gin, whiskey, rum, brandy, and liqueurs are from 40 per cent to 50 per cent alcohol.

Alcohol does not have to be digested. It is diluted by stomach juices and enters the blood very quickly through the walls of the stomach and intestines. The rate of absorption depends on which beverage was drunk and how full the stomach is. Absorption takes longer when there is food in the stomach, especially fatty foods. However, carbonated beverages speed up the absorption rate. The blood transports the alcohol to the organs of the body, including the brain.

Alcohol affects the brain in two ways. First, it is a depressant on the central nervous system. As the concentration of alcohol increases, the depression intensifies, leading to sedation, passing out, and coma. It puts to sleep some of the cells in the hypothalamus, a part of the brain having to do with the regulation of the vital processes such as breathing and heartbeat. Consequently, *the person cannot react as quickly as usual because the alcohol has slowed the body's reflexes.* An intoxicated person is unable to use full intelligence or exert self-control.

Secondly, alcohol is a stimulant which causes the person to feel exhilarated, lose control, talk excitedly, change moods, and become hysterical.

Some 90 per cent of the alcohol is disposed of by the liver. The rate at which the body can dispose of alcohol is limited. An average-sized man can dispose of one-half ounce of alcohol per hour. That is equivalent to an ounce of whiskey, a 12-ounce bottle of beer, a 4-ounce glass of dry wine, or 2.4 ounces of fortified wine. If someone drinks more than their body can burn up, the alcohol accumulates in the organism, resulting in intoxication.

Teenagers and Intoxication

When youngsters become evenly mildly intoxicated, their perceptions are affected and they cannot make clear decisions. As they go on drinking their awareness is also affected, they are unable to see clearly, and their reflexes grow sluggish.

As far as we know, small amounts of alcohol, even when taken regularly over a long period, have no pathological effect. In the case of occasional drunkenness, the body returns to normal after suffering a temporary chemical disturbance. When teenagers drink heavily and frequently, however, the organs of the body may be damaged. The central nervous system, including the brain, is affected.

People typically pass through four stages in their response to increasing amounts of alcohol. The numbers on the following chart refer to the level of alcohol in the blood.

> *Stage 1* (0.05 per cent): Some inhibitions are removed, the person is sociable and confident, but skill and judgement are impaired.
> *Stage 2* (0.10 per cent): The person tends to overdo things, is talkative, careless, and funny. Skill is further diminished, and the will is weakened.
> *Stage 3* (0.15 per cent): The person sees double, totters, fumbles, is incoherent and boisterous. Feeling and pain are lessened.
> *Stage 4* (above 0.15 per cent): Action is slow, breathing is difficult. The person staggers, mutters, is indifferent and semi-conscious.[38]

Why Do Teenagers Drink?

Adolescents often begin drinking because alcohol helps them to feel grown up. It helps them break their ties within the parent–child relationship, and they feel more in charge of their own lives. 'I am an individual', they seem to say as they take a drink.

The individuality of the young adolescent, the sense of self, is very fragile. Most of the time, the true self is hidden deeply within the soul or far outside the soul, masked by emotions masquerading as the true self. When too much alcohol is taken or when it is taken too often, what occurs is quite different from what the teenager thinks is happening. Instead of strengthening the individuality, alcohol weakens it, leaving the youngster witless in the face of all their confusing emotions and desires.

In Arabic, alcohol means 'The Spirit', and alcohol is sometimes referred to as a 'False God'. So the False God or Spirit doesn't allow the true Spirit to work. Teenagers are not in control of their own conscience. Instead, under the influence of alcohol, they do things they would not do if they had clear heads.

At this most insecure time of their lives, alcohol promises security — but doesn't keep the promise. It helps them feel mature — while hindering their maturation. They look tough and strong and are accepted into certain in-groups, but they risk becoming weak and possibly even outcasts. They feel independent of authority and deliciously rebellious, but they are flirting with a dependency much more demanding.

Drinking alcohol is connected with the party scene, having fun, forgetting problems, and gaining courage to do things they wouldn't ordinarily do. Alcohol makes it easier to approach others. It is also used so that stressed teenagers can forget what's bothering them. They drink because their parents or friends drink. Adolescents want to belong to a group, and if others are drinking it helps them to feel accepted, thus acting as a pressure for them to drink. Alcohol is all around them, and it is neither as dangerous nor as expensive as other drugs. They feel they can handle its effects and are certain they won't become alcoholics. If they depend on alcohol to socialize, to dance, or to face new and frightening social situations, they never develop real social skills or a sense of appropriateness. Using alcohol deprives them of the experience of coming to terms with life and leaves them emotionally immature.

If teenagers do dangerous or foolish things under the influence of alcohol, they can delude themselves by thinking, 'That wasn't me. That was the alcohol.' Projecting blame and not taking responsibility for their behavior becomes a life-pattern which, in time, so weakens their will that they no longer have the courage or determination to do things or face situations. That kind of courage cannot be gained from alcohol.

Some develop a desire for the alcohol, as it tastes good and makes life seem better. Others are in social situation where they dare each other to drink a certain amount; and not wanting to seem like a weakling, they take the dare. Girls may drink to please their boyfriends or to show they can handle the alcohol. They then are at risk of having unprotected sex or being raped. This situation is particularly dangerous when a group of boys take advantage of an inebriated girl. Boys are more likely to get into trouble when drinking in a group with risky behavior, showing off, trying to prove themselves, or by drinking heavily to qualify for membership in a group. Most of all, they drink because they don't have the self-control or thinking skills to make healthy decisions.

The biggest health issue is that the earlier the youth starts drinking, before age 15, the more likely they are to have a drinking disorder compared to those who started at 21.

Is Teenage Drinking a Problem?

In the United States, underage drinking is a serious problem, and it is the most widely used substance American youth uses. Although youths drink less often than adults, when they do drink, they drink more. However, there is some good news in this area.

According to two reports on teenage drinking in the USA, based on an annual survey of students in eighth, tenth, and twelfth grades since 1971, binge drinking and heavy alcohol consumption have declined steadily, reaching the lowest levels in 2018. In addition, overall heavy drinking among college students (defined as five or more drinks in a row at least in the past two weeks) also continues to show a decline.[39]

This is also true in other countries. The National Drug and Alcohol Research Centre in Sydney, Australia has similar results.[40] Alcohol consumption in Australia has reached its lowest point since the early 1960s, which is mostly due to the decline in youth drinking. Rates of heavy drinking have fallen as well; this is for boys and girls, across all socioeconomic groups and in regional and urban areas. A similar situation exists in the United Kingdom, Canada and Sweden.

The German fondness for alcohol seems to be declining as well, although the price of beer is often about the same as a bottle of water. Over the past 30 years, alcohol consumption amongst German teenagers has fallen by half, but binge drinking is on the rise. The average age for the first sip is 14. In line with German laws on consumption, 14-year-olds are allowed to drink alcoholic beverages such as beer and wine as long as they are accompanied by a custodial person. The legal age for drinking alone is 16. The biggest problems are the 18–25 young adults who tend to drink to intoxication. As in other countries, the new generation of German youth is more interested in being active, staying up late, and being fit and showing it. They see that alcohol makes people tired and fat, so they want to avoid that.[41]

What Is Changing with Teenage Alcohol Consumption?

There seems to be a global shift in the youth culture that is driving the change. Rather than relying on alcohol for socializing, the increased use of social media may have changed the way teenagers interact. We really don't know. What we do know from research is that today's youth are interested in exercising, eating well, and avoiding alcohol and other drugs. This lifestyle change may be driving the trend. Other contributing forces may include more restrictive policies, increased public concern, public-education campaigns and school programs, checking identification when young people buy alcohol, making alcohol harder to obtain, increasing the its price, and outlawing driving after any amount of drinking for people under 21. Regardless of what is causing the change, this is good news.

We can celebrate the decline in teenager's use of alcohol. Although frequent binge drinking decreased among American adolescents between 1991 and 2015, it is still a problem, especially as youths get older. This is also a problem in other countries. Most teenagers state that they disapprove of binge drinking, yet it continues to be of concern. According to international data from the World Health Organization, European teenagers aged 15–19 tend to report greater levels of binge drinking than

American teens. In France, Belgium, Denmark, Sweden, and Iceland there is more binge drinking than in the USA.

The 2017 report quoted earlier from the Study Institute for Social Research indicates that binge drinking is a particular concern for girls, African-American adolescents, and people from lower socioeconomic backgrounds. Does this indicate there are fewer resources for helping these youth, or alcohol sellers or bartenders are not as strict about keeping alcohol away from these groups, or parents are not as strict? Are there schools not doing as much education of these groups? Binge drinking is decreasing more quickly amongst economically better-off youth, and among boys. What does this tell us?

Dangers from Underage Drinking

At school or in the family, adults should be alert to signs of underage drinking. These include changes in mood including anger and irritability, academic and/or behavior problems in school, rebelliousness, changing groups of friends, low energy-level, less interest in activities and/or care in appearance, finding alcohol among their things, smelling alcohol on their breath, problems concentrating and remembering, slurred speech, and coordination problems.

The danger from underage drinking is that it causes many deaths from motor-vehicle crashes, homicides, alcohol poisoning, burns, falls, drowning, and suicides. In addition, injuries are caused because alcohol impairs judgement and causes poor decisions to be made. Teenagers under the influence of alcohol get involved in risky behavior, drink and drive, engage in sexual activity (unprotected sex), and act aggressively or violently. Underage youth who drink are particularly at risk of victimizing, or becoming a victim of a physical or sexual assault, than others of their age who do not drink.

Problems with drinking can lead to trouble in school or with the law, and it can lead to the use of other drugs. Beyond what drinking causes under-age youth to do to themselves or others, the most significant issue is that alcohol can alter the development of their brains into their 20s, affecting brain structure and function and thus causing learning problems and creating alcohol dependency.

It is generally agreed that alcohol affects judgement — precisely the area in which the teenager is already weak. Even without drugs the teenager swings to the extremes of the emotional pendulum. Wanting to be accepted already renders the adolescent vulnerable to risks and daredevil feats. Alcohol gives short-term bravado. With alcohol, teenagers may drive without putting their hands on the steering wheel, they may have the courage to jump off a bridge into a river, and they may have sex without thinking too much about it.

Where are young teenagers getting the alcohol? They usually get it from family or friends, and mostly in their own home. Even though older teens have influence on younger ones, parents are the most influential person in a child's decision either not to drink at all or not to drink on occasion. Even though access is easy, most young teenagers do not drink regularly.

Alcoholism

Awareness is growing that alcoholism is a disease, and that certain people do not need to take in a great amount of alcohol to create the need for more. In the words of the old saying, 'For an alcoholic, one drink is too many — and a thousand are not enough!'. Once a person becomes an alcoholic, they deal with the condition for the rest of their life. Alcoholism has become a serious problem in Western society.

Alcoholics Anonymous puts out the following 12-question quiz to help teenager decide whether their drinking is becoming a problem:

1   Do you drink because you have problems? To face up to stressful situations?
2   Do you drink when you get mad at other people, your friends or parents?
3   Do you often prefer to drink alone, rather than with others?
4   Are your grades starting to slip? Are you goofing off on the job?

5   Do you ever try to stop drinking or to drink less — and fail?
6   Have you begun to drink in the morning, before school or work?
7   Do you gulp your drinks as if to satisfy a great thirst?
8   Do you ever have loss of memory due to your drinking?
9   Do you avoid leveling with others about your drinking?
10   Do you ever get into trouble when you're drinking?
11   Do you often get drunk when you drink, even when you don't mean to?
12   Do you think it's cool to be able to hold your liquor?

If the teenager can answer 'yes' to any one of these questions, it is a sign that their drinking is following a dangerous pattern and that help is needed.

Drinking and Danger

I live across the street from a favorite teenage hangout. Teenagers drive into the gravel parking lot and drink a couple of six packs of beer or a bottle of hard liquor. They break bottles, yell, and spin around on the gravel with their cars, kicking up dust, shouting, and arguing. Thoroughly drunk, they speed down the dark street, lights often out, weaving from side to side, challenging friends in another car to race them to the corner. In this condition, they turn on to one of the busiest thoroughfares in Sacramento County. It is not surprising that automobile deaths due to drunkenness have become a national concern.

Drinking is often related to unplanned pregnancy amongst teenagers. I have spoken with girls who had sexual intercourse while drunk and they are not even sure who their partner was. This is not surprising, since alcohol lessens inhibitions and weakens self-control.

Despite all the awareness of the problems stemming from teenagers and drinking, many adults do not take responsibility where they can. I had strong words with a parent about a party where alcohol was served. The parent felt I was unreasonable by suggesting that 13-, 14-, 15-year-olds, and even 16-year-olds, were not able to handle themselves (including those who would be driving home).

Problem drinkers tend to be those teenagers who are impulsive, who over-emphasize their masculinity or femininity, who deny anxiety and dependency, who are compulsive, and who lack self-esteem. How can we prevent them from developing drinking problems? One way is to help them strengthen their personalities. A second way is to take away the status given by alcohol, and a third is to be alert to our teenagers' behavior.

Teenagers with serious drinking problems often describe how their parents didn't notice, even when their drinking became extreme. Some parents did notice that something was wrong, but then allowed their youngsters to avoid the questions or to give vague answers. Few parents like confrontations, and those over alcohol or drugs are among the most feared. If parents fail to induce their teenagers to talk about what is going on, they can insist that counseling begin and see if a neutral person will help the teenager explore the problem.

Denial does not help. The first step in helping these teenagers is parents' admitting their teenagers have a drinking problem, and the second step is getting *them* to admit it. Protecting the teenagers will only help them make excuses for their behavior. Most teenagers with drinking problems are crying out for help. Even though they resist help at first, the seed of recovery occurs at the point where teenagers know that they need help and appreciate the intervention.

Guidelines

For teenagers who are concerned about the effects of drinking or whose parents are concerned about the effects of alcohol on them, there are guidelines with which teenagers can monitor themselves.

They can learn to refuse a drink when it's offered. No apology is needed, no argument or excuse has to be made. They simply must feel clear about the issue to say, 'No thanks'. They can have a ginger ale or mineral water, so that they, too, are drinking and enjoying the social scene without standing out. If they do take a drink, they can nurse it so that it lasts the evening, and they can eat while drinking.

They can have arrangements with their parents to pick them up at a party if they or their date has been drinking and is unfit to drive. Friends can help each other by being sure that the driver doesn't drink. They can cultivate the image that it is OK not to drink. Only through awareness and a change in attitude will teenagers take control of their lives rather than handing over the power to the False God.

There are many different groups working to help educate teenagers to overcome substance abuse. One is called Natural High (naturalhigh.org) that is a drug-abuse prevention non-profit 'that inspires and empowers youth to find their natural high and develop the skills and courage to live well'. It is a free program available on the internet which works to bring together the kinds of people teenagers look up to as role models who use storytelling as a way of helping teenagers with these issues.

How Can Teenagers Be Influenced Not to Drink?

The higher legal drinking age does play at least some role in reducing teen drinking and its harm. After the drinking age in the USA was raised nationally to 21 in the 1980s, the number of fatally injured drivers with a positive blood alcohol concentration decreased by 57 per cent among ages 16–20. New Zealand reduced its drinking age from 20 to 18 in 1999, which led to significant increases in drinking among ages 18 to 19, greater increases amongst those 16–17 years old, and an increase in alcohol-related crashes among 15 to 19-year-olds.

Communities can help teenagers resist drinking alcohol by spreading the knowledge about its effect in public campaigns, including posters, statements on radio, television, and movies, and social media. They can help by listing places to go for help if teenagers think they are having a problem.

Because the average age when teenagers begin to drink is 14 or 15, it takes the efforts of schools, youth groups, parents, and other community organizations to work together to address this issue.

Since parents have a strong influence on teenagers, they should set and enforce clear rules against drinking, have more conversations at home in which they speak about the dangers of drinking, and about drinking responsibly. Parents should serve as positive role models, not making it available, knowing their children's friends, connecting with other parents about sending clear messages about not drinking alcohol, and supervising all parties to be sure there is no alcohol. If their child has a serious alcohol problem, they should make an intervention to get help. Parents can encourage participation in healthy and fun activities that do not involve alcohol.

Schools can help by having classes showing the effects of alcohol, including the changes in the brain. They can have counselors who help students who are on the way to having a drinking problem, including intervention to help those teenagers who are severely affected. Supporting youth by giving them a motivation to stop drinking is often through a trusting relationship with an adult who doesn't judge them, but offers ways of getting help. The school should have referral services that can help teens who are drinking.

Doctors can help by screening during health-care visits, asking questions that elicit information on alcohol consumption.

It is best not to drink or to use any substances. However, for those who are drinking, they should be encouraged to reduce the amount that they drink and drink less often. They need to take care of themselves if they are drinking, especially regarding safe rides home, protected sex practices, and mental health. Under no circumstances should they drive after drinking.

Adults help teenagers develop their budding egos and wills by involving them in decision-making. If they are spared having to make decisions, their egos are dulled, and the opportunity to develop consciousness and character has been forfeited. The young person is left directionless, at the mercy of whatever the group does. All aspects of the community need to be involved in education, support, and treatment of adolescents who are involved in drinking alcohol.

In a Nutshell

Teenagers and alcohol

- Although small amounts of alcohol, even when taken regularly, have no pathological effect, when teenagers drink heavily and frequently, the central nervous system, including the brain, is affected.
- Adolescents often begin drinking because it helps them feel part of the crowd and grown up, and it takes away their sense of insecurity.
- Under the influence of alcohol, teenagers do things they would not do if they were sober.
- Alcohol consumption is a problem world-wide, yet it seems to be in decline — possibly because youth today are interested in exercising, eating well, and avoiding alcohol and other drugs. Also, more restrictive policies, educational programs, checking identification, and driving limitations may be having an effect.
- Binge drinking is still a problem with older teenagers, and is of particular concern for girls as it affects judgement.
- There is growing awareness that alcoholism is a disease, and adults should take behavioral signs seriously.
- Different groups try to encourage teenagers to find ways of a 'natural high' rather than relying on alcohol.

Chapter 20

Use of tobacco and drugs

Turn on, tune in, drop out.
               Timothy Leary

This chapter on teenagers and drugs should be read with the awareness that the drug scene is constantly changing, as new drugs are introduced. If you have questions and need more information, do not hesitate to get drug advice from professionals.

Cigarette Smoking and Vaping

Alcohol and tobacco are the most commonly abused drugs by teenagers, followed by marijuana. We discussed alcohol in the previous chapter, so now let us look at tobacco use. Use of tobacco has decreased overall as it has been barred in public places. This generation does not experience what it was like to fly in airplanes, attend concerts, dine in restaurants, and all the other places where people congregate and where we were assaulted by smoke and pungent smells. I was so disappointed when I traveled to Ireland, hoping to enjoy the music in pubs, only to find they were smoke-filled. That has changed, and now we can go from pub to pub, enjoying the fiddling and singing that are such a part of the Irish experience.

It was satisfying to know that cigarette smoking has been in decline in the past ten years in all high-school grades. However, in its place daily nicotine vaping is threatening progress. It is not unusual to find teenagers vaping in school bathrooms or in other places. Advertising has spread the word that vaping is safe. However, according to the Center for Diseases Control and Prevention (CDC), vaping or e-cigarettes was first used in 2018, peaked in September 2019, and then declined.

> Reasons for the decline are likely multifactorial and may be related to the following: Increased public awareness of the risk associated with THC-containing e-cigarette, or vaping, product use as a result of the rapid public health response, removal of Vitamin E acetate from some products, and law enforcement actions related to illicit products.[42]

Why do teens vape? Some like the flavor; others are experimenting, doing it for social reasons or just to feel good. Some feel sophisticated, while others think they may be avoiding the health problems of tobacco; and still others like embracing the latest trend.

> Findings from the 2019 *Monitoring the Future* (MTF) survey demonstrate the appeal of vaping to teens, as seen in the increased prevalence of marijuana use as well as nicotine vaping… Past year vaping of mari-juana, which has more than doubled in the past two years, was reported at 20.8% among 12th graders, with 10th graders not far behind at 19.4% and eighth graders at 7.0%… Past year rates of any illicit drug use, other than marijuana, remain relatively low among 12th graders. …Other drug use, including the misuse of prescription medicines and the use of alcohol as well as tobacco cigarettes, continues to decline.[43]

Marijuana and Other Drugs

Today's teenagers are confronted almost daily with the drug culture. It is expressed in album or CD covers, rock music or hip-hop lyrics, in overdoses among friends or relatives, in the death of entertainment stars or athletes, in burnout-damaged friends or siblings, in burglaries and muggings committed by users needing money for drugs, in students selling drugs on campus, in social interaction, and in experimentation. Hardly a family is spared the tragedies of drug experience and damage.

Too many teenagers have been diverted from meaningful and responsible adult lives, spending instead the golden years of adolescence and young adulthood in drug rehabilitation therapy, committed to institutions with brain damage and apathy. Too many young people have lost their teenage years in drug addiction.

Those of us who have been teaching, counseling, and parenting for decades have experienced the waste of many young people. The drug scene is no longer tied to political and social revolution. The idealism is gone, but the hard reality of drug use remains with us.

Drugs have moved down from the high schools to the middle schools and elementary schools. Children of 10, 11, and 12 are now drug-conscious. The good news is that their drug consciousness includes awareness of its dangers as well as a sense of its allure. Teenagers have seen their heroes die because of misuse, and they are more aware of the dangers than were their predecessors of a few decades ago.

Millions of teenagers have experimented with drugs. They have experienced changes in their minds and their moods. Many try drugs a few times and quit, but many others continue and become addicted. Once they become dependent, they move from one drug to another.

Rather than smoking, young adolescents prefer inhalant substances (such as breathing the fumes of household cleaners, glues, or pens), whereas older teenagers are more likely to use synthetic marijuana and prescription medications — particularly opioid pain relievers like Vicodin and stimulants like Adderall. The survey of adolescent drug use and attitudes shows that prescription and over-the-counter medications account for a majority of the drugs most commonly abused by high-school seniors.

On the streets, the picture is mixed. Marijuana cultivation and use are widespread, tolerated, and now legal in parts of the USA and of Europe. At the same time, however, the accumulated experiences with a generation of users, plus insights from scientific studies which steadily trickle in, enable us gradually to understand the dangers more clearly. Even as we learn, however, the devastation continues.

As with alcohol, marijuana produces a high. It is available everywhere, on campus, on the streets, in schoolyards — used to relax, generate

Chapter 20 — Use of tobacco and drugs

euphoria, or induce a pleasant distortion of time and space. In small doses, this is what it does. Users have the illusion that they are merging with other people or beings. They experience a feeling of community. Unfortunately, it has no real basis, as the feeling of community is a product of chemicals rather of conscious relationships.

By twelfth grade, more than three-quarters of US teens have tried alcohol, nearly half have used marijuana, and 21 per cent have abused prescription medication. These figures make clear that every adult who supports a teenager should be concerned about drugs and alcohol. The issue is especially pressing for LGBTQ teens as they cope with stigma, harassment, and even rejection by their families, and they are more likely than their non-LGBTQ peers to abuse drugs and alcohol.

Club drugs such as ecstasy and others tend to be used by teenagers and young adults in nightclubs, concerts, and parties. New club drugs, commonly called 'designer drugs', are often being designed, and tempt teenagers to be 'cool' in front of their peers.

Whereas prescription drug misuse such as Adderall has decreased in tenth and twelfth grade, there has been an increase in damage to their health, as well as causing emotional, financial, and other problems. They need more and more to feel the sense of reward, as when the brain is flooded with dopamine. Other daily activities or times with family or friends are not as pleasurable as what they get with the drug. Help is needed.

Is Your Child Using Drugs?

Some signs of drug use are physical, some behavioral, and some are unusual occurrences that should alert parents to possible drug use.

When confronted with the question of whether they are using drugs, teenagers will often deny that they have a problem. Parents, teachers, or others caring for the adolescent need to be persistent and insistent on their seeing a professional who can assess the situation. Teenagers will often protect their peers who are struggling with drugs until the problem becomes too noticeable, and the teenager is in harm's way.

There is denial within the drug community as to whether drugs such as marijuana, alcohol, or tobacco can really do serious damage to the person's health.

However, the National Institute on Drug Abuse reports the following.

> The brain continues to develop into adulthood and undergoes dramatic changes during adolescence. One of the brain areas still maturing during adolescence is the prefrontal cortex — that part of the brain that enables us to assess situations, make sound decisions, and keep our emotions and desires under control. The fact that this critical part of an adolescent's brain is still a work in progress puts them at increased risk for making poor decisions (such as trying drugs or continuing to take them). Also, introducing drugs during this period of development may cause brain changes that have profound and long-lasting consequences… Using abusable substances at this age can disrupt brain function in areas critical to motivation, memory, learning, judgment, and behavior control.
>
> Nora D. Volkow, MD[44]

Meanwhile, we cannot wait until such a study is completed to step in and help teenagers who are becoming addicted.

How Do I Recognize My Teenager Is Using Drugs?

Physical signs
These signs may point to drug use or some other physical problems. It is recommended that the adolescents see a doctor if any of the following persists:

- Inability to concentrate
- Loss of weight and appetite, increased craving for sweets
- Blackouts
- Red eyes
- Persistent colds or coughs

- Chest pains, vomiting

Behavioral signs

As with the physical signs, the following may indicate drug use or other disturbances and should be taken seriously:

- Inability to organize anything
- Paranoia
- Restlessness, irritability, nervousness
- Sudden hostility, vagueness, apathy, secretiveness
- Lying
- Strange phone calls, late hours, change of friends

Unusual occurrences

These signs should alert parents:

- Prescription drugs missing from the closet
- Smell of incense in teenager's room to mask marijuana
- Drug paraphernalia around the house or in teenager's room
- Money or things of value disappearing from the house
- Drug use is seldom a problem in itself. Adolescents who abuse drugs usually suffer from other conditions such as depression, anxiety disorders, attention-deficit hyperactivity disorder (ADHD), oppositional defiant disorder, and behavioral problems. Each teenager is unique, and there is no treatment solution that is right for all of them.

There are indications that gender differences may influence drug addiction. For example, girls are more likely to have had depression or experienced physical or sexual abuse which drives them to taking drugs. Boys are more likely to have been identified in school with disruptive behavior and learning problems. They are often suspended or expelled, but the deeper issue is ignored.

Minority racial adolescents may be more subject to taking drugs because of discrimination, bullying, and feeling ineffective in their daily life. Lesbian, bisexual, transgender, and queer (LGBTQ) teens may be twice as likely to be bullied, excluded, or assaulted at school. So it's of no surprise that they may be twice as likely to experiment with drugs and alcohol. Schools need to make sure they have equal access to support for all teenagers.

> The University of Pittsburgh has conducted studies on the substance abuse rates of gay teens, and… according to research, LGBT teens experience exponentially higher rates of cigarette, alcohol, and marijuana abuse; other frequently abused substances include cocaine, methamphetamines, and injection drugs such as heroin. On average, gay teens are 190 percent more likely to resort to substance abuse to cope with the minority stress of homosexuality. Interestingly, teen girls who identify as lesbian are at the highest risk for addiction; studies show that lesbian teens are 400 percent more likely to abuse drugs than heterosexual females. Additionally, when gay teens use drugs as coping mechanisms, mental health issues — such as depression and anxiety — can be exacerbated and made significantly worse. LGBT youths, and males in particular, resort to criminal behavior (i.e. prostitution and selling drugs) to feed their addiction. In such cases, using drugs to deal with the minority stress of homosexuality can lead to being expelled or dropping out of school, running away from home or homelessness, and further rejection by family and friends.
>
> Dane O'Leary[45]

Treatment for Drug Addiction

First of all, family members need to urge the adolescent to go into treatment, and they should support them through the process. In addition, therapists who get to know the teenager will be able to suggest the kinds of therapies that will best serve them.

Rather than focusing only on the drug addiction, it is essential to evaluate the teenager as a whole person. Providing incentives for abstinence by itself may not be enough. The teenager needs to work *from within outwards*, wanting to make the change. They need scripts and skills to help with resisting and refusing substances.

Additionally, there has to be the determination to go through the entire treatment program, making a strong enough commitment that will make a serious difference. Treatment options vary from Outpatient/ Intensive Outpatient, partial hospitalization, and residential/Inpatient treatment. Special summer camps also offer opportunities to help teenagers with addiction.

What Can Parents Do?

Don't wait until your teenager has a problem. Make it a point to find out about the different kinds of drugs, and learn to spot symptoms. Share what you learn with your teenagers and pre-teenagers. Leave published material lying around the house. You would be surprised how many teenagers read educational material on drugs, sex, and alcohol if their parents don't force them to.

Examine what kind of an example you are to your children. Do you take pills as soon as you have a problem? Do you use sleeping pills, stimulants, or sedatives? Are you aware of what programs on drug education are offered by your child's school or by the community? See what you can do to support the program. If you think your teenager is involved with drugs, be awake and aware. Keep a close watch. Go to your child and express your suspicions. Try to speak about it. Ask questions that may help them speak about it. Speak in a concerned manner rather than lecturing them.

When we find our youngsters in trouble, often our first impulse is to accuse, and vent our own frustrations and embarrassment. What is our real goal? Do we want to punish the teenager for causing us stress, or do we want to get help? Be aware that teenagers often lie when they are questioned about drugs. Their loyalty goes to the drug. If your suspicions are strong, do persist.

Adolescent substance abuse needs to be identified and addressed as soon as possible. Many adolescents who abuse drugs have a history of physical, emotional, and/or sexual abuse or other trauma. Addiction interferes with family, positive peer relationships, and school performance.

While a teenager is involved in drugs, steps necessary for their development are not happening. As we know, adolescence is a painful time. They need to learn to deal with stress, with feelings, with disappointment and frustration. During adolescence, people develop patterns of coping with success and failure. Running away is not the answer. How do we help a youngster develop those life skills after having used drugs as a crutch?

Teenagers involved with using drugs need to strengthen their will so they can be disciplined. Security has to develop within the self, to replace dependency on a substance. The teenager has to learn to delay gratification, resist temptation and develop inner strength. Learning to trust adults, developing self-confidence, and understanding the need for rules and limitations are major steps in the teenager's release from drug dependence. We cannot pretend that this is easy. Getting off drugs, and then staying off them, is one of the most difficult tasks the teenager may ever face.

Most drug programs are step-by step programs. As the teenager learns to handle small responsibilities, larger privileges are granted.

The long road to recovery involves honesty and training of the will. The teenager has learned to lie to parents, teachers, and themselves. Their will has been crippled and needs to be strengthened. That is only part of the treatment. The problems that led to drugs in the first place need to be explored and examined.

Strengthening the Individuality

If we use drugs to enter another kind of consciousness, or if we use drugs to have a spiritual experience, we have not earned these experiences. We also have no control over them. Instead of moving us forward in our development as human beings, opium, LSD, and marijuana push us backward.

The human being is fighting for freedom in the midst of many forces in society that want to enslave, such as advertising, the distorted image of the human being, and the denial of anything spiritual. Teenagers feels trapped in their physical body. In a drug experience, the adolescent is freed, and it feels good even if it's only temporary.

Teenagers today have a thirst for imaginative pictures. The dry thinking that goes on in so many schools, the bizarre posters and images on tee-shirts, the sick humor that fills so many comic books — all create an inner longing for something higher, something that affirms the human spirit. It is not surprising that some teenagers turn to drugs for pictures. In the LSD consciousness, another world is revealed. The three impressions common to many drug experiences are: disappearance of boundaries leading to a false connection with the world; a heightened rapture; and a split sense of the self and the world. These are ways in which the teenager is lifted out of the body into an artificial universal experience.

Rudolf Steiner gave exercises for strengthening the soul. For example, one exercise is to observe a plant, its budding, its growing, its blossoming. Then observe its fading, decaying, withering. If this is done repeatedly, the person develops a strong experience of life forces. To heighten the experience, bring strong feelings into the perceptions. This helps the person relate to the growing and dying forces in nature and in the self, thus strengthening the core. A teenager doing these exercises then sees that the world of nature and the world of the self are similar processes. In this inter-relationship, the human being and nature are one. Such a strong feeling helps them to retain a centeredness in life.

Another exercise is to observe one's thinking, becoming aware of how thoughts randomly flow in and out of their minds. Try concentrating on one thought for one minute, then two, and so on. See if you can keep your peripheral thoughts from wandering in. Don't permit free association to take over this concentration exercise. Work on concentration every day for a few minutes until you are able to discipline your own thinking.

Still another exercise has to do with feeling. Deepen your gratitude or appreciation for what others do for you. Learn to notice small gestures, the smiles, the hands reaching to help. Observe your own feelings from the outside. What gave rise to sudden anger? Why do you feel sorry for yourself? What caused the hysterical laughing? As you begin to observe your feelings, you master them.

Many of the exercises Rudolf Steiner gave had to do with developing moral life. He said that a person should take three steps forward in moral development for every step forward in spiritual development.

Conscious self-development is a much slower path than the unconscious path of drugs. However, conscious development develops concentration and will power. The person is active in the process rather than passively being at the mercy of whatever appears in a chemically induced brain-storm. Doing the exercises develops a new soul-being created by the person's own activity which does not threaten the soul with annihilation in the way that drugs do.

These exercises are particularly helpful for adults who have their full consciousness, but adolescents can also work with them. They can help develop focus, concentration, and gratitude, all of which help teenagers be more productive and more at peace.

Teenagers are hungering for imaginative pictures. When they receive stones instead of bread, when they find dry fact after fact instead of living images, their longing builds to bursting. Using drugs to feed this longing is understandable, but it is dangerous for both the individual and for society.

Artistic activity also provides a safe path of developing an inner life. Through engaging in painting, sculpting, poetry, and music, teenagers awaken new capacities in their souls, strengthening their feelings, sharpening their observation, focusing their concentration, and creating moments of expectation and joy. The experience of working artistically involves taking risks, working with the unknown, and creating something that is new.

Let us love and support our young people who have struggled with drug addiction as they struggle to transform themselves.

In a Nutshell

Use of tobacco and drugs

- Alcohol and tobacco are the most commonly abused drugs by teens, followed by marijuana.
- Cigarette smoking has been in decline in the past ten years, but nicotine vaping is increasing.
- Drug use continues to be a serious issue as millions of teenagers have experimented with drugs. Prescription and over-the-counter medications are the most commonly abused by high-school seniors, according to a 2013 study.
- Marijuana, the most common drug, is widespread and is tolerated in parts of the US and in parts of Europe. Club drugs such as Ecstasy tend to be used in night clubs, concerts, and parties.
- Drug addiction affects the brain and behavior, changing teenagers' health, emotional life, and family relationships.
- Treatment can work even if teenagers are mandated or enter into it unwillingly.
- Strengthening individuality so that the teenager doesn't rely on drugs is an important way to help.

Chapter 21

Sex and pregnancy

I thought if I had a baby I would feel needed and have someone to love.

16-year-old girl

Teen Pregnancy and Parents

'Mom, I'm pregnant.' Have you ever wondered whether your teenage daughter would say those words to you? If other parents in your circle of friends have had to deal with teenage pregnancy, what has your reaction been? You may have breathed a sigh of relief, glad that this wasn't happening in your family. As with other difficult life situations, we are confused and frightened when they actually happen to us, no matter how many times we have thought about them. Most of us carry mental images of the way we hope our lives and those of our children will turn out. When something disrupts those hopes and dreams, we become disoriented and scared.

How we handle a teen pregnancy depends on a number of considerations, such as the teenage girl's age, how the pregnancy happened, the nature of her relationship with the father, and whether marriage is a viable option.

Although pregnancy doesn't fit neatly into the normal picture of adolescent life, much joy and closeness can come of it if the family supports the young couple. The father of the coming child should be involved in decision-making as much as possible. Ultimately, however, the young woman must decide whether to have or abort the baby, and whether to keep and raise the child. It is her body, she will carry the child, and she will be chiefly responsible for it for at least the next 18 years.

How much of a problem is teenage pregnancy? When a family is confronted with the challenge of a pregnant teenager, it becomes a deep concern, and decisions have to be made. Yet there is some good news for society at large.

> In 2017, a total of 194,377 babies were born to women aged 15–19 years, for a birth rate of 18.8 per 1,000 women in this age group. This is another record low for U.S. teens and a drop of 7% from 2016. Birth rates fell 10% for women aged 15–17 years and 6% for women aged 18–19 years.[46]

Making the Big Decision

You, with your daughter, must consider the possibilities. If abortion is an option, time becomes a pressure. You cannot ignore what is happening.

Trying to make decisions, feeling insecure, and feeling pressure all affect the young woman's ability to cope unless she has the strong love and support of her parents.

Every human being is a spiritual individuality — a miracle — the product of the weaving together of physical heredity and spiritual individuality. The young woman has to decide whether to welcome this heavenly being on to the earth, or block its incarnation. If she decides to have an abortion, she must then bear the decision within her own conscience.

The first reality is that teenagers, with all due respect to their nascent sophistication and experience, are still children. They are not yet ready to assume the responsibility that comes with parenthood. Because they are preoccupied with themselves and still learning to be responsible, they have difficulty making the shift into taking care of a child.

If she keeps the baby, the young mother has two possibilities, marriage or raising the baby as a single parent. In either case, she will need proper pre-natal care. She should see a doctor, find out how advanced her pregnancy is, and receive advice on diet and health care.

If she marries, the question will be — is there deep enough love and caring to sustain the challenges that face all marriages, and especially a teenage marriage? If she decides to give up the baby for adoption, she will have to live with the unfulfilled yearning of not knowing how her baby is, what kind of person her baby has become, and whether she will ever again see him or her.

No decision is easy. The family should consult friends, religious leaders, a doctor, a social worker, or anyone who will help the family think through the choices. Advice is very helpful, but in the last analysis the young woman must decide in the intimacy of her family and in the privacy of her heart and conscience. Whatever she decides, parents have an opportunity to give their daughter love and support, guidance and clarity — all of which she will need in this situation.

What about her schooling? Will she remain in school until she is ready to give birth? Some schools have special programs which include classes on child care as well as pregnancy counseling and support groups for pregnant teenagers. Some teachers feel threatened by having a pregnant girl in class, and some parents feel that a mother-to-be serves as a poor model for their daughters, and that the school is implicitly condoning the pregnancy by allowing her to attend school. They are concerned about the attention she receives, and they confuse support and friendliness with supporting premarital sex. (When I was dealing with such a situation with one of my students, I was surprised that the parents who were most upset about having a pregnant student in class were the mothers and fathers of more sexually active teenagers. Was the situation coming a bit too close?)

What about the girls' friends? Will they continue to support her? She needs their friendship very much at this time. And her friends' parents? Will they allow their sons and daughters to be close to a pregnant teenager? Frightened parents have been known to forbid their sons and daughters from being too close to a young unmarried, pregnant woman. Needless to say, the teenagers find ways of seeing their friend and assuring her of their loyalty.

What will the father's role be? Will his family be involved? Will the couple continue to see each other? It is not unusual for the girl's parents to forbid the couple to date, or to allow them to see each other only in certain situations. Does this not remind us of the old proverb about locking the barn door after the horse is stolen? Pressure will be placed on both the young man and the young woman because fear and anxiety are inherent in such situations. The young father's anxiety is heightened because he is legally obligated to support the child for the next 18 years unless the child is legally adopted. This may be a hardship. Who will pay the costs of medical care and delivery? Will the couple be able to live together, if they wish? To what degree will the parents make decisions about the young parents' lives? Often, the young mother is still a minor.

A teen mother may have many reasons for keeping the baby. If the reasons are not sound, or if parent support is not there, even the young mothers who keep their babies may decide to give them up for adoption after they are born, sometimes even two or three years later. Always, it is a difficult decision. One young friend told me that several of her girlfriends had been pregnant at the same time she was — all at around 15 years old. After the excitement of the delivery and the cute baby days were over, the girls were overwhelmed. Two of her five friends eventually gave their babies up for adoption, after the babies were a year old.

Often the teenage mother is emotionally immature, and she is not willing or able to accept responsibility, yet she is assuming the most significant responsibility of her life. She is often frightened and unable to cope with the situation by herself. Regardless of how parents feel, they must consider what their daughter is experiencing.

A good prenatal care program is essential for teens, and parents should ensure that the young mother participates. With diet and medical guidance, the young teenager can have a successful and healthy pregnancy. Without guidance, however, problems can and do occur, such as birth injuries, infant death, illness, or mental retardation. Low birth weight is often a result of drugs, alcohol, tobacco, and poor diet. Anemia and toxemia are also common when the mother does not receive proper medical care. A higher death rate exists for younger mothers who do not take adequate care of themselves.

Everything possible should be done to help the teenager prepare herself physically, psychologically, and spiritually for the birth and care of the child. If she can appreciate the wonder and awe of the incoming being, she may be able to prepare herself to receive the child in quite a different way than if she perceives childbirth and childrearing as purely physical responsibilities. Experienced and loving mothers in the community may be able to help her by inviting her into their homes, talking about the care of the child, sharing hints, and welcoming her into motherhood.

The decision to marry because of teenage pregnancy is very sensitive. Clearly it would be better for mother and the child to be in a secure, protected, and nurturing relationship if that is what the marriage would bring. Unfortunately, most teenagers have enough trouble handling the complexities of romantic relationships, and would be unable to carry the seriousness of marriage. The question of marriage should be considered carefully. The scars of divorce may be as traumatic as the task of being a single parent until one is mature enough for marriage. Teenagers who are at least 17 years old have a better chance of developing a mature relationship.

Parent Responses to Real Situations

There are many alternatives. In one case, the parents insisted that their 15-year-old pregnant daughter live at home, continue going to school, and have the baby. She and her boyfriend could continue their relationship and, after graduation from high school, could marry. She followed through in this way, despite some difficult times, and the couple married and began their life together. They have been married for 16 years and have two children in what appears to be a stable and happy marriage.

In another case, the pregnancy was the result of a summer romance. After much consideration, the couple decided to marry. They received strong support — both financial and moral — and have become independent and solid as a family. They, too, now have a second child.

Another young woman wanted no connection at all with the father of her child. She moved in with her parents, who were saddened by the situation but supported her, and received the grandchild with loving attention. They have helped the young mother stand on her feet, continue her education, and be a good mother. As she said not long ago, 'Even with all the support I've had, life has been very hard'.

Most young teenage mothers who return to high school leave before graduating unless they have a strong parent, sibling, or friend standing behind them. It is difficult to be a high-school student and then go home and deal with a tired or sick baby. In addition, being out of touch with high-school life may result in alienation from peers. School friendships tend to drop off and new ones are made with other young mothers. The young mother is now more concerned with the baby's colic than about solving the quadratic equation.

Teenage mothers who are punished by their parents and made to live with harsh consequences of their actions often haven't enough education or income to take care of themselves and the child. In addition, they suffer from isolation. Who is the parent punishing? And what lesson is being taught? The young mother often ends up on welfare, or marrying prematurely for companionship and security — and soon after, pregnant again and possibly abandoned by the husband.

Marriage may be the right decision for the young couple, but it should only be made after a great deal of careful thought, and with sensitivity to the couple's age, the quality of their relationship, and the kind of support the two will receive from their families.

In some families, the girl's mother chooses to take care of the baby while her daughter continues at school. In situations where the young mother has psychological or mental issues, it is not uncommon for the grandmother to raise the child.

Adoption

If the pregnant teenager considers adoption, she has to think about dropping out of normal life for a year, usually losing a year of school unless she can take online courses. There will also be changes in her social life and challenges to her self-esteem. As she carries the child, she comes to feel a connection with it, yet she knows she will be giving it up. She may feel guilty about giving up the baby, but on the other hand, there is a serious shortage of adoptive babies and large numbers of couples yearning to adopt a child. These people offer care, love, attention, security, and a home. In such cases, adoption may be a choice that solves the predicament in a selfless way — assuring life and love for the child she is carrying, and offering the opportunity of parenthood to deserving people.

With the liberalization of regulations concerning the confidentiality of adoption records, many biological parents and children are finding each other, years after the adoptions. These reconciliations can be embarrassing in cases where the mother has not told her husband or family, but they can also resolve guilt and offer new possibilities for family bonding.

Adoption is a great sacrifice; it is also a responsible way to resolve the situation of the young woman who is not ready for marriage or for motherhood, and who treasures the life of the child and doesn't choose abortion. In the past, a family friend sent her pregnant daughter to live with our family for a few months. The young woman gained support and warmth by being with a family during that lonely time, even though her sense of loss was great whenever she thought of giving up her child. After the baby was born and the adoption proceedings complete, she returned to her home, resumed her job, and after several years she married and had a family of her own. As far as I know, she has had no connection with the child she gave up for adoption. When she married at 20, she was mature and more ready for a deep relationship than she would have been at 16.

Abortion

Once a teenager learns that she is pregnant she usually has trouble believing it. More than anything, she wishes the whole situation were a dream and would disappear. Taking the life of the fetus is not what she wants, but she may feel it is her only option. Abortion for most young women is seldom chosen without serious thought and feeling. Her dilemma confronts the young woman with her actions. She cannot be sexually active without consequences. For those who have been having casual sex, the actual experience of having an abortion may shock them into realizing the serious consequences of their behavior. Regardless of why the young couple did not use contraception, the reality of an abortion may force them to consider it in the future. Of course, if the situation includes rape, that is a different issue.

If a teenager uses abortion instead of contraception as a regular means of birth control, and a few do, she is being irresponsible. She is not considering the moral issue involved in abortion with appropriate seriousness. If she continues to be sexually active and does not take precautions, she may be developing a calloused attitude toward life which will affect her relationships in other areas of life, too.

The considerations are legal, physical, psychological, moral, and spiritual. The physical danger is especially acute for young teenagers. Girls under 16 are more likely to suffer damage to their cervix than women over 20 because the cervix in younger girls tends to be small and inelastic. Many teenagers make the risks greater by waiting until after the 13th week before seeking abortion. This is especially true of younger teenagers who are most likely to stall before telling their parents. Younger teenagers also are less likely to seek help from a doctor or agency.

Abortion is an intimate matter, deserving serious consideration and weighing of responsibility. The decision to abort may not seem all that grave at the time, but as the young woman matures, she is likely to reach a deeper understanding of its gravity.

In this chapter, we have been concentrating on the young woman's situation with pregnancy. What about the teenage or older father? If you are the parent of a son in this situation, some important questions should be asked. Have you been as frank with him as with a daughter? What has he been taught about responsibility, about consideration and respect for girls? Do you feel that it's the girl's problem if your son is responsible for her pregnancy?

Boys tend to get less involved in pregnancy decisions, especially if the relationship has been casual. Few boys, for example, accompany girls to find out about birth control. Society stereotypes the man as the provider and the woman as the one concerned with bearing and caring for the child. Should that stereotype continue? Is birth only a woman's business?

Girls become aware of their passage into womanhood rather dramatically through the onset of menstruation. For boys, it is not as clear. Rarely does the ability to have an erection confront the boy with the image of fatherhood. The models presented to young men show them as conquerors or controllers far more than as caring, feeling partners. One common image is the conqueror who leaves the woman, who takes, uses, and discards. Is it any wonder that many young men feel no responsibility when a pregnancy occurs?

One teenage father told me that his parents resented the pregnant teen, felt she was responsible for the pregnancy, and that she had trapped him. He didn't want to marry the girl, and his parents didn't want that either. At his construction job, other 17-year-old fellows made remarks about his being 'caught'. When he visited the baby at the girl's house, he felt ill at ease. He was the baby's father and had to support the child, yet it was difficult to feel that the baby was really his. He wasn't a member of the family, and his relationship with the girl wasn't the same any more. He felt intensely isolated. When he thought about continuing in this way for future years, he became depressed.

Some young men have babysat or have taken care of younger siblings, but many are far removed from little children and feel intimidated by them. The prospect of fatherhood leaves them feeling trapped and scared. The young woman has the advantage of being able to work out of instinct, but the young man does not. He is not ready to settle down and give up dreams of adventure. The adjustment varies with each teenage boy but, with support, he may come to appreciate and make the best of his new situation. Which boy becomes sexually active and takes into account that he may be responsible to support a child for 18 years? As with the girl, he needs to be fully prepared to understand and use birth control.

Teen pregnancy is a complicated and serious problem. Whatever decision the adolescent girl makes carries consequences. Decisions are often made at such times solely on the practical level, without considering the spiritual at all. Courage and vision are needed at this delicate time, and considering the spiritual aspects of bringing a child into the world can add another dimension to the decision-making.

Chapter 21 — Sex and pregnancy

In a Nutshell

Sex and pregnancy

- When a teenage daughter becomes pregnant, the parents' responses can have a powerful impact on the family.
- The pregnant teenager has serious decisions to make, and needs the love and support of those around her.
- The involvement of the father-to-be should be thoughtfully considered.
- The spiritual aspect of the incoming child adds an important aspect to the decision.

Chapter 22

Teenagers and food

I'm not hungry. Stop trying to make me fat.

16-year-old girl

'I'm too fat' must be three of the most spoken or thought words of teenage girls and women. Boys are becoming increasingly weight conscious, too.

Food is a part of our everyday needs, necessary for survival all over the world, a significant part of each culture in the way in which it is served and shared. It represents a social gesture of coming together to share in the bounties of the earth. In countries where there are food shortages, even famine, teenagers struggle just to have enough to survive. In countries where food is abundant, one would expect people to enjoy preparing and sharing meals, grateful for the opportunity to sit together around the table and give thanks.

Yet food is an issue for many teenagers. It is not about scarcity, but a mental-health issue in which food has become a psychological expression of the teenagers' deeper needs, even a question of life and death. Instead of many teenagers enjoying food through taste, texture, and smell, some use food to control their lives or that of others. What is it that has created such an imbalance in their lives?

The Role of Body Image in Girls and Boys

As children grow up they take in cues from their families, friends, and the culture. One look is considered beautiful or handsome, another one is ugly. We use expressions thoughtlessly. 'How pretty you look today!' 'That doesn't look good on you.' 'Smile for the camera even if you feel sad.' Emphasis on superficial appearance rather than on character tells the child what is highly valued.

How comfortable or uncomfortable are girls or boys with their own body? With the avalanche of images on social media, in magazines, advertising billboards, and so on, the fragile teenager is confronted with the so-called perfect body. The majority of girls in middle school are unhappy with their bodies.

Common Sense Media reports that the average teenager spends about nine hours per day using media for their enjoyment. They are bombarded with thousands of messages about the 'ideal' body. Underweight models and Photoshopped images of perfection are everywhere. Diet products and beauty items emphasize that being thinner and more attractive is the key to happiness and success. Teenage girls crave validation from their peers. When a friend tells them they look great, they feel justified in what they are doing. At the same time, cyberbullying makes comments on their thigh gap and the shapes of their bodies.

Boys are also being affected as they look at superheroes and action figures where they see unrealistic body types. Teenage boys strive for the perfect body through dieting and compulsive exercise. The perfect image is thin and more muscular, attractive-low body fat and lots of muscle, narrow waist, large shoulders with v-shaped torso — the idealized male body. The 2016 Monitoring the Future report cited anabolic steroid use in teenagers as a way of bulking up.

Girls often respond by trying different diets, aiming to get the perfect weight. Boys work out to develop big muscles or even resort to taking steroids. Both try to force their body into a mold that is shown as perfect.

> Leading health experts from many countries now believe that the problem arises from putting our focus on the wrong thing; we shouldn't be focused on weight, because weight is not as important as health. Their research shows that if we shift our focus onto health, and enjoying eating and exercising our bodies, we would be far better off.[47]

For many years I taught art history to ninth and tenth graders. They are barely comfortable with the proportions of the ancient Greek sculptures of women and the Renaissance Madonna paintings, but they react strongly in a negative way when the fleshy and curvaceous women painted by Renoir and Degas are shown. Some laugh, some become nervous, some indignant, others mocking. They find it hard to imagine such women as beautiful. They have formed an image of what is a beautiful body from outer influences.

Every culture has its ideal of beauty. The Western view has been 'Skinny is beautiful'. Or more currently, 'Skinny is best', especially if she is curvy in the right places. 'If I look like Kim Kardashian, having large breasts and rear, I'm sexy.' One teenage girl told me she liked to do yoga, but she was concerned because it was making her butt smaller. In the race to look sexy and seductive, a small butt isn't going to make it.

Boys worry about being too skinny, too fat, or too soft, too tall, not tall enough, not enough muscles or six-pack abs. They worry about whether they are strong enough to defend themselves. The models of boys in magazines don't display any acne. They are always perfect.

The glut of advertising, magazine pictures, television and movie heroines, and You Tube videos present the teenagers with the ideal woman or man. Even before their body starts to change they know what they want to look like. The 9- and 10-year-old teeny-boppers already have their vision internalized. As their body changes they are determined to force it into a shape most acceptable by their peers (and by social media). The easiest way to do this is by not eating.

I will focus more on girls in this chapter as they are experiencing eating disorders in greater numbers than boys. However, we need to help the boys as well. 'It is estimated that 8 million Americans have an eating disorder — seven million women and one million men.' Other statistics show even higher numbers. According to the National Eating Disorder Association, in the United States 20 million women and 10 million men will suffer from an eating disorder at some point in their lives.[48]

An estimated 10–15 per cent of people with anorexia or bulimia are males. Many clinicians believe that this figure is underreported because many men are ashamed to admit that they may be suffering from something widely thought to affect only women.

According to the Child Mind Institute:

> Estimates vary, but it is believed that a quarter to a third of those struggling with an eating disorder are male. And disordered eating behaviors are increasing at a faster rate in males than females. ...Girls with eating disorders are typically obsessed with being thin. While boys with anorexia are driven by a similar motive, the majority of them tend to be more focused on achieving a muscular physique... To achieve what they perceive to the 'ideal' physique, boys may work out excessively, or use steroids or over-the-counter supplements to minimize body fat and increase muscle mass and definition. An obsession with 'clean eating' — cutting out carbs, increasing protein, or adhering to restrictive fad diets — is another common feature.
>
> Christina Frank[49]

Teenage girls are diet conscious, even diet obsessive. Yet in spite of that, many of them gorge themselves on fast food, cookies, potato chips, and soda.

It is hard to resist wanting to have the ideal body. How can teenagers know how magazine advertisements are made, or how magazine advertisements are made and Photoshopped, or how YouTube videos are edited? How can they know what models go through to stay skinny? Certain body types are naturally thin, and others never will be. You don't usually see short models being photographed because clothes photograph best on tall, flat-chested girls. The message is 'tall and skinny are good, short and rounded are not, but tall and rounded in the right places are great'.

> The more girls are exposed to images that celebrate the 'thin-ideal' female form, the more likely they are to be dissatisfied with their own bodies.... Where visual media leaves off, peer culture kicks in. Girls talk with one another about weight, dieting and appearance, and research tells us they are more likely to feel dissatisfied with their bodies and flirt with eating disorders. If they have these conversations frequently.[50]

Body image problems can affect the girl's exercising because if she is rounder than she thinks she should be, she doesn't want to wear tights or spandex tops. Everyone will look at her. In this way she shames herself. Body image affects self-esteem. She romanticizes that if only her body were perfect, more people would like her.

There are other pressures placed on the teenager — the pressure to be popular, to be liked, to be accepted, to dress appropriately, and to do well in school. Most adolescents are affected by pressure, but some are more vulnerable to one way or another of escaping it. We have already spoken about alcohol usage as one way of dealing with the pain of growing up. Some of the other dangerous means to alleviate pain are eating disorders, drugs, promiscuity, and suicide.

The body image problem is world-wide. Some countries are passing laws to counter the diet industry and the additives put into food

Eating Disorders — Both Ends of the Scale

> Eating disorders, at their core, are not about weight, but are mental disorders about control that manifest themselves physically.[51]

Some teenagers focus their problems on food — either by eating too much or too little. Food is a symbol of love, and some turn to food as comfort, a pacifier to soothe the hurt they feel; others use it as a way of gaining control over those they want to hurt.

Food is one area that is almost completely within the teenager's power to regulate. When carried to an extreme, it becomes an illness, an addiction. Diet fads are a mild form of illness, whereas the binge-and-purge cycles of bulimia and self-starvation, or anorexia, are serious health hazards.

The South Carolina Department of Mental Health says that eating disorders have the highest mortality of any mental illness. The mortality rate associated with anorexia nervosa is twelve times higher than the death of all causes for females 15–24 years old.[52]

Lydia Jade Turner and Sarah McMahan, both involved in clinical work with eating disorders, title their article 'Burning the candle at both ends', referring to the two extremes of body weight — those who are over-weight (they quote that one-quarter of school-age children are reported to be overweight) and those who are unhealthily skinny. Parents behave desperately at both ends, feeling pressurized to put their girls on diets and those who are horrified by watching their girls refusing to eat and becoming super skinny. 'Despite all the anti-obesity rhetoric, children are getting fatter and despite warnings about eating disorders, more girls are falling prey to them. We are doing something wrong.'[53]

Eating disorders typically begin in adolescence or early adulthood. Stressful events of adolescence, including self-consciousness, puberty, and peer pressure, can play a big role in triggering these conditions. They often start with a stressful life event such as exposure to violence, family conflicts, stress at school, or loss. Young athletes, gymnasts, runners, body builders, rowers, wrestlers, jockeys, dancers, and swimmers are vulnerable to these disorders. In most of these competitive sports there is often a weight requirement.

Eating disorders are not associated with a person's race or their socio-economic status.

> Rates of minorities with eating disorders are similar to those of white women. 74% of American Indian girls reported dieting and purging with diet pills. *Essence* magazine, in 1994, reported that 53.5% of their respondents, African-American females were at risk of an eating disorder. Eating disorders are one of the most common psychological problems facing young people in Japan.[54]

Anorexia Nervosa

Anorexics can starve themselves to death. They are compulsive about becoming extremely thin.

'The mortality rate associated with *anorexia nervosa* is 12 times higher than the death rate of all causes of death for females 15 to 24-years old.'[55]

Many others develop health problems which they live with for the rest of their lives.

The anorexic has a fixation on food. She collects recipes, likes to prepare gourmet meals for others, but she doesn't eat. She is very particular about food, and when she does eat she has no sense of what her body needs. She exercises frantically because no matter how skinny she is, she is still convinced she is fat. She occasionally goes on a binge, but then vomits to keep from gaining weight. She drives herself unmercifully, and wants to be a good person.

The anorexic may drop 20–40 per cent of total body weight, becoming skeleton-like. Her hair will drop out. She will stop menstruating, have low body temperature and low blood pressure. No matter how gaunt or skeletal she becomes, she sees herself as fat. Her image of herself is so distorted that she will do anything to keep losing weight. We are used to connecting this kind of thinness with concentration camp victims or victims of famine, but it is a shock to see young people in our society look like this. What is even stranger about anorexia is that it is not a disorder that comes from inability to buy or know about good food.

The pattern of the typical anorexic is surprisingly clear. From a middle- to upper-middle-class family, most are super-achievers who have high expectations from their parents and from themselves. They have usually been easy children to raise, seldom getting into trouble, doing whatever they needed to do to please their parents and be approved of. Some have been doted on, especially by their fathers. Others are ignored most of the time, receiving attention only when they receive good grades or recognition of some kind. In both cases, approval is coming from outside, while the girl secretly feels insecure. She takes life seriously, and often internalizes problems between her parents or siblings.

As she enters her teenage years, she needs to break away from her family. She develops negative feelings, but is afraid to express them. People are counting on her, especially her mother. She doesn't want to hurt anyone. Her father is usually busy and preoccupied, but he pays attention to her when she achieves something. She adores him. He may have commented that she was starting to put on a little weight. He may only have been teasing her, but she wants to please him. She feels empty inside. She feels insignificant and unable to control her own life. She may stop eating as a way of showing this control, or she may stop eating because of her father's comment. She may connect putting on weight with failure. She may fear not being popular or not having a boyfriend.

Chapter 22 — Teenagers and food

For whatever reason, she starves herself. Early signs are loss of appetite and loss of weight. If the subject is raised, the anorexic usually denies that there is a problem and tries to change the conversation.

However, the problem is even more serious, as it is not just a family issue. The impact of social media affects girls of all ages in their feeling of being content with their bodies. Because teenagers feel they are the center of their world, they are especially sensitive to what others think about them.

Bulimarexia (Bulimia)

Instead of starving herself, the bulimic young woman eats plenty, but then vomits up the food. She is not as easy to notice as the anorexic, because she is not skeletal in appearance. She tends to be of normal weight, even slightly overweight. She enjoys food, appreciates a good meal, enjoys socializing in restaurants. She is fixed on food as much as the anorexic, but her fixation leads her to gorge. In one sitting, often at night and in secret, she may eat as much as five or six meals, but then she takes a laxative or induces vomiting. She maintains her weight by binging and purging.

A *New York Times* article called bulimia 'the secret addiction' which leads epidemic numbers of young women to consume up to 5,000 calories in an hour or two, induce vomiting, and repeat the behavior up to four times a day. Others use large quantities of laxatives to prevent the retention of such enormous amounts of food.

What kind of teenagers develop bulimia? Again, they are mostly female. About 50 to 75 per cent are former anorexics, and this is their way of maintaining their weight because they have not worked through their food fixation. Many teenagers under great pressure to be thin use this method to maintain their weight, especially those who want to be models, dancers, or gymnasts.

They are similar to the anorexics in that they want to be perfect in everything they do. They tend to be compulsive about their work, their clothes, their bodies. Their food intake is an area where they can exert control and be in charge without worrying about someone else's standards.

In anorexia, the danger is death through starvation, as well as damage to the gastro-intestinal system. In bulimia, the danger is mainly to the gastro-intestinal system. Other problems are severe tooth decay (due to destruction of the tooth enamel by acidic vomitus), constant sore throat, esophageal inflammation, swollen glands, liver damage, nutrient deficiencies and rectal bleeding (from extensive use of laxatives). In both cases, the emotional damage is considerable.

Signs of Eating Disorders

A young woman at college sneaks into the bathroom at night to eat. Her roommate can hear her crinkling the foil around the brownies her mother had sent her. She throws up constantly. Her hair is falling out. In the dining room she eats nothing. Occasionally, she takes a blueberry muffin and slowly picks out the blueberries, eating them and throwing away the rest. For four years, she has acted like this, growing thinner each year.

Another girl can hear her room mate gagging in the bathroom every night. The girl seems to be normal during the day, but she has a secret life at night. Secrecy and obsession distort the teenager's personality.

Because so many teenage girls are obsessed with being thin, it is easy to accuse them of being anorexic or having bulimia. Teens who are struggling to stay thin have much in common with those in the first stage of anorexia or bulimia. What is different is the degree of emotional stability that keeps one adolescent in balance and allows another to get out of control. Accusations only worsen the situation. If parents suspect their daughter may be struggling with an eating disorder, they should speak about it, but not push. Youngsters want control over their own lives, and parental pushing is part of what they are trying to escape.

If caught in its early stages, anorexia can be cured. The girl should see a doctor who specializes in treating adolescents with eating disorders. However, those in advanced stages urgently require help. Even if treated, they may have anorexia for life and need help in dealing with their feelings and problems. There is no quick cure, and health will return very slowly, even after the youngster has dealt with her attitudes and changed her habits.

For many parents, food is a loaded issue. Arguing, nagging, or lecturing about food backfires as the teenager becomes stubborn and unyielding. This stubbornness cuts off communication on important issues and insures that the teenager will not listen.

Compulsive Overeating/Obesity

Some teenagers react to the emphasis on the ideal body by finding a safe non-judgemental place in their lives, namely the realm of food. When they were little and hurt themselves, mommy gave them a cookie and everything felt better. Now they are hurt too, and food still makes them feel better. It is better to go to the refrigerator and eat a ham-and-cheese sandwich or to pig out on a bag of potato chips than speak with someone who is intimidating. They become obsessed with food, even to the point of dreaming about it.

When they feel afraid, they eat; when they feel anxious, they eat; when they feel relieved of stress, they reward themselves by eating; or if they want to celebrate something, they eat. When their parents fight, they eat; if they are worried about an exam, they eat; when they feel disappointed, they eat; when they are successful, they eat.

One of the great fears of adolescence is the relationship with others, either of the opposite or the same sex. If they get fat they don't have to deal with it. Most heavy boys and girls are looked down upon. If they are funny, if they play the clown, they will be appreciated as entertainment, but not as dates. Through their heaviness, they can postpone having to face intimacy, relationships, and sexuality. Especially when teenagers have had a traumatic experience in early childhood, they seek safety in food because reaching out may result in another trauma. Feelings are frightening to them, love is frightening, any kind of relationship built on vulnerability is scary. Food is a safe, dependable source of pleasure.

Another reason that teenagers over-eat is depression. When they feel bored and empty about their lives, when they lack interest in what is happening around them, they fill their emptiness with food.

Others over-eat in order to rebel. They use it to punish those around them and themselves. If a parent has overemphasized thinness and good looks, they may try to get even by eating more.

Whatever the reason teenagers over-eat, one common factor is that they feel worthless. Their self-image is so low that they sabotage themselves and make the situation worse. They feel low to begin with, achieve a temporary high after eating, but then feel worthless again.

It is difficult for those with no weight problem to understand the frustration of the obese person. Occasional attempts to diet do not bear results, and the person gives up. When all the advertisements show skinny people having fun, skinny people finding dates, skinny people modeling clothes, the heavy teenager feels shut out. This intensifies the need for comfort, and food fits the bill.

Medical researchers say that fat children and teenagers often become fat adults because fat cells formed during childhood can be reduced in size but not in number. Just as anorexia is a life problem that needs attention, even in adulthood, so too is obesity. A change in eating habits and exercise is necessary to maintain any weight loss.

What Can Parents Do for Daughters with Body-Image and Weight Issues?

Most teenagers, boys, and girls will at times be concerned about their weight and their bodies, but the path into eating disorders is different. It is a mental disorder that needs attention and help.

Remember that the teenager already feels uncomfortable about weight. If parents communicate judgement, the youngster will usually rebel. Weight has to do with control and self-image.

It is much more helpful to ask adolescents how they feel about their weight. Do they want to do something about it? Are they comfortable with it? Are there things they want to do which the weight prohibits?

Parents can get a sense of how much the teenagers want to talk about it and respect them as people. If the teenagers indicate that they want help, parents can contact a group such as Weight Watchers or a diet center. Give strong support and encouragement.

Parents can do things with the teenager that encourage exercise, whether it is going to the gym, hiking, swimming, bicycling, etc. They can examine their family's eating habits and see what can be done to support the teenager's needs. Make eating together a pleasant time when you are sharing ideas of the day or week.

Check how many boxes and prepared foods are in your closet, filled with unhealthy oils and preservatives. What food is in the house? Snacks, sodas?

Is the teenager a purist, so that some foods are good and others are bad? If they go out with friends and they eat some bad foods, will that leave the teenager feeling a failure?

Most of all, mothers should be a role model. If you are obsessing about your weight, your daughter will take that on as well. If you try diet after diet, she will see that as the right behavior. The advice to a mother is the same as to a daughter. Accept your body, like your body. Find something you like, what can your body do? Eat healthy foods, have good sleep, be active, have a healthy weight.

In her book *Untangled*, Lisa Damour writes:

> A research study with one of my favorite titles — 'Adolescent girls with high body satisfaction: who are they and what can they teach us?' — found that girls feel good about their bodies when their parents focus on positive ways to maintain a healthy weight, as opposed to encouraging dieting. Specifically, the girls in the study who reported high levels of body satisfaction had parents who exercised, encouraged their daughters to be fit, and emphasized healthy eating…. And try to stay clear of value judgments when it comes to food. Labeling foods as good or bad can make 'bad' foods (or worse, forbidden foods) particularly alluring for some girls and can contribute to eating disorders in perfectionistic girls who refuse to eat anything but 'good' foods. The terms healthy and unhealthy can have the same effect.[56]

If the problem is deeper than concern about weight, and parents sense that their daughters are having an eating disorder, they need to speak to counselors who can recommend professional help. Dealing with a daughter with eating disorders is very time consuming and exhausting. It takes a lot for the teenager to admit to having a problem. This is where professional help can intervene. Care is expensive and takes a lot of time — there is no quick cure. 'About 80% of the girls/women who have accessed care for their eating disorders do not get the intensity of treatment they need to stay in recovery — they are often sent home weeks earlier than the recommended stay.'[57]

Parents would benefit from joining a support group for those who are supporting their daughters dealing with eating disorders. It is a long haul and very worthwhile to interact with others facing this challenge.

Other Eating Problems

Although teenagers may not be affected by eating disorders as serious as anorexia or compulsive eating, they may be developing poor eating habits.

Many teenagers exist on junk food: snacks made up of sugar and empty calories, and fast-food items. Girls usually combine junk food with diet fads, whereas boys eat constantly and whatever is around.

A steady diet of empty, junk-food calories causes a thiamine deficiency and a beriberi-like disease, as well as personality problems. Drinking coffee, cola, and cocoa — the three Cs — leads to nervousness, anxiety, sleeping problems, and irritability. It is always surprising at the amount of candy and soft drinks teenagers consume. Although their junk-food consumption is a sensitive issue, they need to be made conscious about it. So much of the teenage scene takes place over hamburgers, sharing a pizza, or having a can of soda. Advertisements romanticize these events, and teenagers feel they are in the swing of things when they participate in the junk-food ritual, especially soft drinks. The adverts that are particularly well designed are the ones in movie theaters. The size of the popcorn box is shocking.

Chapter 22 — Teenagers and food

It is difficult to eliminate junk food completely from a teenager's diet. If one succeeds in raising teenagers' consciousness about good nutrition, one then has to be careful not to go overboard in that direction. Some teenagers become fanatical about good nutrition, and they avoid socializing because they don't want to be contaminated with poor food-choices. They can develop a sensible attitude toward food and nutrition, mostly by example. Their meals at home should be nutritious, and healthy food should be available for them to take for lunches and snacks. Having salad items, milk, fruit juice, vegetables, raisins, and nuts available sets a good example, and fills the need of the growing teenager who constantly asks, 'What's there to eat? I'm hungry.'

More teenagers are choosing particular diets or attitudes toward food, such as being vegetarian or vegan. With the increase in food allergies, many teenagers have become very careful about what they eat.

Schools can play an important part in developing attitudes toward food. Offering salad bars and healthy choices says a lot about a school's values. Michelle Obama tried to change the attitude about school lunches. While she was partially successful, there was a lot of resistance from food suppliers who claimed that students threw away the healthy food and requested chicken nuggets, tater tots, and pizza. It takes time to change food choices. Some schools have a successful program by having a garden in which students are involved in growing food, learning about soil, and composting. When students are involved themselves, they are more apt to transfer their learning to their own habits.

In a Nutshell

Teenagers and food

- The feeling about food has become a mental-health issue for many teenagers because they eat, overeat, or diet for different reasons.
- Images in advertising, magazines, and social media affect teenagers' feelings about their bodies, which they then transfer to their attitude toward food.
- Eating disorders are not associated with a person's race or socio-economic status, although body image is regarded differently in different societies.
- Eating disorders affect boys and girls, although they are more prevalent with girls.
- Young athletes are vulnerable to eating disorders, as in most competitive sports there may be a weight requirement.
- Parents should pay attention to the signs of eating disorders and gain help for their teenagers because if caught in the early stage, treatment is often successful.

Chapter 23

Teenagers and the media

Media such as newspapers, telephones, telegraph, television, and movies have been around for a long time. As the media has become more sophisticated and more affordable, it has moved from the adult population to the teenage population, and even down to children under 3 years of age.

As soon as one form of media is introduced, another comes along and creates a new fad. The forms of media include: television with cable, DVDs, cell phones, digital cameras either on cell phones or self-contained, video games, and internet computers.

Why is Media So Interesting to Teens?

These new forms have increased the possibility of connecting people in different parts of the world, simplified research, allowed businesses to reach huge numbers of customers, allowed soldiers to communicate home from the battlefield, and inspired endless advances in medicine, manufacturing, and distribution. Today's teenagers and pre-teens are the biggest population for media use. They are the pioneers finding their way in an unknown land, not having been discovered before.

We can ask why this is. From a developmental viewpoint, it makes a lot of sense. Pre-teens and teenagers are trying to figure out their identity. They like to find out what is new, try on different identities, meet new people, and communicate what they like and don't like. They like the instant response that comes with text-messaging, and they like the creativity of blogs and profiles. They like the chat rooms in which they can express themselves and say whatever comes to mind. The social-networking craze with such programs as MySpace began with young adults, spread to college students, and became popular with the 12 to 13-year-olds. It is not surprising. This is true with every new form of social media. Face Book was once *the* form of communicating amongst teenagers, but is now passé, and is mostly used by the older generation. The younger ones prefer Instagram, but that, too, is waning in popularity as new programs come on the scene.

A key developmental need of pre-teens and teenagers is to figure out relationships, both in their immediate environment and those far from home. Rather than develop pen-pals across the globe, the online community is more instant and satisfying than waiting for letters to be sent by plane. Teens look for ways to secretly communicate outside of their parents' earshot. They look to make friends who do not have to be scrutinized by their parents' eyes. Online contact has become a place for freedom.

On the broader front, important questions arise. What is the long-term effect of the impact of digital media on our youth, how they learn, and how they think? Does online use of social networks mean that people are less social? Teens are communicating regularly, possibly more than any previous generation. Does it have the same effect as speaking to next-door neighbors or friends from school?

Different Aspects of the Media

In the past, parents were concerned by the influence of television. The box with the screen was like a stranger who inserted itself into our family life, bringing in influential images and introducing values that were different from what parents taught. The struggle was to limit the amount of television children watched, not just from the content but also from the flickering screen.

Today, the television is like a ghost from the past. We can access what is on television on our computer, iPad, or phone, not just in live time but whenever we choose. Young teenagers can watch what they choose, away from the presence of their parents.

Movies and Video Games

Movies pose similar challenges as TV, either in the theater or at home. Here, violence and sexual imagery are the strongest issues. One only has to go to the movies and watch the previews to sense what the industry is producing. The sensory overload de-sensitizes youngsters to the images and foul language, the objectification of women, and the feeling of the world being a dangerous place. The conscious manipulation of viewers through subliminal imagery and increased volume exploits young and old adolescents who are vulnerable to this kind of stimulus.

At the same time, the movie industry has expanded its choices to include superheroes, stories of those who overcame difficulties to win awards or fame, and more images of everyday people who show tenderness to those in need. It has also become more cognizant of diversity in many areas. The archetypal description of the quest lies behind the *Star Wars* sequels, as well as Harry Potter. These movies are side by side with the comic-strip characters, space travel, war movies, and thriller shoot-em ups. It's not that movies are bad; it's a matter of selection and guidance.

Video games have become a significant part of the landscape for children. Since the 1970s, when they were first introduced, they have become a popular pastime for children and teens, as well as for adults. The biggest game players are 8 to 10-year old boys, while girls listen more to music.

While watching television was a passive experience, video games offer interactive participation. As with some movies and television, many video games are filled with gross and violent images. But they are also filled with quests, character development, and opportunities for collaboration. It is difficult to compare being part of an exciting team on the verge of eradicating the enemy with paying attention to a class on the subjunctive case.

Boys are particularly drawn to video games because of action. The boy is in charge, and he holds the power. Girls are not as attracted to them because they are more interested in relationships, in being liked. So they more likely watch videos that show them how to improve their appearance.

Spend time playing the games with your children, discuss the values in the games, and educate yourselves on the ratings of video games. As young teenagers struggle between resisting form which their parents lay out for them, and the freedom of deciding for themselves how much time they will play and what they will play, they need guidance, but ultimately they have to come to balance.

As they move into the next phase, as 16- and 17-year-olds they understand the effect of being immersed too strongly in video games, and they begin to set limits for themselves. Healthy teenagers tend to leave their obsession with video games behind as they become interested in other activities. However, others become addicted and lose their way.

The question to consider is, what is the effect of video games on teenagers. Dr Leonard Sax writes:

> …researchers find that the more time you spend playing video games, the more likely you are to develop difficulties maintaining sustained concentration on a single item. Conversely, researchers find that boys who already have difficulty concentrating and focusing tend to gravitate to video games, where their distractibility is an asset rather than a liability.[58]

Cell Phones

Telephones have been a pre-teen and teen obsession for years. However, the cell phone (or 'mobile phone' in the UK) makes contact immediately wherever they are. It has also offered parents a way of keeping in touch with their children and brought a sense of security. The cell phone extends the time youngsters can be in contact with friends in any place and at any time. Texting is like an extension of the teenager's thinking, and the phone an extension of the teen's brain. Cell phones with cameras can be used to record wonderful events, but it can also involve taking embarrassing pictures of a classmate and putting it out virtually, as well as cheating on tests.

As with all media, the problem comes with overuse so that teenagers aren't getting other things done, have interrupted sleep, and are anxiously awaiting the next text to arrive. Another issue is the use of the cell phone while driving. The highest mortality rate for teenagers is due to accidents while driving.

Let us remember that the cell phone is actually a miniature computer, and everything available on the computer can be accessed on the cell phone. Through Amazon Prime and Netflix, movies can be streamed on to the cell phone. It is more difficult for parents to have an influence on the teenagers' choices, as the cell phone is often in the bedroom or in the youngster's pocket.

Internet

Computers are becoming a universal presence in our lives. They far outpace the use of TV. As with TV, however, one of the main issues is parental guidance. How much time the teenager spends on it, the games, the email contact with strangers, and more importantly, the way a teenager can email opinions about a classmate that can be harmful. 'Flaming' of other teens is a term that has been used, although such terms change quickly in time and place. It refers to saying things online that they would never say to someone's face.

Teenagers, especially those under 17 or 18, still have trouble fully understanding the consequences of their actions. Because email is instant, there is no time to reflect on what they are going to say. Ruining someone's reputation, using foul language, being inappropriately gross or mean are ways teenagers have caused harm. The harm is intensified because they can download the email on to a website or email it to hundreds of people, most of whom did not request it.

The monster in the media is the prevalence of pornography that has become a shadow overlaying the understanding and experience of sexuality. It has colored many boys' images of sexual relations, infused their comments in texting and the way they speak about girls and speak to them, and influencing how they act with girls. Under the influence of those images and messages, boys consider their own and others' bodies as object purely for their own satisfaction. Pornography has snuck in to the images of how girls regard their own bodies, how they dress and portray themselves on social media by modeling themselves after celebrities who are actually porn stars.[59]

Social Media

Online social networks are the craze. Teenagers love the creativity of creating a profile, placing photographs, their favorite stars and bands, and sharing their inmost thoughts. In short, they create a persona. In fact, social media is where teenagers, especially girls, live.

> In 2015, 88 percent of American teenagers 13 to 17 had access to a mobile phone, and 73 percent had a smartphone, according to the Pew Research Center. 92 percent were going online from a mobile device daily, and 24 percent were online almost constantly.[60]

Visitors to the site can make comments or contact the person directly. This interaction expands the teen's community of friends. Just as teenagers have always looked for a place to hang out, meet friends, put on a persona, flirt, and test their limits, these networks offer this. It's just like a big community where people can talk and hang out. Why does it have a special allure for young teenagers?

Developmentally, they are becoming aware of their own identity. Who am I? What do I like? What do my friends like? What do they think of me?

They can try on different identities and change them from day to day. Instead of going to the local drive-in of my youth or even writing letters, it's a place to meet new friends and strangers. Even though programs set up an age-limit, young teenagers lie about their age in order to develop their profile.

When boys ask girls to please post nudes, it seems another way of sharing themselves, not only to watch porn but to actually produce porn. When girls get mean with each other, they have a way of getting back by commenting hatefully on pictures they post.

It isn't only girls who are doing this to themselves and each other. Boys post 'dick pics' which are commented on by other boys and by some girls. Girls are not generally excited about this form of sexualizing, and it does cast a shadow on their romantic sense of relationship.

During the middle-school years, girls develop a sense of self, who they are, and who they will become. The girl is focused on a superficial view based mainly on her looks or what she has bought. How she interacts with other girls becomes the primary way for her to know who she is. The early identification of beauty and sexuality which creates behavior becomes internalized over time and affects her high school years, often overshadowing more subtle aspects of her personality.

There is no doubt that the various media can be addictive for young and older teenagers, as well as for adults. Girls are more involved with social media; in their own words they are obsessed, meaning 9–11 hours of the day.

Why is social media so addictive? In addition to the satisfaction it gives in establishing connection with others, social media stimulates the reward centers in the teenagers' brain, especially when they receive 'likes', or the feeling of being let down when the response is negative.

In her book *American Girls, Social Media and the Secret Lives of Teenagers*, author Jo Ann Sales points out that the culture of social media where girls are spending so much of their time is a product of the culture of Silicon Valley, a male-dominated, frat-boy culture focusing on judging girls as to whether they are 'hot or not'. They set the standard for whether a certain girl is attractive or not. Their idea of what is funny or not, the misogynistic attitudes and comments, and the emphasis on appearance have made their way into teenage girls' psyches.

The APA (American Psychological Association) surveyed multiple studies which found links between the sexualization of girls and a wide range of mental health issues, including low self-esteem, anxiety, depression, eating disorders, cutting, even cognitive dysfunction. Apparently, thinking about being hot makes it hard to think: chronic attention to physical appearance leaves fewer cognitive resources available for other mental and physical activities.[61]

Chapter 23 — Teenagers and the media

The major concerns with online social networks have to do with how much information and what kind of information is put on the site. Young teens have little sense of their effect on other people, on how public the site is. One teacher received MySpace, and within a few minutes he knew who was drinking and what was going on at parties with his students. This lack of realization can cause problems when older visitors visit the site and arrange to meet the youngster, exchange sexual imagery and connotations, and where the teenager gives away too much information about their residence. It is important for them to understand that the information they give can be accessed by others, such as when high-school students are applying to colleges or for jobs.

Unfortunately, they do not realize that these are public documents: even with passwords, they can be entered. In their innocence, they may give their address or phone numbers, and make contact with viewers who may be out to do them harm.

With education about social media, girls, especially older girls, are waking up to how they are being affected by social media. They are starting to see the sexism aimed at girls and how it is even affecting the way they are treating each other.

What Is Needed for Healthy Teenage Life?

The biggest antidote is parental awareness. Parental attitudes and increased communication with their teenagers are the strongest means of bringing balance to their involvement with media.

- Strengthen face-to-face relationships, especially long-lasting relationships, as anxiety has become one of the most common problems.
- Develop communities in which teenagers have a place, and people are committed and connected to each other over time, and are role models of moral behavior.
- Set limits on time and content of media. Explain the dangers of putting personal information on social media. Emphasize respect toward their classmates and friends in the use of social media.

Let them know that if there is something unsafe or harmful they encounter, you are there to support them.
- Schools should set limits on cell-phone usage and text messaging in class.
- Parents and teachers should help find a balance in media usage.

Parents have to self-regulate as well. The constant posting of images of their children has created a similar reaction to the 'likes' that teenagers look forward to. All a parent has to do is tell the children to pose for the camera, and they adopt a pose that is an immediate reaction with the fake smile. Without thinking, parents use their children to bolster their own popularity. As children become teenagers they post for each other, not intending for the posts to go viral.

We live with the media. It is not going away. It is up to the adult world to understand what is going on, how it affects child and adolescent development, find ways to work with teenagers to use it effectively, and to model ways in which the media does not negatively invade family life.

Ben Klocek has spoken to parents about ways to do this. He looks at two areas — personal life and family life. The first is looking at ways in which adults can make changes to control the influence of technology in their own lives, such as choosing a tech-free day; taking time to sit away from screens, even for a few minutes; acknowledging that adults are models for children; and being ethical in the use of the phone. The other is how to develop healthy family habits, not saying technology is bad, but moderating its use. Some good suggestions include no phones in the bedroom, no phones on the dining-room table, putting away your phone when you are speaking with another person, having a place in the home where technology can be used and easily supervised, and the understanding that all screens will be monitored.[62]

Neil Postman hit the nail on the head when he titled his book *Amusing Ourselves to Death*.[63] All technology can be used for information as well as for entertainment. It is up to us to be conscious of our behavior, recognizing our responsibility as parents and teachers, and choosing to work for the health of our children.

Chapter 23 — Teenagers and the media

In a Nutshell

Teenagers and the media

- Although media has been a way of historically connecting with each other, teenagers and pre-teens are the biggest population for media use today.
- The media meets the needs of adolescents who are trying to figure out their identity, their relationships, and how they fit into the social scene. However, they typically lack the developmental maturity to handle it in a healthy way.
- Boys tend to be more drawn to video games for their interactive participation, while girls are attracted to videos that show them how to improve their appearance.
- Obsessive use of media can affect concentration, isolation, and attention.
- The use of social media can have negative effects on how teenagers treat each other.
- Some strong ways to balance involvement with the media include strengthening face-to-face relationships, interacting in communities, limiting time and content of media, and helping adolescents self-regulate their media usage.

Conclusion

We shall not cease from exploration
And the end of all our exploring
Will be to arrive where we started
And know the place for the first time.
                                    T.S. Eliot, 1942

The times have changed, and since the second edition of *Between Form and Freedom*, the life of young and older teenagers has undergone influences we could not have imagined. The sophistication of technology and consumerism, pornography, and the domination of the cell phone and its use in social media have crept into our lives like a many-headed fire-breathing dragon. Teenagers are courageously finding their way in this world, asking powerful questions about their own identity, about the future of the planet, and the nature of life itself. Will robots replace human beings? Will love still guide us in our relationships? What does it mean to be a parent today? What is the role of a teacher?

I feel so grateful that teaching and parenting have been significant parts of my life. We are never prepared for the journey when we start out. Now, six decades later, I can say, 'If only I knew at the beginning what I know now!', as T.S. Eliot says in the above lines from his poem *The Fire and the Rose*, when the whole journey is over, we are back where we started and know the place for the first time.

As a parent, that is certainly true. I look back over those years when my daily life was filled with the needs of the family, and I felt stressed and confused, doing everything for the first time. Yet I remember when I felt that being a parent was the most important work I could ever do. Despite the heartaches, challenges, and joys, I know I would do it all over again. Knowing what I know now, I would do it so much better. But I don't fool myself, because it wouldn't be the same. Life isn't like that.

Conclusion

It is similar with teaching. In the beginning we are carried by enthusiasm and a certain degree of innocence. Over time, we gain skills and capacities as we learn to meet our students and serve their needs. As with family life, every day in the classroom is a new day. Another chance to be more sensitive, more responsive, and more confident. Yet there were many times, when I was close to retiring from full-time teaching, that I said to myself, 'Finally, I'm learning to be a teacher'.

Between Form and Freedom has been part of my personal journey, from its conception in 1978, through the first edition (1988), the second edition (2009), and now in its third edition (2021). Each time I have edited and rewritten parts of it, my life has been enriched by new experiences, the world we live in has changed, and the needs and challenges of adolescence have been significantly different.

Life as a parent never really ends, although the conversation takes on a different tone. The cultural influences that have made parenting challenging have also made their mark on teachers' lives.

Parents are there from the beginning of a child's life. Teachers are present at a particular moment, and they have the opportunity to make a significant difference in whichever phase of the child's development they are present.

Rudolf Steiner indicated that the teacher uses the capacities of a particular soul quality to help a child or adolescent. When we work with young children we use our life forces to strengthen their physical development towards health and balance. As we take the children through the elementary school years, it is our soul body that surrounds them with beauty, enthusiasm, and hope. In the challenging years of adolescence, we teachers rely on our capacities of objectivity, empathy, and intellectual questioning to guide their recently awakened soul life.

The connection between teachers and students is a deep karmic relationship in which each brings something to awaken the other. I am deeply grateful that I have been able to continue connections with many of my former students and experience how they have ripened into adulthood and are making the world a better place.

We, along with our adolescents, are struggling to live in a world between form and freedom. We cannot do it alone. We need to help each other. Something we all need today is courage — courage to develop meaningful relationships within our own lives, to respect our children's individuality, to stand by decisions when we feel alone and weak, and to do so without knowing all the answers, or even being able to ask all the questions. We need the courage to participate in the evolution of tomorrow from today even when we know that what we hold most firmly cannot escape change. We need courage to be thankful for adversity, to make statements that are neither popular nor generally supported, to explore the unseen world of human evolution, to form a vision of a better world, and to live our lives in gratitude for freedom.

In closing, I share a poem I wrote for the graduation of the first senior class of the Sacramento Waldorf School in 1978.

Teaching

What is teaching?
Keys to barred doors.
Rusted, squeaking — opening,

First a narrow shaft of light,
Then widely swinging –
The glimmer illuminates
As broad swaths of clarity.
The door, once opened,
is never closed again.

Facing the future in becoming,
Tiptoeing behind,
Penetrating the veil,
Lifting the corner of the gossamer curtain
Until the statue of Isis stands revealed
To those with eyes to see.

Discovering metaphor
and layers of thought!

Conclusion

The joy of shifting from layer to layer.
As a musician plays his scale,
I tune my consciousness.
The mind expands
Carried on the wings of the surging soul
And the ever-pounding heart skips a beat,
THUNDERS;
At the thrill of an idea,
Or the feel of a greater reality
Floods the being of the seeker.

The Tree of Life, The Tree of Knowledge
Stand beckoning on either side
Of the twisting path.
Which crossroad?
Why only one?
Each yields to one-sidedness.
Instead —
Unite, synthesize, merge!
Union within Union.

Live and Learn.
Be in the moment …
Know of the past
but SERVE
the will of the future!

The teacher is …
the Key, made of metals,
forged in the fires of the Alchemist.
Mysterious, selfless,
guiding the emerging guide
within the other.
The musician intoning the harmony of the spheres
in earthly density.

The magician creating what never could be in a
sleeping soul,
Waving the wand of the Word,
Dispelling clouds at dusk
To dawn's awareness and
Tomorrow.

In a Nutshell

Conclusion

- Earlier in our adult years, we could not have predicted how teenagers' lives would change in the 21st century.
- Teachers and parents have opportunities to make a significant difference in an adolescent's life.
- The connection between teachers and students is a deep karmic relationship.

Notes and References

Chapter 1

1 J. Chilton Pearce, *The Biology of Transcendence*, Park Street Press, Verm., 2002, p. 46.

Chapter 5

2 Rudolf Steiner, *Intuitive Thinking as a Spiritual Path*, Steiner Books, Hudson, NY, 1995, p. 102.

Chapter 6

3 Rudolf Steiner, *Observations on Adolescence*, AWSNA, Fair Oaks, Calif., 2001, p. 23.

Chapter 7

4 Robert Shmerling, The gender gap in sports injuries, Harvard Health Publishing, 3 December, 2015; available at https://tinyurl.com/y5v6z82z (accessed 20 November 2020).
5 L. Sax, *Why Gender Matters*, Broadway Books, New York, 2005, p. 14
6 Ibid., p. 18.
7 S. Biddulph, *Raising Boys: Why Boys Are Different and How to Help Them Become Happy and Well Balanced,* Celestial Arts, Berkeley, Calif., 1999. pp. 47–8.
8 R. Steiner, *Observations on Adolescence*, AWSNA, Fair Oaks, Calif., 2001, p. 111.

Chapter 8

9 R. Steiner, *The Four Temperaments*, Anthroposophic Press, New York, 1944, p. 39.

Chapter 9

10 Rilke, *Letters to a Young Poet*, p. 69.
11 R.W. Emerson, *The Heart of Emerson's Journals*, ed. Bliss Perry, Dover Publications, New York, 1939, p. 39.

Chapter 10

12 C. James, *Beyond Customs: An Educator's Journey*, Agathon, New York, 1974.

Chapter 11

13 L. Damour, 'Untangled: guiding teenage girls through the seven transitions into adulthood', *New York Times*, 18 February 2020.
14 2015 US Census, published 2018.

Chapter 13

15 Rilke, *Letters to a Young Poet*, p. 35.
16 D. Pope, *Doing School: How We Are Creating a Generation of Stressed out, Materialistic, and Miseducated Students*, Yale University Press, New Haven, 2001.
17 Dr Allegra Alessandri, interview, February 2020.
18 Source: US Centers for Disease Control and Prevention.
19 M. Flannery, 'As suicide rates climb among American teens, educators need to ask and listen', *NEA Today*, 17 January 2020; available https://tinyurl.com/yyn8lv3y (accessed 20 November 2020).
20 R. Wiseman. *Queen Bees and Wannabees: Helping Your Daughter Survive Cliques, Gossip, Boys, and the New Realities of the Girl World*, 3rd edn, Harmony Books, New York, 2016, p. 272.

Chapter 14

21 R. Steiner, *Education of the Child in the Light of Anthroposophy*, Anthroposophic Press, Great Barrington, Mass., 1996.
22 K. Avison and M. Rawson (eds), *The Tasks and Content of the Steiner Waldorf Curriculum*, Floris Books, Edinburgh, 2018.

Chapter 15

23 R. Steiner, originally in R. Steiner, *Wahrsprachworte*, Dornach, Switzerland, as quoted in Hildegard Gerbert, *Education through Art*, Verlag Freies Geistesleben, Stuttgart, 2006, p. 24.

24 Rilke, *Letters to a Young Poet*, p. 35.

25 V. James, manuscript, *Painting with Hand, Heart, and Head*, 2019.

26 Rebecca La Clair, 'Why teens need their music, Part I: 4 secrets for parents, backed by research', *Huffington Post*, 2 February 2017; available at https://tinyurl.com/yyhqz8g2 (accessed 20 November).

27 William J. Cromie, as quoted by Rebecca La Clair, *Huffington Post* (note 26).

Chapter 17

28 Rilke, *Letters to a Young Poet* (note 10), pp. 68–70.

29 Wiseman, *Queen Bees and Wannabees* (note 20), p. 163.

30 M. Gurian, *A Fine Young Man*, Jeremy Tarcher, New York, 1999, p. 111.

31 L. Sax, *Girls on the Edge*, Basic Books, New York, 2016. p. 12.

32 Sax, ibid., pp. 12–13.

33 Sax, ibid., p. 16.

Chapter 18

34 D. Elkind, *All Grown up and No Place to Go*, Addison and Wesley, Reading, Mass., 1984, p. 33.

35 Preventing suicide: a global imperative', World Health Organization, 2014. R. Bergeron, CNN, 12 August, 2019.

36 L. Johnson, *San Francisco Chronicle*, 8 February 2009.

Chapter 19

37 Chaim Ginott, *Between Parent and Teenager*, Avon Books, New York, 1969, p. 192.

38 Shirley Schwartzrock, 'Facts and fantasies about alcohol', American Guidance Service, Circle Pines, Minnesota 55014-1796, 1984.

39 National Survey on Drinking Use and Health — NSDUK — and the Monitoring the Future Survey, Institute of Social Research at

the University of Michigan, 2018; available at https://tinyurl.com/yycm7lxp (accessed 20 November 2020).

40 Michael Livingston, UNSW and Amy Pennay, Univ. of Melbourne, National Drug and Alcohol Research Centre, Sydney, Australia.

41 Federal Center for Health Education, DPA/ The Local News; see https://tinyurl.com/y489knbd (accessed 20 November 2020).

Chapter 20

42 Centers for Disease Control and Prevention, CDC24/7: *Saving Lives, Protecting People*, December 2019, www.cdc.gov; available at https://tinyurl.com/yyoujne9 (accessed 11 December 2020).

43 'Vaping of marijuana on the rise among teens', Adolescent and School Health, Monitoring the Future Survey,18 December, 2019; available at https://tinyurl.com/ybxn6rja (accessed 11 December 2020).

44 Nora D. Volkow, MD, *Drugs, Brains, and Behavior: The Science of Addiction*, NIH pub no. 14-5605, April 2007, revised July 2014; available at https://tinyurl.com/y3o9x5kr (accessed 11 December 2020).

45 Dane O'Leary, 'Are gay teens at higher risk for addiction?', American Addiction Centers, 4 November 2019; available at https://tinyurl.com/y6nugfeg (accessed 11 December 2020).

Chapter 21

46 Center for Disease Control and Prevention, 'About teen pregnancy', available at https://tinyurl.com/ya937fa9 (accessed 11 December 2020).

Chapter 22

47 S. Biddulph, *Raising Girls*, quoting from Linda Bacon, *Health at Every Size: The Surprising Truth about Your Weight*, BenBella Books, San Francisco, 2010, p. 160.

48 National Eating Disorder Association, 'Our work' available at https://tinyurl.com/y2jeolmz (accessed 11 December 2020).

49 Christina Frank, *Boys and Eating Disorders*, Child Mind Institute; available at https://tinyurl.com/y6zfl75g (accessed 11 December 2020).

50 L. Damour, *Untangled: Guiding Teenage Girls through the Seven Transitions into Adulthood,* Ballantine Books, New York, 2017, p. 243.

51 Wiseman, *Queen Bees and Wannabees*, (note 20), p. 192.

52 South Carolina Department of Mental Health, 'Eating Disorders'; see www.State.sc.us.

53 Biddulph, *Raising Girls*, Harper Thorsons, London, 2013, p. 159.

54 Essence Magazine, 1994, quoted by South Carolina Department of Mental Health, www.State.sc.us.

55 Alternative Eating Disorder Treatment Center, Arizona. www.Mirasol. net.

56 Damour, *Untangled* (note 50), p. 243.

57 South Carolina Department of Mental Health, Eating Disorder Statistics; see www.State.sc.us.

Chapter 23

58 L. Sax, *Boys Adrift*, p. 80, quoting from Edward Swing and colleagues, 'Television and video game exposure and the development of attention problems', *Pediatrics*, 126, 2010, pp. 214–21.

59 B. Staley, *Tending the Spark: Lighting the Future for Middle School Students*, Waldorf Publications, Hudson, New York, 2019, pp. 146–7.

60 J. Sales, *American Girls, Social Media and the Secret Lives of Teenagers*. Alfred A. Knopf, New York, 2016.

61 Ibid., p.14.

62 B. Klocek, 'Transforming tech habits: creating a world that reflects the heart: a presentation and discussion for schools & parents'; available at https://tinyurl.com/yxoa7jtv (accessed 20 November 2020).

63 N. Postman, *Amusing Ourselves to Death*, Viking, New York, 1985.

Appendix I

Bibliography

Aeppli, Willi, *Rudolf Steiner Education and the Developing Child*. Anthroposophic Press, New York, 1986.

Anderson, Craig, and others, 'Violent video game effects on aggression, empathy, and prosocial behavior in eastern and western countries: a meta-analytic review', *Psychological Bulletin*, 136, 2010, pp. 151–73.

Avison, Kevin and Martyn Rawson (eds), *The Tasks and Content of the Steiner-Waldorf Curriculum*, Floris Books, Edinburgh, 2018.

Bartholow, Bruce, and others, 'Chronic violent video game exposure and desensitization to violence: behavioral and event-related potential data', *Journal of Experimental Social Psychology*, 42, 2006, pp. 532–39.

Bartlett, Christopher and Christopher Rodeheffer, 'Effects of realism on extended violent and nonviolent video game play on aggressive thoughts, feelings, and physiological arousal', *Aggressive Behavior*, 35, 2009, pp. 213–24.

Biddulph, Steve, *Manhood: An Action Plan for Changing Men's Lives*, Hawthorn Press, Stroud, Gloucestersire, 2002.

Biddulph, Steve, *Raising Boys*, Ten Speed Press, Berkeley, Calif., 2013.

Biddulph, Steve, *Raising Girls*, Harper Thorsons, London, 2013.

Brizendine, Louann, *The Female Brain*, Morgan Road Books, New York, 2006.

Damour, Lisa, *Untangled: Guiding Teenage Girls through the Seven Transitions into Adulthood*, Ballantine Books, New York, 2016.

Easton, Stewart C., *Man and the World in the Light of Anthroposophy*, Anthroposophic Press, Spring Valley, New York, 1975.

Elium, Jeanne and Don, *Raising a Daughter*, Celestial Arts, Berkeley, Calif., 1994.

Elium, Jeanne and Don, *Raising a Son*, Beyond Words Publ., Hillsboro, Oreg., 1992.

Elkind, David, *All Grown up and No Place to Go*, Addison-Wesley Publishing Co., Reading, Mass., 1984.

Elkind, David, *The Hurried Child*, Addison-Wesley Publishing Co., Reading, Mass., 1981.

Elkind, David (ed.), *Jean Piaget: Six Psychological Studies*, Harvester Press, Brighton, 1980.

Freed, Richard, *Wired Child: Reclaiming Childhood in a Digital Age*, self-published, 2015.

Garbarino, James, *Lost Boys*, Anchor Books, New York, 2000.

Ginott, Dr Chaim G., *Between Parents and Teenagers*, Avon Books/ Macmillan Company, New York, 1969.

Greenspan, Louise and Julianna Deardorff, *The New Puberty*, Rodale, San Francisco, 2014.

Gurian, Michael, *A Fine Young Man*, Jeremy Tarcher/Penguin, New York, 1999.

Gurian, Michael and Patricia Henley, *Boys and Girls Learn Differently*, Jossey-Bass, San Francisco, 2001.

Harwood, A.C., *The Recovery of Man in Childhood: A Study in the Educational Work of Rudolf Steiner*, Hodder & Stoughton, London, 1958.

Healey, Jane M., *Endangered Minds*, Simon & Schuster, New York, 1990.

Hinshaw, Stephen, *ADHD: What Everyone Needs to Know*, Oxford University Press, New York, 2016.

Hinshaw, Stephen and Rachel Kranz, *The Triple Bind: Saving Our Teenage Girls from Today's Pressures and Conflicting Expectation*s, Ballantine Books, New York, 2009.

Hymowitz, Kay S., 'Tween: ten going on sixteen', city-journal.org, New York, Autumn 1998.

Icard, Michelle. *Middle-school Makeover: Improving the Way You and Your Child Experience the Middle-school Years*, Bibliomotion, Mass., 2014.

James, Charity, *Beyond Customs: An Educator's Journey*, Agathon, New York, 1974.

James, Van, *Painting with Hand, Heart, and Mind*. BookBaby (self-published), 2020.

Jensen, Frances E. and Amy Ellis Nutt, *The Teenage Brain: A Neuroscientist's Survival Guide to Raising Adolescents and Young Adults*, Harper Collins, New York, 2015.

Kessler, Rachael, *The Soul of Education*, ASCD (Association for Supervision and Curriculum Development), Alexandria, Virg., 2000.

Lievegoed, Bernard, *Man on the Threshold: The Challenge of Inner Development*, Hawthorn Press, Stroud, Gloucestershire, 1985.

Lynn, George and Cynthia Johnson, *Breaking the Trance*, Central Recovery Press, Las Vegas, 2016.

Pearce, Joseph Chilton, *The Biology of Transcendence*, Park Street Press, Verm., 2002.

Pollack, William. S., *Real Boys' Voices*, Random House, New York, 2000.

Pope, Denise, *Doing School: How We Are Creating a Generation of Stressed out, Materialistic, and Miseducated Students*. Yale University Press, New Haven, 2001.

Postman, Neil, *Amusing Ourselves to Death*, Viking, New York, 1985.

Rilke, Rainer Maria, *Letters to a Young Poet*, W.W. Norton, New York, 1934.

Sales, Nancy Jo, *American Girls: Social Media and the Secret Lives of Teenagers*, Alfred A. Knopf, New York, 2016.

Sax, Leonard, *Boys Adrift*, Basic Books New York, 2016.

Sax, Leonard, *Girls on the Edge*, Basic Books, New York, 2010.

Sax, Leonard, *Why Gender Matters*, Broadway Books, New York, 2005.

Siegel, Daniel J., *Brainstorm: The Power and Purpose of the Teenage Brain*, Jeremy Tarcher/Penguin, New York, 2015.

Staley, Betty K., *Adolescence: The Sacred Passage, Inspired by the Legend of Parzival*, Fair Oaks, Calif., Rudolf Steiner College Press, 2006.

Staley, Betty K., *Soul Weaving: Understanding and Transforming Ourselves*, 2nd edn, Fair Oaks, Calif., Rudolf Steiner College Press, 2012,

Staley, Betty K., *Tending the Spark: Lighting the Future for Middle School Students*, Waldorf Publications, Hudson, New York, 2019.

Steiner, Rudolf, *Education for Adolescence*, Anthroposophic Press, Great Barrington, Mass., 1996 (translation of lectures given in 1921 in Suttgart, Germany).

Appendix I — Bibliography

Steiner, Rudolf, 'Education of the child in the light of anthroposophy', now included in *The Education of the Child*, Anthroposophic Press, Great Barrington, Mass., 1996.

Steiner, Rudolf, *Human Values in Education*. Rudolf Steiner Press, London, 1971.

Steiner, Rudolf, *Observations on Adolescence: The Third Phase of Human Development*, ed. David Mitchell, AWSNA, Fair Oaks, Calif., 2001.

Steiner, Rudolf, *Soul Economy and Waldorf Education*, Anthroposophic Press, Spring Valley, New York, 1986.

Steiner, Rudolf, *Study of Man*, General Education Course, Rudolf Steiner Press, London, 1966.

Stibbe, Max, *Seven Soul Types*, Hawthorn Press, Stroud, Gloucestershire, 1992.

Wiseman, Rosalind, *Queen Bees and Wannabees: Helping Your Daughter Survive Cliques, Gossip, Boys, and the New Realities of the Girl World*, 3rd edn, Harmony Books, New York, 2016.

Appendix II

Study questions

The questions that follow can be used by the reader as a kind of 'self-examination', or for the purposes of paired and/or group discussion. You can use any of the questions as a way of evaluating yourself with the children who are in your care. The questions can be taken in a general way, or very specifically in relation to your own children.

Part I: The Nature of Adolescence

Chapter 1: How do you get to be an adolescent?

1. What are the characteristics of each seven-year period between birth and age 21?
2. In each phase, what is the nature of the child's thinking?
3. In each phase, how does the child best learn?
4. What are the signs of the 7 to 14-year-old-phase beginning and ending?
5. Why is it important to differentiate between the phases?
6. What are some of the ways the parent would relate to the child in each of these phases?

Chapter 2: Stages of adolescence

1. What are the characteristics of the period of negation?
2. How do young adolescents relate to adults during this period?

3. What is the basis of these actions?
4. How does the crush help the adolescent overcome his or her negativity?
5. What kind of pressures are on the teenager during the period of transition?
6. What role does self-esteem have in the transition from negation to affirmation?
7. Give examples of the kinds of changes we might see in a teenager's behavior from early adolescence to later adolescence.
8. What are some of the beneficial ways young people can spend the time from 18 to 21?
9. What are the results of not having close friends or intense interests during this period of transition?
10. What kind of activities will balance eroticism and the will to power?
11. How do drama and world events help teenagers gain perspective?

Chapter 3: The search for the self

1. Characterize the major crisis within each seven year period.
2. How does self-awareness change during each seven year period?
3. How does the nine year change affect adolescence?
4. How does the child's relationship to adults change during the nine year change?
5. What are the losses and compensations that occur around the nine year change?
6. What aspects of the child's life help him or her to work through the nine year change in a positive manner?
7. What kinds of questions are being asked during the 16–17th-year change?
8. What are some ways that teenagers confront their mortality? Why is this important?
9. What is the role of loneliness in becoming self-conscious? Is it necessary?
10. In what way is the captain a useful image of the ego that comes to birth at 21? Can you think of other images?

Chapter 4: The birth of intellect

1. How does a young teenager build his or her world view?
2. In what ways is thinking related to power?
3. Discuss the similarities and differences between the thinking of 16 to 17-year-olds and adults.
4. How is thinking related to eroticism? Can you think of any examples?
5. Examine Plato's image of the charioteer. How is this helpful in understanding teenagers?
6. What is meant to awaken the intellect gradually?
7. How does intellectual consciousness relate to imaginative consciousness?
8. In what way does materialism enter into the thinking of adolescents?
9. What are some of the ways youngsters can awaken lively thinking? Why is this important?
10. Why is it important not to rush youngsters into intellectual thought?
11. What are the dangers of keeping a youngster in imaginative thinking too long?

Chapter 5: The release of feelings

1. How do children in the nine year experience change with regard to their feelings?
2. How does the feeling life differ before and after puberty?
3. How does the development of emotional maturity relate to the development of thinking?
4. How does the astral body express itself in adolescence?
5. What is the role of the I and the soul body in the maturing of feelings?
6. How does dopamine influence the young teenager's behavior?
7. What is the importance of separation during adolescence?
8. How do different teenagers relate to the teen culture at this time?

Chapter 6: Strengthening the life of will

1. How is imitation related to unconsciousness? Give an example of a young child's unconscious will.

2. How do children begin to develop conscious will in the elementary school?
3. How do adults help children develop their will?
4. How does the will change during puberty?
5. What kind of adults help middle-school children during this time?
6. What is the vulnerability gap?
7. What kinds of activities help young teens discipline their will?
8. What does Steiner mean by intentions that are smaller than the deeds? Why is it important that intentions be wider than the deeds?
9. What is the relationship between thinking and will in adolescence?
10. What kinds of activities help the teenager to direct the will?
11. How are different aspects of love an important experience in adolescence?

Chapter 7: Understanding our sons and daughters

1. What is changing in the way young people today look at gender and identity?
2. What are different ways in which society has influenced sexual identity?
3. What is the most important attitude adults should cultivate toward children exploring questions of identity?
4. What are some of the ways girls experience puberty and adolescence?
5. Why is it important for coaches to understand differences in the structure of females?
6. What is the effect of testosterone on a boy's mind and body?
7. What is meant by 'a spectrum of male and female responses'?
8. What are some of the differences in the ways boys and girls express their emotional life?
9. How can teachers be helpful in relating to their adolescent students?
10. How do boys and girls relate to power and morality?
11. How do teenagers you know express their individuality? How do they express their sexuality?

Chapter 8: Temperaments and soul types

1. What are the four temperaments?
2. Are there good and bad temperaments?
3. Which temperaments are more inward, and which more outward?
4. Which is your strongest temperament? Give examples of how it is expressed.
5. How can parents nurture the positive aspect of each temperament?
6. What happens to the temperament at puberty?
7. What are the seven soul types?
8. How are they different from the temperaments?
9. Which soul types are strongest in your personality?
10. What is the best in each soul type?

Chapter 9: The development of character

1. How does character develop?
2. How does character connect with the civilizing mind in middle-school students?
3. What are some character traits?
4. How does the ego/I form character from within?
5. What are some examples of teenagers showing character in their community?
6. What is the role of the adult when children or adolescents make mistakes? Why?
7. What happens when teenagers set their own punishment?
8. How do adults influence the character development of adolescents?
9. How can leadership positions in high school help teenagers develop character?
10. What is special about the 18½-year rhythm?

Part II: The World of Adolescents

Chapter 10: The needs of teenagers
1. What are the basic needs of teenagers?
2. Why is there tension between the needs of teenagers?
3. How can parents help teenagers balance the need for physical activity and the need for stillness?
4. How can the family balance the need for intensity and the need for routine?
5. How can the adults help teenagers to feel needed? Give examples from your experience.
6. How can teenagers bring about change?
7. What needs is the group that my youngster belongs to fulfilling a need? What needs does my teenagers' group of friends fulfill?
8. Does the teenager depend on the group for self-esteem?
9. What is the teenager's role in the family? What does the teenager contribute to the family's well-being?
10. How is the teenager's need for facts being satisfied?
11. Is the teenager's need for imagination being nurtured?

Chapter 11: Teenagers and family life

1. How does the image of the volcano and the mask relate to teenagers?
2. What are some of the ways teenagers view parents?
3. What are some of the stresses placed on teenagers, according to their birth order?
4. What special burden is on the oldest child?
5. How do children handle being caught in the middle of a divorce? How can parents help them?
6. What fantasies may develop for a teenager regarding an absent divorced parent? How can the teenager be helped with this?
7. Teenagers of a divorced family often lack the guidance they need. How can parents be aware of not vying for the teenager's approval?
8. Is the teenager carrying too much responsibility in the family after a divorce?
9. How can remarriage of a parent help a teenager? What extra pressures does it put on the teenager?

10. What are some of the patterns of teenagers and their step-parents that you are aware of?

Chapter 12: Teenagers and friends

1. What is the special role friends play in a teenager's life?
2. What stresses do teenagers experience in friendship?
3. What role does conformity have in a teenager's life? Give examples.
4. What kinds of cliques are in your child's school? How does he or she relate to the cliques?
5. What is the special blessing of a platonic relationship?
6. How do teenagers support friends who are coming out with a new identity?
7. How can parents handle a situation involving their child which they consider negative?
8. How can parent restrictions actually help a teenager feel cared for?
9. What can be done when a teenager feels lonely and without friends?

Chapter 13: Teenagers and school

1. How does the social life at school affect the adolescent?
2. What does 'doing school' mean?
3. Why are there so many pressures in some upper-class schools? How can that be met in a different way?
4. What kind of students are attracted to Carver High School? Why?
5. How does Carver High School help students in poverty?
6. What issues of mental health are of concern for high-school students?
7. How can schools help students manage the pressures of social media?
8. What pressures are parents dealing with today? How are they putting pressure on the teachers?
9. How can parents be supportive of teachers in middle and high schools?

Chapter 14: Waldorf education

1. When did Waldorf schools originate? Where? In what situation?
2. What children first attended the Waldorf school?
3. What happened to the Waldorf schools under the Nazi regime?
4. What are the basic principles of Waldorf education?
5. What is the stage of consciousness of the 9-year-old? What image describes this?
6. Why is history so important in fifth grade?
7. What is the basic approach of the Waldorf kindergarten? How is that different from other kindergartens?
8. How is the artistic approach carried into the Waldorf high school?
9. How would you characterize the 9th, 10th, 11th, and 12th grades?

Chapter 15: Teenagers and the arts

1. What is the ancient Chinese character for art? What does it mean to you?
2. What is the special gift of the arts to teenagers?
3. How does art relate to thinking and feeling?
4. How does imagination change during the adolescent years?
5. What does copying works of the Great Masters do for the teenager?
6. How does art touch teenagers in their soul life?
7. How is imagination different before and after the 14th year?
8. How is art included in the curriculum in a Waldorf school?
9. Why is craft power? Give examples.
10. What is the special role of music in the teenager's life?

Chapter 16: Power and loyalty

1. What is the teenager trying to prove through power? Can you relate to this?
2. Why is power such an issue between teenagers and their parents?
3. How do teenagers have power over adults?
4. How do we feel when we think we are powerless?

5. What areas are negotiable with your teenagers? Are there areas where you will not let your teenagers make a final decision? Why?
6. How is loyalty expressed in your family?
7. Are there situations you know of where the teenager is caught between loyalty to friends and loyalty to parents?
8. How is the I–Thou relationship relevant to teenagers?

Chapter 17: Love, relationships, and sex

1. How do youngsters become conscious of their sexuality as they enter puberty?
2. How do teenagers form thoughts of ideal love?
3. What does 'cisgender' mean? Why has that become a term in adolescent life today?
4. How do adolescents struggle with questions of identity?
5. How do boys come through puberty? What are their challenges?
6. How do girls come through puberty? What are their challenges?
7. What is the danger of young girls hanging around older boys?
8. How is sex education taught in your children's school?
9. How is sexual activity different today from when you were a teenager?
10. What is the difference between relationships during middle school and high school?
11. How does egotism show itself in teenager's experience of love?
12. How do teenagers' experiences of love change?

Chapter 18: Self-esteem

1. What is self-esteem? How does it affect the teenager?
2. How does advertising affect self-esteem? Give examples.
3. What makes teenagers vulnerable to self-esteem issues?
4. How do teenagers cope with parental expectations?
5. Can expectations be positive? Negative? Both? Explain.
6. Why is it normal for teenagers to have periods of depression?
7. What are the signs of depression?
8. What are some of the ways teenagers relate to separation and loss?
9. What are some of the reasons for the high suicide rate in adolescence?

Part III: The Challenges of Adolescence

Chapter 19: Teenagers and alcohol
1. Why is alcohol the drug of choice amongst teenagers?
2. How does alcohol affect judgement?
3. What are some of the reasons teenagers drink?
4. How have alcohol rates changed in different countries? Why?
5. What is binge drinking? Why is it so dangerous?
6. What can adults do if they suspect a teenager has a drinking problem?
7. What are some of the guidelines that can help teenagers monitor their drinking?

Chapter 20: Use of tobacco and drugs

1. How has tobacco use by teenagers changed?
2. What are the common drugs in your community?
3. Why do teenagers take drugs?
4. What are the physical signs that your teenager may be using drugs?
5. Why do teenagers lie about drugs?
6. How do drugs affect a teenager's development?
7. How does rehabilitation help teenagers with drug addiction?
8. What are some of the soul-strengthening exercises given by Rudolf Steiner?

Chapter 21: Sex and pregnancy

1. Why is teenage pregnancy so common in life today?
2. What kinds of consideration should a pregnant teenager think about before making a decision?
3. In what way can a teenage mother experience success?
4. What is the responsibility of the father of the child? Is it being handled maturely?
5. How can the young woman be prepared to accept the spiritual responsibility of the child?
6. What are the advantages and disadvantages of the pregnant teenager marrying the father?

7. What kind of support system needs to be around the young couple?
8. Who makes the final decision on the question of birth, adoption, abortion, marriage?
9. How is birth-control information shared in your community?
10. What are some of the dangers of teenage pregnancy?

Chapter 22: Teenagers and food

1. What is our culture's idea of beauty? How is it shaped?
2. What are some of the ways teenagers turn to food to solve their problems?
3. What is the condition of anorexia nervosa, and what is its typical pattern?
4. What is bulimia? What is its pattern?
5. What are the dangers of each condition?
6. What is a common factor in teenagers who over-eat?
7. How can teenagers get support in changing their eating and exercise habits?
8. How can parents encourage healthy nutrition in their teenager's diet?

Chapter 23: Teenagers and the media

1. What are some examples of media today?
2. How have the media helped teenagers connect with each other?
3. How does the media affect relationships?
4. Why is the media so alluring for young teenagers?
5. How are video games different from television?
6. Why do teenagers, especially boys, favor video games?
7. How can overdoing video games be a problem for boys?
8. Why is the cell phone so problematic for a teenager's life?
9. How is the cell phone helpful in a teenager's life?
10. In what ways has internet use on the cell phone affected the social life of teenagers?
11. How has pornography influenced teenagers' relationship to sex and relationships?
12. How can parents and schools regulate the use of the media with adolescents?

Other Titles by Hawthorn Press

The Parenting Toolkit
Caroline Penney

This unique and valuable resource offers simple skills for developing healthier relationships with children of all ages. The author also has advice on how to manage parents'/guardians' own stress and ensure they are getting the self-care that they need.
176pp; 250 × 200mm; paperback; ISBN: 978-1-91248011-1

Simplicity Parenting
Using the power of less to raise happy, secure children
Kim John Payne

Here are four simple steps for decluttering, quieting, and soothing family dynamics so that children can thrive at school, get along with peers, and feel calmer, happier, and more secure.
352pp; 234 x 156mm; paperback; ISBN: 978-1-912480-03-6

Ordering Books

If you have difficulties ordering Hawthorn Press books from a bookshop, you can order direct from our website www.hawthornpress.com, or from our UK distributor BookSource: 50 Cambuslang Road, Glasgow, G32 8NB: Tel: (0845) 370 0063, E-mail: orders@booksource.net. Details of our overseas distributors can be found on our website.

Hawthorn Press

www.hawthornpress.com